W9-BXO-516

Praise for

How Iceland Changed the World

"*How Iceland Changed the World* is not only surprising and informative. It is amusing and evocatively animates a place that I have been fascinated with for most of my life. Well worth the read!"
—Jane Smiley, Pulitzer Prize–winning author

"Egill Bjarnason has written a delightful reminder that, when it comes to countries, size doesn't always matter. His writing is a pleasure to read, reminiscent of Bill Bryson or Louis Theroux. He has made sure we will never take Iceland for granted again."
—A. J. Jacobs, *The New York Times* bestselling author of *Thanks a Thousand* and *The Year of Living Biblically*

"Egill Bjarnason places Iceland at the center of everything, and his narrative not only entertains but enlightens, uncovering unexpected connections."
—Andri Snær Magnason, author of *On Time and Water*

"Icelander Egill Bjarnason takes us on a high-speed, rough-and-tumble ride through one thousand–plus years of history—from the discovery of America to Tolkien's muse, from the French Revolution to the NASA moonwalk, from Israel's birth to the first woman president—all to display his home island's mind-opening legacy."
—Nancy Marie Brown, author of *The Real Valkyrie* and *The Far Traveler*

"I always assumed the history of Iceland had, by law or fate, to match the tone of an October morning: dark, gray, and uninviting to most mankind. This book challenges that assumption, and about time. Our past, much like the present, can be a little fun."
—Jón Gnarr, former mayor of Reykjavík and author of *The Pirate* and *The Outlaw*

"Rich with entertaining anecdotes and helpful pronunciation guides, this is a winning introduction to a unique and fascinating culture."
—*Publishers Weekly*

PENGUIN BOOKS

HOW ICELAND
CHANGED THE WORLD

Egill Bjarnason reports on Iceland for the Associated Press and frequently writes for *The New York Times*, *Al Jazeera English*, *Lonely Planet*, and *Hakai Magazine*. Prior to covering his native Iceland for the international news media, he reported on the rest of the world for Icelandic readers, publishing features and photographs from Afghanistan, Uganda, and West Africa. As a Fulbright Foreign Student grantee, he earned a master's degree in social documentation at the University of California, Santa Cruz, and currently lectures at the University of Iceland. This is his first book.

How
Iceland
Changed the World

The Big History of a Small Island

EGILL BJARNASON

PENGUIN BOOKS

PENGUIN BOOKS

An imprint of Penguin Random House LLC
penguinrandomhouse.com

Internal illustrations © 2021 The Heads of State

LIBRARY OF CONGRESS CONTROL NUMBER 2021932814
ISBN 9780143135883 (paperback)
ISBN 9780525507468 (ebook)

Printed in the United States of America
6th Printing

Set in Mercury Text
Designed by Chris Welch

Fyrir Val & Frey

❀

CONTENTS

INTRODUCTION

The town of Selfoss is a rare find. Nearly all of the sixty-three towns and cities in Iceland were first established out of nautical convenience, in sight of approaching ships, but Selfoss sits inland, away from the stony coast. I grew up there, landlocked.

The town is on the eastern banks of the Ölfusá River, the country's largest, streaming from a glacier 105 miles inland. For the first nine hundred years of Selfoss's settlement, the area saw few travelers because crossing the river on horseback or rowboat was a life-threatening endeavor and, let's be honest, not worth it. Finally, in a symbolic gesture, Icelandic and Danish authorities joined forces on the construction of a suspension bridge. Completed in 1891, thirteen years before the arrival of the first automobile, the bridge connected western and southern Iceland. Selfoss became a rest stop for long-distance travel—the place to dry your clothes and catch up on weather conditions from travelers heading in the opposite direction. Today, people stop for a hot dog.

The bridge still brings plenty of traffic through town and serves as the central landmark around which everything else is oriented, just as a harbor would in a seaside town. Where other towns have a fish factory, we have a dairy plant. And instead of watching ships sail in and out of port, we can watch our cars drive around and around and around—the main roundabout is impressively big. "Big city" big—after all, with about eight thousand people, Selfoss is one of Iceland's largest towns. So don't be intimidated by its size if you walk around; and don't be alarmed if you find yourself alone out there— walking in Selfoss is practiced solely by children and the odd drunk driver with a suspended license.

Along Selfoss's Main Street are, among others, five hair salons, three bank branches, a bookstore owned by my parents, a store for yarn, a store with only Christmas items, and a supermarket named Krónan. At the entrance of that store, I began my career as a reporter, holding a notebook and the cheapest camera I could borrow from *Sunnlenska*, a local newspaper. Every day I waited to snag passersby for "The Question of the Day," a column in which innocent pedestrians were prompted to articulate, for the record, a view on a contemporary issue they usually knew next to nothing about and—after guaranteed intellectual embarrassment—have a portrait taken to accompany the answer.

Over time, I worked my way up to the news desk. THESE MASKS ARE NOT FOR SWIMMING: A BAG OF SEX TOYS FOUND AT THE SWIMMING POOL, read an early headline. Another was a crime story about a tomato farmer who turned to growing marijuana in an abandoned slaughterhouse. Being a secret drug kingpin in a small community was very stressful, he confessed. So he consumed most of the weed himself.

Sunnlenska stayed in business through my early twenties, thanks to its very resourceful owner. Among his fine ideas for survival was a reliance on the barter system: he liked to pay people in things rather than money, the kind of stuff local businesses might trade for advertising. Christmas bonuses, for instance, consisted of fireworks and a stack of books given to the paper for review. For one payday in spring, he came riding to work on a twenty-seven-gear Mongoose bicycle, a touring bike with fat tires and a rear rack. "It's yours," he said with enthusiasm, prompted more by this apparent advertising deal. Zero paper money this month.

To properly enjoy my salary, I was obliged to take it for a spin. And one of the very best things about Selfoss, as one guidebook is quick to note, is how easy it is to leave. Route 1, the famous Ring Road, plows right through town.

Loaded up with a tent and an impressive amount of couscous, I cycled past the dairy plant and around the roundabout, headed east.

Officially, the Ring Road is an 821-mile loop that connects most towns and villages in the country. Done in one stretch, that's a little more than fifteen hours of driving. Cycling takes a bit longer. The landscape of Iceland is famously uneven, and along the coast the wind blows hard. On top of that, statistics and meteorological patterns simply cannot explain how often the wind blows directly against you while bicycling. Always, I tell you. Always.

Cycles around Iceland.

My bartered bicycle held up admirably, but between the fickle headwinds and the long uphill climbs, by the time I got halfway around the country, I was exhausted. I decided to rest for a bit in the town of Húsavík.

Húsavík sits on the north coast, overlooking the wide Skjálfandi Bay. The bay's mouth gapes toward high north, toward the Iceland Sea, the Greenland Sea, the Arctic Ocean, and, beyond that, the North Pole.

While strolling around the harbor on a sore knee, I struck up a conversation with the captain of a wooden schooner whose crew was one person short. Soon I learned that "one person short" meant that the crew was just one man: him, Captain Hordur Sigurbjarnarson, a cartoonish version of an old skipper, the classic image minus the wooden pipe (he was vehemently opposed to smoking). Raspy voice, gray hair, grim face, strong handshake. Warm smile.

I told him about my theory on wind direction, how it magically never works in your favor. He did not seem to follow.

"So, do you get seasick?" he asked, his opening question in a sudden job interview.

How would I know? This was like asking if I'd be prone to space sickness (motion sickness for astronauts). The high seas were beyond my experience, so my body had never been put to the test. I had no idea that knowing how to tie a bowline was an essential life skill.

He scratched his head and rolled it to the side as if he were attempting to pour water out of his ears. "Come this afternoon and we'll see what happens."

As it turned out, I do not belong to the 35 percent of people highly susceptible to seasickness. I locked the bike and called the newspaper to say I would not be back that summer. The owner was about to land a big advertising deal with a new Jacuzzi distributor. After weeks of cold days out at sea, I did sometimes question my choice: owning a hot tub would have been nice.

I got a crash course in knots and halyards, worked twelve hours at a stretch in freezing conditions, and wore the bright-yellow fleece hat the captain had given me. "It's the first color the eye detects, in case you fall overboard," he explained reassuringly.

The captain was a seafarer through and through. His five

favorite pizza toppings were five different things from the ocean—essentially, a fish buffet served on bread—and he could always point in the direction of north, even when standing on land in a hardware store. My own lack of orientation puzzled him. He'd been sailing the *Hildur* out of Húsavík for twenty-five years, taking passengers on whale-watching voyages and pleasure cruises.

After that first serendipitous summer, the ship's cabin became my annual summer home. Each year I would travel out to Húsavík in early May, and we'd sail in and out of the harbor with passengers who were eager to watch whales and puffins from beneath nearly 2,700 square feet of taut sails. Each day we told the same stories, the same jokes, and watched the same horizon, from spring to fall, until the whales swam out of the bay, from Iceland to all corners of the globe.

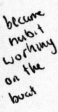

because nubit working on the boat

It was my first time at sea, but it was my first time, too, witnessing Iceland's strange position as both a marginalized curiosity and a global hub. Well-meaning tourists asked questions that ranged from baffling to mildly insulting, like whether the country had enough educated people to run a functioning government. Each visitor seemed to have a preconceived narrative of what Iceland was. Iceland the alien planet. Iceland the frozen wasteland. Iceland the expensive playground. Iceland the Viking fortress. The captain and I, while we scouted the sea for whales, sometimes tried to untangle these myths or figure out which felt most true.

"Whales capture people's imagination," the captain once told me. "All it takes is a tiny glimpse and people feel like they've seen an entire whale, mouth to fluke." That's Iceland too.

interesting

This book tells the story of Iceland by taking a second look at the canon of Western history. At first sight, it may seem bold to position Iceland as a central player on the global stage. After all, Iceland has never had a military. Never shot at another country. Never plotted against a foreign leader, nor fought proxy wars, nor laid claim to being a hegemonic power of any kind. But how, then, to explain its fingerprints all over Western history? Without Icelanders, no one would have recorded Norse mythology and the medieval history of Nordic kings. Without Iceland, the world from England to Egypt would not have suffered a major famine, cultivating a fragile political climate that culminated in the French Revolution. The anti-imperialist struggle would have been one hero short. Neil Armstrong would never have practiced the moon landing on earth. A Cold War–defining chess game would have had nowhere to take place. The world would have had to wait years longer to see the first woman elected head of state. And the North Atlantic might have wound up under the control of the Nazis instead of the Allies during World War II, with all the fallout that would entail.

Here I present a new perspective on Iceland's history, one that revolves around the lives of various known and unknown Icelanders, in order to tell a story built on both the latest research and neglected narratives. Together the chapters chronicle the remarkable history of Iceland: 1,200 years of settlement that began when a frustrated Viking captain and his useless navigator ran aground in the middle of the North Atlantic. Suddenly the island was no longer just a layover for the Arctic tern. Instead, it became a nation of diplomats and musicians, sailors and soldiers, who found themselves suddenly faced with enormous responsibility, and who quietly altered the globe forever.

Captain Hordur wound up becoming a lifelong friend, one who enabled key research for this book as we sailed to Greenland, Norway, Sweden, and Denmark.

On our first voyage abroad, three years after that initial meeting, a small crowd of twenty-some people stood on the harbor's quay waving goodbye. It was a bright summer day. The first mate's wife blew kisses from the dock. Swept up in the moment, some tourists wandered over from a nearby hot dog stand to join in the farewell. The spring line loose, the vessel drifted off, and the captain's five-year-old grandson raised his voice louder and louder the farther away we sailed, with such eagerness I was afraid he might suffer a heart attack. Goodbye! Goodbye! Goodbye!

Life at sea was simple, if incredibly unpredictable. The only constant was worry—about winds and weather patterns. Tailwinds might push the vessel ahead eight nautical miles; unfair winds and currents might slow our progress to four or five knots. Time unspooled strangely, measured less by hours than by the slow course we plotted across the water. That water stretched on and on, in every direction, endlessly, day after day. Water. Water. Water. Land!

We'd reached our destination: the coast of Greenland. There we sailed passengers around Scoresby Sound, the longest fjord in the world and one of the largest natural areas in the world not yet touched by mass tourism. Large icebergs calve from the outlets of Greenland's massive ice cap. Toward the end of summer, melted ice waters down the ocean's salt ratio to the point where it can be used in cooking, to boil pasta or potatoes. As the cook on board, I could even use the sea for dishwashing and bread making, kneading dough for a "seawater loaf." Captain Hordur ate the bread with enthusiasm, despite its ridiculously salty taste, because the man loved thrift.

The captain sincerely struggled, therefore, with watching our vacationing passengers. Watching people stand on the deck and do nothing made him uneasy. Unless people were manic photographers, or compulsive knitters, or were engaged in some constant and productive activity, he tended to come up with tasks for them. By the end of each eight-day trip, everyone on board would typically have been assigned some nautical responsibility, answering to the captain on evening iceberg watch and the morning anchor heave.

The fjords we sailed and the mountains we hiked generally had two names: one from the time the area was initially charted by Europeans, and one used by the local Inuit. The local Inuit names were descriptive—the Fjord with the Red Mountain, the Twin Peak Ridge—enabling locals to guide travelers with verbal directions. Our European nautical charts, however, were a monument to stuffy long-dead explorers and sailors who named the area after themselves, their mothers, and everyone they (nominally) respected. Carlsberg Fjord. Liverpool Land. Charcot Bay. One English whaling ship, zigzagging the coastline a century ago, exhausted its list of names all the way down to the deck scrubber.

It's a stunt as old as Greenland.* Erik the Red, forced into exile from Iceland, led others from Iceland to establish the first European colony in Greenland, one he dubbed Eriksfjord. One of the people who joined him for this venture into a

---

* The name of the country in the indigenous Greenlandic language is Kalaallit Nunaat, the Land of the Kalaallit. Passport stamps at border control use this name.

strange new land was a remarkable woman, one of the greatest explorers in Iceland's history: Gudrid Thorbjarnardóttir.

In Eriksfjord, having just settled into life in southwest Greenland, Gudrid heard rumors of a richly forested landmass across the sea, a land even farther west, past the edge of any map they'd seen. After two separate failed attempts, Gudrid finally completed that voyage west, though the attempts had cost her a husband each. She reached North America five hundred years before Columbus, and there she gave birth to the first European American.

Icelanders found uncolonized America somewhat disappointing, though, and they ditched it, more or less forgetting about the vast continent for the next eight centuries. History books, in turn, forgot about Gudrid and her bravery. Ultimately, she sailed back to Europe. She traveled to Rome. She finally returned to her farm in Iceland, and there she died. The American settlement disappeared, rotted away by time, and sank under the grass.

When Captain Hordur and I finally sailed back into harbor two months later, the same crowd of people stood around, still waving, as if they had never left.

At sea, when every day is an endless set of twists and risks, two months is a long time. But as the daily life I had abruptly left behind resumed, my memories of icebergs the size of skyscrapers and roaming polar bears felt less like recent events and more like a vivid hallucination as described by an eccentric. With maps and satellites and photographs at our disposal, it was easy to trace where we'd been, but it's difficult to imagine Gudrid's experience, returning to Iceland after years away, trying to tell others about this continent, far across the sea, that no one else had ever seen.

Here we'll attempt to uncover and reclaim Gudrid's story, along with other key threads of Iceland's history that have been neglected and lost in time. To understand Iceland's role also means to undo certain beloved myths of the heroic explorer, the eccentric chess genius, or the noble-hearted northerner—but it leaves us with a historical tapestry that is richer and far more complex. And it starts—no surprise—with a ship.

How
Iceland
Changed the World

The Discovery of the West

Iceland from Settlement—AD 1100

> The Icelanders are the most intelligent race
> on earth, because they discovered America
> and never told anyone.
>
> —OSCAR WILDE

Somewhere in the vast northern ocean, between Iceland and Norway, Thorsteinn Olafsson got himself involved in the biggest mystery of the Middle Ages by making an honest mistake: he turned his ship a few too many degrees west. His passengers would have preferred to arrive in sweet home Iceland, but instead they had to settle for an iceberg. They got nice and close. Closer. Closer: *wham*. The wooden ship made a sound like a massive tree branch wrenching and splitting. There was no fair fight here between the ship and the iceberg; frozen glacial water is older and far stronger. Damaged and doomed, the ship's direction was suddenly the same as the iceberg's: wherever the currents pulled and the wind blew, there the ship went. Adrift.

Lucky for them, the winds and currents eventually blew them to land, albeit not the one they were hoping for. "By winter," a loose and pretty all-encompassing term in the Arctic, "the ship made it to the East Village of Greenland," according to a short report written roughly five years later.

The ship had arrived at the world's biggest island. From an administrative point of view, Thorsteinn had technically delivered his passengers to Iceland: this was Iceland's colony of southern Greenland.

Despite rolling around the northern North Atlantic for months, the folks on board apparently continued to enjoy one another's company. Over the next four years, none of them chose to hop on a boat to Iceland (although it remains unclear whether there were any ships available to be hopped on). Thorsteinn, probably a decent guy despite his poor sense of direction, developed a crush on a lady passenger, Sigrid Bjornsdóttir. So he asked her uncle for her hand, and they decided to marry inside that massive stone church the Greenlanders so prided themselves on.

When Sigrid Bjornsdóttir walked inside the stone church one calm September morning, her future looked as steady as the turn of the seasons. The grand arched window of the majestic fieldstone church cast light onto the crowd of "many noble men, both foreign and local," as noted by local authorities. With "a yes and a handshake," the two happy castaways were presented as husband and wife.

The wedding certificate, signed by Greenland's pastor Pall Hallvardsson, was later delivered to the bishop of Iceland and stored in Skálholt for centuries, until some historians dug it out and did a double take at the date: September 16, 1408. This was the last-ever day on record in Erik the Red's Greenland. Shortly thereafter, following roughly four hundred years of Norse settlement, the entire vibrant community disappeared. Vanished. To this day, no one knows exactly why.

Icelanders in the Viking age had discovered Greenland in the search for more land and had turned its stock of walrus and narwhals into a global enterprise. Hungry for wood and wheat, the Icelandic Greenlanders had then launched even farther west, and thereby discovered sailing routes from Europe to North America five hundred years before Columbus. Greenland hadn't just hosted a single flimsy settlement; it had been the burgeoning site of a trade empire, a crucial link between the raw resources of North America and the powerful Viking civilization in Norway. Archaeological evidence today suggests a far bigger presence than we'd initially assumed from written records.

So how did a community of thousands, after five centuries, simply disappear without a trace? How could an entire island nation become a ghost town? And what was it like in that early America?

To unravel the mystery, we'll follow Iceland's three most famous explorers—Erik, Leif, and Gudrid—through the bizarre, violent, and lucky events that shaped their lives. Many of us know the simplified versions of their stories, but, as usual, the truth is a lot more complicated. Our heroes murdered people, got lost a lot, converted to Christianity, got lost again, murdered some more people, rescued castaways, lied, benefited from bribes, murdered a few more people, and finally died on a farm. What's more, despite what you've heard about the legacies of Erik the Red and Leif Eriksson, the true explorer here is the neglected heroine Gudrid Thorbjarnardóttir, who left behind a comfortable life and bonded with the natives in North America while the men tossed rocks at one another. Incredibly, all these explorers were part of the same family by blood or marriage. Their family tree is the starting point for our Greenland mystery.

The story ends with a disappearance. But it begins with exile.

⌘

Like many people, I used to romanticize stormy ocean crossings. Waves crashing over the deck. Scissors flying through the galley. Sailors straining to save their ship in the face of the ocean's immeasurable power. *Reef the main! Stretch the sheet! Ten degrees starboard!* During my own sea crossing a few years ago, I found storms considerably less romantic.

The mayhem forces you to raise your voice and scream, even during face-to-face conversations. Your fingers grow numb as they grip your shipmate's shoulder. *Get some damn rest!* Down in my cabin, I discovered I couldn't undress without completely lying down. Late in the night, I woke up with cold seawater dripping through the deck and onto my bed. A drop landed on my cheek and slowly traveled inside my ear. I gave up on sleep. I heaved myself up, constantly gripping the railing, the ladder, anything. Up on deck, I nearly stepped on the sea chef who was "just getting some fresh air" while unable to stand upright. When we'd first sailed from the harbor mouth in northern Iceland with spirits high, we'd joked that it would make for exciting television to film a cooking show inside the galley of a rocking ship. Now, looking a bit green, he seemed very unlikely to host such a show. "The worst thing about seasickness," he told me from his hands and knees, "is knowing that you are not going to die." Food was canceled for the day.

This antiromantic venture took place during the crossing from Iceland to Stavanger in Norway. Coincidentally, we were sailing the first voyage of Erik the Red in reverse, tracing the route he had taken a millennium earlier, to bring our wooden schooner, the *Opal*, to the dry dock of Scandinavia's finest boat builders. Erik the Red is, of course, the founder of the first Icelandic settlement in Greenland—but his story didn't begin very nobly.

When Erik was just a toddler, he was forced to flee Norway along with his father, Thorvald, who was exiled after committing "some murders." They fled west to Iceland, boarding a knarr, a broad-beamed ship designed for a small crew and large cargo, and spent about a week making that stormy ocean crossing. Knarrs were the crucial tools for Viking voyages in the open North Atlantic. Much, though, was still left up to Njördur, the god of the sea. The captain could maneuver with a rudder attached to the starboard side, but ultimately the wind of fortune dictated his journey. A single strong gust, and the one-masted boat could lose its most important piece of wood. No wind, and the crew could spend days watching the coast of their destination without getting any closer. Fair wind at last, and the knarr could reach a top speed of eight knots (for comparison, a harbor seal's top swimming speed is about ten knots).

Erik and Thorvald headed west across the Norwegian Sea. When the wind was harsh, Erik got cold. When it rained, he got wet. When the boat broke the waves, splashing them over the deck, he hardly slept. A knarr has limited space below deck, nowhere to hide from the elements. Assuming the journey went normally, he would have reached Iceland after seven to ten nights. The knarr averaged 6.5 knots on long journeys—modern rebuilds of knarrs by curious archaeologists have established the vessel's efficiency—but speed, of course, was not the only determinant of his journey's success.

The schooner I sailed hundreds of years later was no faster than the knarrs; after all, the wind still blows the same way after a thousand years. In good weather and fair winds, the ship sailed at eight knots. In swell and currents, we were down to four or five nautical miles per hour: Jogging speed, running speed, jogging speed, running speed. Of course, we had the benefit of cabins below deck, waterproof jackets, and a nauseated chef—but our greatest advantage was being able to navigate without looking for Norwegian birds, whales, leading stars, or the position of the sun. For we—lucky modern sailors—had a compass.

To say that Iceland, Greenland, and mainland North America were initially discovered by men blown off course assumes that a course could be *set* in the first place. These men invented sailing centuries before the art of navigation was anything more than an educated guess. Just as the Icelandic dictionary has 156 entries describing wind, the early seafarers had their own word for getting lost at sea: *hafvilla*. Old texts don't tell us how Iceland's first settlers navigated without a compass. Did they use a quadrant and a sundial? If they did, this would have been challenging in a part of the world defined by long dark winters and cloudy skies. Stars? In summer, when most crossings to Iceland were made, the stars would have been hidden by the midnight sun.

This limited yet impressive degree of navigational ability was crucial to the course of history. Had Erik the Red and his father been unable to find Iceland—had they aimed just a few degrees too far south and missed the island completely—hundreds of years of settlement in Greenland and North America may have gone down differently. This balance, between pinpoint navigation and finding oneself unavoidably lost at sea, was the determining factor for much of the way Nordic history occurred. No two sailors had the same degree of success. As we shall see, Erik sailed straight to his destination, Leif followed someone who was lost, and Gudrid was shipwrecked mid-ocean: each a random stroke of maritime luck, each crucial for what came next. *LUCK in NAVIGATION*

❀

Iceland is the only country in Europe that remembers its beginnings as a nation, as noted by author Magnus Magnusson, as the founding is "enshrined in the works of her early historians." The remote North Atlantic island had existed for millions of years, serving merely as a festive bird colony for its only terrestrial mammal, the Arctic fox, when humans suddenly figured out a way to get there. Half the size of the United Kingdom and the same size as the state of Ohio, Iceland was the last major territory to be settled in the Northern Hemisphere. When New Zealand was settled by the Maori population some centuries later, the entire world was occupied by humans, minus a few small islands (Cape Verde, for example) and places of extreme weather conditions (Svalbard).

First, the country was visited by three explorers, arriving one after the other, who had each come to Iceland mostly out of curiosity and the desire to verify one another's boasts about finding a vast empty island. Flóki Vilgerdarson, the third explorer to arrive, allegedly gave Iceland its name while standing on top of a mountain overlooking the wide Breida Fjord, packed with sea ice. Other proposed early names included Snowland, Gardar's Isle, and Thule.

But those explorers showed up, looked around, and then left.

walked?

The real day number one in Iceland's history—the beginning of actual settlement—was a summer afternoon in AD 874, when Norwegian farmer Ingólfur Arnarson, his family and slaves in tow, walked from Cape Ingolfshofdi to modern day Reykjavík (Rayk-ya-veek) in the Southwest. Iceland's first history book, *The Book of Settlements*, tells the story of Ingólfur, and then goes on to detail the names and farm holdings of the thousands of settlers who came after him. This was a kind of Viking VIP list written by the country's first nerd, Ari the Learned, to highlight the country's respectable genealogy—to show that it was populated by more than slaves and murderers. Iceland, as Ari explains in 102 chapters, was the land of brave Norwegians.

But in a brief aside in the prelude, thrown out like a hand grenade for modern scholars to toss around, Ari mentions that prior to Norwegian settlement "there were those men" *first?* called Papar—Irish monks. Ari repeats the story in the later *Book of the Icelanders*, claiming that the monks abandoned Iceland because they didn't want to live alongside Norse heathens, leaving behind "Irish books and bells and canes."

Historians and archaeologists have tried hard to verify Ari's testimony, but as of today the jury remains out. Certain old place-names, such as Papar Island in the East, do suggest that early settlers believed certain areas had initially been occupied by the mysterious monks. And in the early twentieth century, three silver coins dating back to Roman times were discovered at three different locations on the southeastern corner of Iceland, a place that would serve as the most convenient landing spot for an Irish ship. What's more, some English texts, penned by an Irish monk half a century before Iceland's settlement, speak of a religious community on a northern island called Thule, which had eternal summer light.

But critics of the pre-Viking settlement theory suggest that the word *Papar* had more than one meaning, in this case referring to uneven landscapes. They dismiss the coin findings, saying it only proves that old coins indeed travel—just check your own sofa cushions. And the description of Thule, the skeptics argue, could easily refer to the Faroe Islands, the Shetland Islands, Saaremaa (an Estonian island), Greenland, or Smøla, Norway, where residents claim to inhabit the mysterious northern land. But one element of the monk notion is certainly no myth: Icelanders have significant Irish heritage. In 2018, scientists at the Reykjavík-based genetic company deCODE were able to sequence the genome of twenty-five ancient Icelanders, preserved at the National Museum, and compare them with those of Celtic Britons and Scandinavian populations. According to the results, the early settlers were of 57 percent Norse origin; the rest were of Celtic and "mixed" origin. The mixing is believed to have taken place in Britain and Ireland, and women of the time were more likely than men to have Celtic Britons' origin. This could mean that some Vikings stopped over in Ireland on their way to Iceland, where they may have kidnapped women for a voyage west. One British tabloid interpreted the results in a headline that read: VIKING SEX TOURISTS LIVED HAPPILY EVER AFTER WITH BRITONS.

It's impossible to tell from gene sequencing alone, however, whether a part of the early Icelandic population consisted of Irish people who couldn't outrun the Vikings. It's fully possible that Irish women were in fact charmed by the roaming Scandinavians who had mastered the art of sailing the northern seas. For one, they had steep personal hygiene standards, based on excavations of burial sites that have turned up tweezers, razors, combs, and ear cleaners made from animal bones and antlers. They spoke Old Norse, arrived with their own cultural habits, and, perhaps most important in pagan Ireland, did not believe in Jesus.

Scandinavia—Denmark, Norway, and Sweden—remained Europe's last heathen region. A lack of religions was in fact the primary definition of *Viking*, a word whose strict meaning remains unknown, though there are plenty of educated guesses. How one interprets the term depends largely on our view of the Vikings' primary calling. If we view them mainly as bandits, the definition of "a pirate who stays close to shore" seems logical, as *vik* is the Norse word for creek. But the Vikings also established an advanced trade network running through Western Europe and the Baltic. The evolution from raiders to traders over time could be due to many factors, including the scarcity issues that accompany villainy: there is only so much land that one can grab, and people one can kidnap.

Unless, of course, one discovers new territory.

Thus, about one hundred years after the Viking age began, Iceland became a hot spot for the Viking sprawl. By the time Erik the Red and his father arrived, around AD 960, all the best agricultural land in Iceland had already been claimed. They were fifty years too late to snag prime real estate.

At the time, in the Viking economy, a man's territory was determined by a peculiar method: to claim land, the sagas say, the early settlers would set fire to it when the sun was in the East. Then they would walk until the sun was in the West and set a new fire. In this way, no one could claim more land than he could cross on foot in a day. This was an effective way to balance land ownership—it prevented one person from taking it all—but it also meant that when all the resources were utilized, the last settler to arrive was out of luck. When Erik and his father stepped off their knarr, soaked to the bone and exiled to a strange new island, they discovered that they had to eke out their existence near Hornstrandir, the last place in Iceland to be inhabited. Their farm sat on a cliff by the ocean. Seaweed was more or less the only vegetation around. Snow and thick fog could descend throughout the year. Polar bear attacks were not unheard of. Erik the Red, our hero, was stuck in the Icelandic boondocks, bored to death. He was not having it. The moment his father passed away, Erik started looking for a way out.

The details of our story come from two books, *Erik the Red's Saga* and *The Saga of the Greenlanders*. The stories are written by two different authors, neither aware of the other's version of the oral history, and both were recorded about 250 years after the events they describe. *The Vinland Sagas*, as the two stories are jointly known, are part of the famous Icelandic literature genre called *The Sagas of the Icelanders*, settlement stories penned over a period of two centuries, from about 1200 to 1350. Altogether, the Íslendingasögur (ees-lehnd-eeng-ah-sö-khör) are thirty-eight separate family stories that remain an intrinsic part of the Icelandic identity. To read them all, according to one man who lived to tell about it, takes a solid four weeks of hard work; the narrative is often drowning in dry pages of genealogy and serial murders that the reader struggles to make sense of. Most Icelanders are only familiar with the more stylistically sophisticated and entertaining sagas, such as *Njáls Saga*, *The Laxdæla Saga*, and *Egil's Saga*.

Professor Sigurdur Nordal once said that the sagas (a word Iceland has contributed to the English language) began as science but ended as fiction. *The Vinland Sagas* are penned relatively close in time to the actual expeditions, "only" some three generations apart, and two distinct versions exist. There is reason to believe that the combined *Vinland Sagas* are *truer* than many of the other sagas, somewhere between a saga with a narrative arc and the "historically accurate" documentation of Ari the Learned's settlement history. So we can be relatively confident that the story of Erik the Red is based in truth. Even Ari, in fact, mentions Erik the Red's travel to Greenland in his lengthy tale of name-dropping, and some experts believe him to be the author behind *Erik the Red's Saga*. One last interesting element that sets *The Vinland Sagas* apart from the rest is that the characters are actual Vikings—sea dogs embarking on bloodthirsty voyages. The "Vikings" in most other sagas are really just farmers fighting with other farmers.

Unlike most people with sagas named after them, Erik the Red is not introduced to the reader with a page-long genealogy and a vivid description of his physical attributes, and this is unusual. The author of *Njál's Saga*, for example, repeatedly brings up Njál's lack of a beard, almost as if to explain why a man named Gunnar fought his battles. Gunnar, the author notes, could swing his sword so rapidly "that there seemed to be three swords in the air at once." The peculiar-looking Egil, from *Egil's Saga,* is described in such detail that modern doctors suspect he had Paget's disease of bone. We even know that he could, charmingly, touch his nose with his tongue as a child.

Erik the Red, on the other hand, is a blank slate. The saga does not even mention his hair color, from which his nickname is believed to be drawn. The reader has to judge the man entirely through his actions. Was he brave? Cunning? Cruel?

Dense? Was he an intrepid explorer, or a really lucky exile? What we do know is that he bailed on his miserable far-flung plot of land and managed to marry Thjodhild, the daughter of a rich farmer in western Iceland. Tall, dark, and smooth-talking? Shortly after Erik moved to a farm overlooking the Hvamms Fjord, two of his slaves were killed by his neighbors. The neighbors claimed the slaves had used witchcraft to start a landslide. Erik promptly walked over and stabbed his neighbors to death.

that's crazy

The idiot! Erik the Fool! In tenth-century Iceland, there was no eye-for-an-eye justice when slaves were involved. Guilty of an uneven retribution, Erik was forced to flee (yet again) to a nearby island. At this point, drawing from what we know so far, we can assume that Erik was either short-tempered and politically immature, or that he held the bizarre belief that all men are equal. His next move supports the first conjecture.

Now living on the small island of Brokey, Erik tried to start over. In a friendly fashion, Erik asked his new neighbor to hold on to some settstokr, ornamented beams of mystical value, brought over from Norway by his father. When he finished building his new house and went back to fetch his magic beams, they "could not be obtained." Naturally, Erik then killed his neighbor, and his neighbor's friend, along with "a few others."

murder

At this point, the authorities condemned Erik as a fjör-baugsmaður, an outlaw, for three years. If seen in Iceland within the next three years, he could be assassinated without consequence. Erik was a man without a country. Again. Whatever his character, his next move was momentous.

Back when he lived in the Northwest with his father, Erik had heard the tale of a man named Gunnbjörn Úlfsson, who had gone astray and seen land in the West. And so, just as his own father had grabbed him by the wrist after getting blood on his hands, Erik now carried his two sons, Thorsteinn and Leif, on board a knarr. They set off for a mysterious land they knew nothing about, across more than four hundred nautical miles of rough seas. A strange island of extremes awaited them.

❀

In retrospect, the death penalty may not have been such a bad deal for Erik. It would have been less risky for his family and the crew who accompanied him. Rates of survival for the journey were, after all, roughly fifty-fifty, as evidenced by the convoy of twenty-five ships that departed for Greenland after Erik returned from his three-year exile—eleven ships either sank or retreated back to Iceland.

On this foolhardy expedition, the group could only hope that the small boat would not come too close to a breaking wave, or a skerry (a lonely rocky outcrop in the middle of the sea), or an iceberg appearing from the fog. If the ocean grabbed them, it would never let go. In the open sea, the number of degrees the water temperature registers on the Celsius scale is roughly equal to the number of minutes it takes you to reach hypothermia. Crossing to Greenland one summer, I measured the water temperature as a balmy 6°C. That's six minutes for a person to tread water until it's all over.

At the first sight of land, Erik and his crew saw alpine mountains capped with ice, far higher than anything in Iceland. Besides the mountains, the country looked a lot like the farm where Erik had grown up in the West Fjords, the place he was determined never to return to. With nothing to lose, the ship slid along the coast farther south.

Due to ocean currents and Greenland's ice pack, the southern part of the island is in fact much colder than latitude would indicate. While being significantly farther south than Iceland, average summer temperatures do not exceed 50°F in Greenland, the bare minimum for trees to grow. In Iceland, the average summer temperature is around 60°F and in January, 32°F; people thus sometimes joke that Iceland really has just two seasons: high winter and low winter. In South Greenland, the seasons have sharper contrasts. You would feel a difference between the occasional 70°F summer day and a minus 40°F day in winter. At minus 40°F, bare skin exposed to the air will freeze in minutes.

In the summer of 983, Erik the Red sailed his ship past Greenland's southern cape. He sailed into a wide fjord, sixty miles inland, until he jumped out of his knarr and promptly named the country (which is 80 percent ice) after the color of grass. Was the name just one man's deception? Was Erik the Red a con man for the ages? Alive today, would he be the one to stamp Chinese-made woolen sweaters as "knitted from Icelandic wool"? According to the saga's authors, "he believed people would be attracted to go there if it had a favorable name." But in fact, Erik had sailed with a small group of men around the southern tip of Greenland and arrived at the greenest part of the country, on the west coast. They settled on an island at the bottom of Eriksfjord (a fjord he named after himself, today Tunulliarfik Fjord), which would have been considered valuable land in Iceland, at least during summer. And so, at the time, the name of Greenland was in fact a sincere advertisement.

Incredibly, for the first hundreds of years that Norsemen wound up living in Greenland, they most likely never realized that they were not alone. Hundreds of miles north, Inuit lived in conditions no other society was able to handle, thriving on a diet of raw fish and blubber. Trying to replicate the lifestyles to which they were accustomed in Norway and Iceland, Vikings stayed in the South, where they could graze livestock and launch ships.

Erik grew rather lonely. It's a lesson in human desire that the man who had the nasty habit of killing his neighbors could not bear to live without them. After three years of exploring north and west of Eriksfjord, bestowing place-names left and right, Erik returned to Iceland to gather more settlers. *A fjord with your name on it awaits you in Greenland!* Erik traveled around West Iceland appealing to folks like himself—late settlers, reduced to farming the grimmest outposts of the nation, hungry for a better life. About two hundred people eventually departed from West Iceland with their livestock in tow. Those who made it went on to settle two areas of southwestern Greenland: West Village, where the capital Nuuk is located today; and East Village, near present-day Narsarsuaq, which today boasts the unique Greenlandic Arboretum, an Arctic botanical garden where stands of dwarf willow are called forests.

In the sagas, you'll find understatement used to great effect. Listen hard, and you'll even detect a sense of humor. The first pages of *The Saga of the Greenlanders* introduce a man named Bjarni Herjolfsson as he was returning from Norway to his home in South Iceland. Fresh off the boat, he learns that his father has left Iceland for a new life in Greenland, a country people had just heard of. "Bjarni thought this was quite the news," the saga says. Quite the news! He was completely thrown; enraged; ballistic, even. The old man had left their estate, given to them by his cousin and Iceland's first settler, Ingólfur Arnarson, for a voyage led by murderer-turned-colonialist Erik the Red. This called for an intervention! Fuming, Bjarni turned to his shipmates and announced that they were heading to Greenland. One crewman awkwardly pointed out that none of them had ever sailed the Greenland Sea, calling it unwise, just as they pushed the ship back out to sea.

For days and days, Bjarni and his crew sailed west without seeing anything but the open ocean and the occasional seabird. On the fourth day, a northerly wind blew hard, and by the time the weather had calmed, the crew noticed unknown species of birds all flying in the same direction, toward land. Was this Greenland? Bjarni told the crew to sail along the coast so they could scout the area for houses, livestock, smoke—whatever clues they could find. He was mildly skeptical of what they saw, the trees and low-lying mountains. That's not Greenland, he concluded, "because Greenland has large glaciers." The crew wanted to get on land, just the same, for water and wood. But for Bjarni, their mission was to find his father, not some silly unexplored continent.

Three times over, the crew noticed land, which, Bjarni concluded, was not Greenland (because what they saw was actually green). Based on the way the trees and vegetation got significantly less spectacular each time they spotted a new landmass, experts think they sailed up the Canadian coast, from today's Newfoundland to the Labrador coast and on to Greenland across the Baffin Bay. For Bjarni, who did not bother naming any of the new territory, all of this was the same country: No-dad-land.

The fourth sighting turned out to be, at last, Greenland.

When Bjarni finally disembarked, mentioning the funny sightings of an unknown continent, the settlers of Greenland had about a million questions. But Bjarni could offer only vague answers because he had merely sailed along the coast. People (understandably) gave him a hard time for this, the saga says, for not being more curious.

In Bjarni's defense, Iceland and Greenland were also first spotted by sailors blown off course, vaguely annoyed by their inconvenient historical findings. Like those explorers before them, members of Bjarni's crew got home and began to spread their news in town. They would have exaggerated with tall tales, lending the gossip wings beyond their circle of drunken sailors. And so we can say there's a good chance that bar gossip changed the course of North American history, as the story of a distant land eventually reached the ears of Leif Eriksson, Erik the Red's oldest son.

❁

Today Leif Eriksson is known as the man who "discovered" America five hundred years before Columbus. His glorification is everywhere in modern culture. Look no farther than Reykjavík's iconic Hallgrímskirkja Church: in front is a statue, a gift from the US government, depicting the larger-than-life Leif "the Lucky" Eriksson. The church's sloping 245-foot-tall concrete facade, resembling gigantic columnar basalt in gray, is visible from all corners of Reykjavík, and gives Leif's statue pride of place. Some say that Leif's luck is in having his statue faced *away* from the church, so he didn't have to watch forty years of construction of the architectural oddity. Nearby hotels are named after him. So is Iceland's international airport. There are more than a couple of statues in North America devoted to him as well. But the truth is that Leif, son of Erik the Red, never really settled on the continent. He just kicked a few stones, like a man testing the tires of a used car, got drunk on fermented grapes, and accidentally rescued a crew of stranded castaways on his way back to Greenland.

The two Vinland sagas, *Erik the Red's Saga* and *The Saga of the Greenlanders*, sometimes, unsurprisingly, contradict each other. In the former, Leif converts to Christianity in Norway and heads to Greenland as a missionary when he accidentally veers astray and finds North America. The latter rendition, however, offers a longer narrative, generally a sign that a document can be considered more reliable, as oral histories tend to become more simplified over time and thereby lose nuance and detail. So in *The Saga of the Greenlanders*, Leif is first introduced to the story when he meets with Bjarni, the stunningly incurious explorer who sailed along Canada's coast and ignored it completely. Upon hearing this story, Leif essentially tossed Bjarni a few Norwegian coins in return for his boat and the navigators from his famed voyage and took off to retrace Bjarni's steps.

Together with forty men and a couple of ships, Leif backtracked Bjarni's accidental route, first arriving at Baffin Island, named Helluland after its bare rocks. The coast remained on their starboard side as they sailed down the Labrador coast (named Markland), the view presenting more and more trees and white beaches. They went to shore here and there but kept returning to the ship, hoping to find something better. After two days of sailing, they did.

Never since has Newfoundland received such glowing

reviews from tourists. "They observed that there was dew upon the grass; and it so happened that they touched the dew with their hands, and raised the fingers to the mouth, and they thought that they had never before tasted anything so sweet," the saga claims in the translation by Keneva Kunz. Wheat, to their amazement, grew wild. This was not Arctic land at all. Newfoundland was mild and rich, with loamy soil and balmy weather that would make a Viking sweat. It's worth remembering here that there was a touch of global warming going on, so Newfoundland was indeed greener and milder than it is today.

Leif's bold expedition crew seems to have mostly walked around, picked up colorful foreign plants, and stuck them in their mouths. The narrative belies the brutal and ferocious depiction of Vikings we're usually given. At one point, the group lost sight of a fellow referred to as Tyrkir the German and later found him wobbling back to camp, in high spirits, mumbling to himself in German. When Leif finally got him to switch back to Norse, he hiccupped with a pink face, "I found grapes!" In other words, he had found berries that were likely fermented grapes, and ate them until he got wasted. Leif asked him if he was sure. "I am," Tyrkir replied, "my homeland has no shortage of grapes." The morning after, Leif ordered his men to stock the boat with grapes and wood. As they sailed away, he named the land after Jesus's favorite drink: Vinland. Wineland.

People often assume that Leif's nickname, Leif the Lucky, derives from his luck in "finding" America. But in fact, in the sagas the name is not coined until he is on his way back to Greenland. Sailing back east triumphant, loaded down with wood, wine, and tales of paradise, Leif suddenly noticed a small skerry. Strangely, there seemed to be movement on these tiny barren islands. What was that? Castaways? One, two, three, four . . . fifteen people waving to the ship. Miraculously, using an unknown sailing route, Leif and his crew had stumbled upon shipwreck survivors. But for the first time on the voyage, the crew questioned his commands. Just leave them, they urged. The group's size was great enough to hijack the ship. Instead, Leif ordered his crew to save the shipwreck survivors. "And was he called Leif the Lucky from that moment on." Of course you could say that it was the castaways who were the lucky ones.

One of them turned out to be our underrated friend Gudrid Thorbjarnardóttir, arriving to the story literally from the middle of nowhere. Scholars think she was on her way from Iceland to Greenland with her Norwegian husband, but the general saga reader is led to assume she may have been stranded on her first attempt to cross to Vinland, a sign of her determination to get there. *The Saga of Greenlanders* should rightfully be named *Gudrid's Saga* in light of the chapters to come. The adventures of Gudrid in the New World span 4,045 words, in both Vinland sagas. Meanwhile, Leif's chronicle is only 1,487 words. For the statue honoring brave Gudrid, look no farther than . . . a lonely parking lot in western Iceland, spotted with the occasional seagull droppings. Made of marble by artist Ásmundur Sveinsson, it's a beautiful work of art, but the four-foot statue does not by any means indicate a person of authority in Iceland's history. Its tallest point extends awkwardly out of Gudrid's hand: A child. Snorri. America's first child of immigrants.

In the macho saga literature, women are depicted as cunning, persistent, and short-tempered. Forbidden from carrying weapons, they get their revenge by provoking their husbands or kin to action by, for instance, brandishing the blood-soaked clothes and murder weapons of loved ones whose deaths demand vengeance. Most famous, in *Njál's Saga* and in *The Laxdœla*, are the battles and assassinations masterminded by legendary female figures. In *The Vinland Sagas*, Gudrid somewhat resembles a Viking Lady MacBeth, steering the narrative without being fully in control as she constantly urges her oft-doomed husbands to sail west. She is vigilant, not violent, and deeply admired by the anonymous writer of her story.

Gudrid was married three times but spent most of her adult life as a widow. What she looked for in a man was, mainly, boat ownership. Her first husband died of illness as he attempted to reach Vinland. Interestingly, once rescued by Leif, she wound up marrying his younger brother, Thorsteinn, who . . . also died of illness as he attempted to reach Vinland. With all these sickly husbands about, Gudrid may never have gotten to the New World if it had not been for Greenland's true savior—a two-toothed brown beast known to other mammals for his laziness and terrible smell—*Odobenus rosmarus*. The walrus.

Walrus ivory was a valuable medieval commodity, used to carve luxury items such as ornate crucifixes or chess pieces. The latest research has found that, for hundreds of years, almost all ivory traded across Europe came from walruses hunted in seas that were only accessible via Norse settlements in southwestern Greenland. So unlike the unfortunate citizens of Iceland, Greenlanders held something the rest of the world deeply desired. Traded along with the occasional narwhal tusk, white falcons, and polar bear fur, the walrus made Greenland a valuable stop in the Atlantic trade route.

Under this flag of toothy commerce, on one autumn day a businessman from Iceland, Karlsefni Thordarson, sailed into Eriksfjord. Erik the Red was still living happily there, in the place he'd named after himself, as was his widowed and landlocked daughter-in-law Gudrid. Karlsefni had a crew of eighty men, and Erik the Red was the only one with a house large enough to host such a crowd. He welcomed them to stay for the entire winter, and their shrugs implied, "Why not?" People never had anywhere they needed to be in those days, it seems.

It requires optimism and a good deal of madness to set sail into the North Sea and onward across the Atlantic, to unknown lands and climates. What's more, in that time of no welfare or insurance schemes, it was risky giving up a comfortable life. You could lose your farm, your ship, your life. Such a leap takes a great deal of optimism. Or love. Karlsefni, the businessman crashing at Erik the Red's place in Greenland, was not such an optimist. He was a sensible trader, and the fabled Vinland was not on his map. Still, night after night he listened to local men tell stories of the unexplored land where "butter dripped from every straw" and the sun rose year-round.

Gudrid, on the other hand, was almost certainly dreaming of Vinland, bored and stuck on the Eriksfjord estate. Then, in the middle of winter, her father-in-law, Erik the Red, announced that they were all celebrating the birthday of some guy called Jesus. Christianity had at last made its way into the palaces of Scandinavia. Denmark had been the first to convert, then Norway and Sweden. Iceland was the next domino: aided and abetted by the Norwegian king, a small band of underdogs was able to terrorize and bribe Icelandic lawmakers to adopt Christian laws in the year 1000. Greenland went the same way, almost by default. Heathen beliefs, from then on, could only be practiced in secrecy.

Over in Eriksfjord, the conversion of the nation didn't have too big an impact. Leif was already a Christian (which arguably made him *not* a Viking by definition), just as his mother, Thjodhild, was. She had tried to blackmail Erik into joining what was then still only a strange cult by refusing sex until he found God. At last, Erik embraced the celebration of Christianity, albeit without completely giving up all heathen practices. After all, any kind of worshipping was welcome in his home, particularly if it meant tapping the barrels of beer Karlsefni and his crew had brought over. During the mead-soaked first Christmas celebration, Karlsefni asked if Gudrid would become his wife. When she said yes, according to *Erik the Red's Saga*, "the party was prolonged, and the guests drank to their wedding."

⊰⊱

Christopher Columbus famously mistook America for India when he discovered parts of South America. The native people were of no surprise to him—they were Indians, of course. But traveling five hundred years earlier, Gudrid and Karlsefni, with their livestock and 140 people, only 5 of them women, assumed they would find an empty wilderness in Vinland, just like Iceland and (as far as they knew) Greenland had been.

Following Leif's route, Karlsefni and Gudrid began sailing north along Greenland's coast, and then made the crossing at the mouth of Baffin Bay. In this way, they hardly lost sight of land and could thread their way down the coast. The crew reached Vinland and settled in a fertile area. They built a little village overlooking a quiet bay, which they called Hóp, and late in the season, Gudrid bore a son named Snorri. Born between 1006 and 1010, he is the first European American on record.

Today there's a great deal of debate over where exactly their village was. The Icelandic meteorologist Pall Bergthorsson estimates—taking into account wind, currents, climate, and vegetation—that Hóp was in modern-day New York. The rivers were full of fish, and as winter passed, the livestock roamed on fields free of snow. Then, one spring morning, a man came running to Karlsefni. Agitated, he told his leader that "skin boats dotted the bay below them, as if pieces of coal had been tossed from the peninsula." Shouts from the boats grew louder as they closed in. Waving sticks above the ships, "they made a sound like flails threshing grain."

Karlsefni turned to one of his men. "What does this mean?"

With a fixed gaze, the man took in the scene. He then proceeded to give a completely irrational assessment of the situation.

"Could be a peace sign," he replied. "Let's take a white shield and face it towards them."

If archaeological findings are consistent with the estimated travel routes of Gudrid and Karlsefni, they would have met with both Native Americans and Dorset Inuits. They called them skræling, meaning, in modern Icelandic, barbarian. According to the sagas, the initial encounters were indeed peaceful, proof of Montesquieu's doctrine that "peace is a natural effect of trade." The natives exchanged rodent hides in return for dairy and colored fabric, particularly red fabric. They were intrigued by the villagers' axes and swords, the sagas say, but Karlsefni refused to make an arms deal. Business boomed—a Viking coin was even found in modern-day excavations of Native American burials.

But on this spring day, as war boats approached, both parties responded with panic and skepticism; a bull bellowed loudly in the distance, and the skrælings ran away. Karlsefni wanted to keep peace, but nevertheless he ordered his men to make a fence around the village. When the time came, he decided, they would meet them on an open field, prepared for a battle. Tensions between the natives and the Viking settlers continued to rise, and it wasn't long before that battle arrived. Gudrid was in her tent, lulling young Snorri to sleep. And for a moment, on this day, she may have come close to brokering peace. As Vikings and skrælings traded outside the fence, a shadow appeared in the door. A woman in a black gown walked inside, toward Gudrid. She was "rather short and with light-brown hair, pale face and very large eyes," according to the saga. "Gudrid had never seen such eyes."

"What is your name?" the woman asked.

"My name is Gudrid. But what is yours?"

"My name is Gudrid," the mysterious woman repeated. She intended to tell Gudrid something. But before they could sit down, a loud noise burst from outside; one of the settlers had killed a native for wanting to take away his weapon. All the natives quickly abandoned the scene, including Gudrid's guest. Why the two of them were able to speak the same language is unclear—but their conversation could have begun to reconcile the two cultures. The act sets up Gudrid as a peace broker, a depiction at odds with how women in the sagas are generally portrayed: angry and vengeful.

Instead, a civil war was brewing. Karlsefni and Gudrid

wanted to live in peace by building a bridge of trade with the natives. An opposing faction of the settlers sought to live in peace by mass killings. Fear drove the colonizers toward warfare. The problem with this approach, besides being an attempt at genocide, was that the natives simply had a better army. There were more of them, they were settled and familiar with the territory, and they had ranged weapons: slingshots, which put the Vikings on the defense with their swords and shields. After one battle, the Vikings watched as a native took an axe from one of the dead Vikings. "They tried to cut wood with the axe, and were impressed," says the saga. Then they chopped at a rock, and the axe broke. Disgusted at a weak tool that couldn't handle rocks, they "threw it away before sailing out on their skin boats."

Snorri was three years old when Gudrid and Karlsefni decided not to spend another winter. Others approved, some presumably with reluctance. On the bright side, back home had more than five women. "We are under constant threat from those who previously inhabited this fertile land," Karlsefni lamented. Gudrid was about to retrace the journey she had made from Iceland as a child. Was this it? She had reached North America, and now she was headed back to the country her parents had once fled. Vinland was too treacherous. She went back east.

Gudrid died a farmer in North Iceland, after traveling more than possibly any other woman of her time (and most men). Her travels did not stop after the Vinland years. After Karlsefni passed away, she sailed to Europe and "walked south," generally interpreted as a trip to Rome. When she returned, Snorri had built a church on their farm. Today her statue stands nearby and in 2011 Iceland's president personally gave the pope a small replica of the monument.

Europeans continued to inhabit Greenland for another four hundred years, and the settlements of West and East Village are featured in sagas that precede the legendary founders: In *The Saga of the Sworn Brothers* (*Fóstbrœðra Saga*), a furious farmer sails to Greenland to avenge a murder (and presumably has an awkward stay with the victim's family as he waits for the next ship back to Iceland). In *Flóamanna Saga*, a southern farmer makes the perplexing decision to uproot his family and move to Greenland. He experiences a series of setbacks and eventually his wife dies. In a flippant twist, the widowed man is capable of breastfeeding his infant son. *The Tale of Auðun of the West Fjords* tells of a poor farmer who arrives at Greenland and spends his entire fortune on a polar bear cub as a gift to the king of Denmark. He struggles to keep the bear fed and alive, but carries it on a ship to Denmark anyway. His life choices remain questionable throughout the story. And in *Króka-Refs Saga*, the lead character, for some inscrutable reason, kills a man and promptly exiles himself to the big island.

North America, on the other hand, is never again mentioned in any of the sagas.

For centuries Icelanders prided themselves on having discovered North America ahead of Columbus and John Cabot (who led an English expedition that arrived years before Columbus), a pride based on no evidence other than old stories in old books. The Greenland legacy, in contrast, had been easy to prove. The ground there was so littered with remains that once the Inuit population migrated into the southwestern regions, they probably scratched their heads over the crumbling church walls and stone structures. By the mid-twentieth century, Greenland's most significant excavations, including the Brattahlid property once inhabited by Erik the Red, had already been studied by Danish archaeologists. Meanwhile, in North America: nothing. Not a scrap of hard evidence to be found.

At the dawn of archaeology in the late nineteenth century, researchers in the United States were incredibly enthusiastic—compared to their Canadian counterparts, at least—about locating the whereabouts of Leif Eriksson's old settlement on the East Coast. Bostonian Eben Norton Horsford, who built his fortune on the invention of baking powder, spent his wealth pushing the idea that Leif had settled Massachusetts and Rhode Island. In his obsession, he commissioned a life-size bronze statue of Leif and got the city of Boston to approve its current location on Commonwealth Avenue, a major thoroughfare. Its installment was followed by a parade and a bunch of other Leif statues set up across the United States. Somewhat conveniently, Horsford later discovered archaeological proof of Leif's presence near Harvard University, and invited two Icelandic historians over to confirm the authenticity of the remains, as Icelanders were generally seen as the lead authorities on Viking voyages. The two Icelandic scientists never commented publicly on the matter, however. And for many decades afterward, news stories would occasionally emerge proving that the alleged Viking visits to Massachusetts were based on pseudoscience and, occasionally, fraud.

Then, in 1960, an adventurous Norwegian couple named Helge and Anne Stine Ingstad, with only limited experience in archaeology, made a groundbreaking discovery on the northernmost tip of Newfoundland, off the Canadian coast: a Norse settlement of seven building complexes and a bloomery (a type of iron smelter) dating to about 1000, which matches the sagas' timeline perfectly. The site, known as L'Anse aux Meadows, is the sole confirmed Viking settlement in North America. In 2016, archaeologists announced, with much excitement in the international media, the discovery of "new sites" in southern Newfoundland, coming to light with the help of satellite technology. But those have since been proven not to be Viking-related.

Historians have speculated that Newfoundland's L'Anse aux Meadows served as a base for exploration or a temporary boat repair facility when Norse travelers went to trade with Native Americans in the Canadian Arctic. That means Icelanders did not simply stumble on North America once—they traveled there regularly and used it as a stopover on their way to other trading posts. That suggests that North American settlements existed in conjunction with the vibrant Greenland community, which was known to compensate for their lack of natural resources with an impressive international trade network. One grave excavation in Greenland, for example, revealed bodies that had been wrapped in cloth because there was no wood for coffins. The cloth was well preserved and turned out to parallel fashionable clothing in mainland Europe from 1250 to 1400. And the fieldstone church in Hvalsey, where Sigrid Bjornsdóttir and Thorsteinn Olafsson got married, resembles monumental buildings from the English Middle Ages; nothing on Icelandic soil comes close to its sophistication and strength. When their wedding was documented in the fall of 1408, there was no sign of a struggling community, as also evidenced by the second-oldest written document from Greenland. In that note, the church announces the death of a man named Kolgrímur, burned alive for trying to seduce a woman with witchcraft. Weddings and funerals—business as usual.

Today, standing in the doorway of the Hvalsey church—now a sheep farm—you can imagine being there on a Sunday, when you could scan the landscape and see people from all directions moving toward the sound of the church's bell. Each week it served as a gathering place for the flourishing Greenland settlement. Until one Sunday, when there were simply no bells. No mass. No people. They were gone.

❦

The disappearance of Greenland's Norse colonies is one of the biggest mysteries of the Middle Ages. Icelanders long assumed that the Greenlanders had been forced out by the Inuit natives. Just as when Gudrid and Karlsefni fled North America. Alleged blue-eyed Inuits were proof that the two tribes had, at some point, mixed together. The black death was another theory on the list of possible cataclysmic events, as was abduction by pirates.

But what really happened was less likely a single devastating blow, and more likely a perfect storm: a variety of exchanges that gradually eroded the Norse economy of trade and agriculture.

To find out what happened to the long-lost Icelandic tribe, I headed out to sea again, moonlighting as a boatswain on a sailing expedition led by Haraldur Sigurdsson. Haraldur has spent much of his adult life as a professor in the United States and speaks Icelandic with a quirky American accent. When I learned how many times he had been married (four), I made a quick note to myself about adopting that accent. Haraldur has a friendly smile and a spry energy; a vociferous learner, he's led the kind of life you may have dreamed of as a child hoping to emulate Indiana Jones. He famously reconstructed the eruption of Vesuvius in Italy; he discovered glass spherules in Haiti that provided proof of a meteorite impact at the time of the dinosaurs' extinction; he uncovered a long-lost town in Indonesia buried by a volcano.

On this trip, we were heading to Scoresby Sound in northern Greenland, where the sea is frozen for all but three months of the year. The community of five hundred people has traditionally made a living hunting on the ice and trading the polar bear furs, narwhal tusks, and walrus skulls that have historically been in demand as pricey living room decor around the world. But no longer. Today, due to a precipitous drop in walrus and other Arctic mammals, international conventions banning the trade of endangered species have limited the market to domestic Greenland alone. Narwhal tusks, once worth their weight in gold, are now offered for as little as seven hundred dollars in local shops. The community's remote location and difficult weather conditions make it hard to reorient the local economy toward another industry.

The Norse colonies suffered in the face of a strikingly similar trend, driven by very different reasons.

In 1234, a British man came home with the teeth of an impossible giant. Elephant tusks had been introduced to the market, and the discovery of this animal by Europeans would devastate the people of Greenland. Their strategy to compensate for the drop in prices of tusks won't come as a surprise: they hunted more walrus. In a 2020 study, researchers from Norway and the University of Cambridge examined sixty-seven walrus tusks taken from sites across Europe, dating from between the eleventh and fifteenth centuries. They detected a change in the tusks' quality around the thirteenth century. By then, the bones were coming from a species of walrus believed to inhabit areas hundreds of miles north of the original hunting grounds; they also came from smaller specimens. This tells us that the hunters of Greenland were digging their own graves by keeping up an unsustainable industry.

At the mouth of Scoresby Sound, we sailed past a place called Walrus Bay, which today has no walruses. Passengers on board were pleased to spot a single seal, at least. The next day, we prepared to go on land, and Haraldur helped me prepare the ship's dinghy. A geologist by trade, he teaches oceanography and volcanology at the University of Rhode Island. No title or discipline fully encompasses his research interests, as more or less all subjects with the suffix -*ology* concern him: geology, archaeology, climatology. Haraldur unfastened the davit lines connected to the dinghy's bow and relaxed them before I was ready. He said he was sorry—ap*ology*.

Our group of six boarded the dinghy and landed on a beach with the remains of stone-made houses that most definitely belonged to an ancient Inuit family. It was most likely just a seasonal residency, as the family traveled in line with seasons and hunting grounds. "For thousands of years, native Greenlanders took incremental steps towards surviving the harsh climate. The Norse arrived fast and never fully learned to adapt," said Haraldur. We know there was a gradual change in the Norse diet. Isotope analyses of the bones of inhabitants show a slow shift, primarily in the balance between seafood (seal, whale, fish) and livestock (sheep and cows). During the eleventh century, sheep and cows, including dairy, were the primary food source. Over time, seafood proportionally grew, and by the 1400s seal and fish had taken over the Norse diet. "The most logical conclusion is a decline in agriculture," said Haraldur. "Gathering hay must have become ever harder, until finally, agriculture completely died out."

The cause of the climate hardship is a more controversial subject of debate. Erik the Red settled in Greenland (and Iceland) during an era of global warming, an era that lasted until the 1600s, when the so-called Little Ice Age began to show up. The Little Ice Age was only an ice age by name, a term used to describe a period of extremely low solar activity, combined with cooling from volcanic aerosols, according to NASA. Did the Little Ice Age wipe out the Greenlanders, as some theories suggest? Haraldur is skeptical because the so-called grand solar minimum, when the sun gives off less energy, appears to have taken place long after the end of Greenland. And while volcanic eruptions have been shown to affect the global climate, they typically only do so for a few years.

The most compelling explanation, according to Haraldur, was laid out by a scholar named William Ruddiman. He argued for a rapid decline in temperatures, prior to the official Little Ice Age, caused by a decline in agriculture in the Northern Hemisphere, and thus a dramatic shift in the rate of release of carbon and methane.

"Many people think greenhouse gases were mainly released into the atmosphere after the industrial revolution," says Haraldur. Ice cores in fact show that carbon dioxide began to appear at greater rates in the atmosphere around eight thousand years ago, parallel to the invention of agriculture and resulting deforestation. Likewise, methane spiked around four thousand years ago, when farmers in East Asia began to use wetlands to grow rice. The agricultural revolution caused

green house gass

massive population growth, and thus the cycle of change grew greater and greater until the world experienced a series of pandemics. The black death and other plagues hit Europe in the fourteenth and fifteenth centuries, and shortly afterward, native people in North and South America were exposed by European settlers to germs completely foreign to their immune systems.

Modern research indicates that these plagues claimed more lives than early documentation suggests. By Ruddiman's theory, these deaths wiped out much of the existing agriculture, reversing the climate trend and eventually causing a temperature decline. By then the Greenland colonies were already struggling, and the sudden shift in climatic conditions delivered the final blow. The black death reached Iceland in 1402 and wiped out nearly two-thirds of the population. The pandemic is not believed to have reached Greenland because no mass graves from the time have been found. And yet "the disease still managed to kill off the Norse population," says Haraldur.

On board the dinghy again, it was my turn to make a mistake. I had loosened the painter rope—a rope used to tie the dinghy to the shore—before starting the outboard engine. This is only an issue if the engine refuses to start right away and, turned loose, the dinghy drifts away, farther and farther away from land. Which is exactly what happened to us. The six passengers stared at the dead engine and then me—their driver—and then the engine again, still dead. "Have you tried opening the ventilation knob?" Haraldur asked in Icelandic, pronouncing the Icelandic word for ventilation, *ventill*, with a *w*. I had not tried that. The engine turned over, and we motored away from shore.

The Medieval Legacy

Iceland from 1100 to 1750

Cattle die and kinsmen die,
thyself too must die,
but one thing never will die,
the fame of one who has done well.

—HÁVAMÁL, AN OLD NORSE POEM OFFERING
ADVICE ON LIVING WELL.

When young Arndis Thorbjarnardóttir arrived in Edinburgh via passenger ship, fresh from Reykjavík, she was prepared to be an au pair for an English family in the countryside. She had never lived away from home before, and the Scottish accent is tough enough as it is. We can imagine her relief, then, when upon finally arriving in Oxford, she was greeted in Icelandic by her new employer, a friendly older man named J. R. R. Tolkien. He picked her up from the railway platform with a smile.

"Gódan dag!" he cried, and the two of them began a rare conversation in Icelandic.

Chatting away, they drove past Oxford University—where Tolkien was merely a professor, not yet one of the most lauded writers of the twentieth century—to Northmoor Road, in the town's leafy suburbs. Earlier in the summer of 1930, the Tolkien family had moved into a grand six-bedroom home there, with enough space to host an Icelandic au pair. Twenty-year-old Arndis would help Mrs. Tolkien with childcare. But in addition to bath time and child wrangling, she would also have the crucial effect of enhancing Mr. Tolkien's already keen interest in the Icelandic folklore.

Tolkien had never been to Iceland—and over the course of his life, he never went—but he admired the nation's medieval stories chronicling brutal kings, brutal Vikings, and brutal mythical creatures. He read the language almost fluently and would chat with Arndis around the house, usually when his wife, Edith, was out of earshot.

"She didn't like to have a secret language spoken around the house," Arndis later recalled. She described Tolkien's wife as "never unkind" but rather unsociable, unlike Tolkien. He was easy and comfortable to be around, and also had a habit of wearing festive colorful waistcoats. He loved nature so ardently that the Tolkiens tore up their house's asphalt tennis court to replace it with grass. And he hated all modern things—even down to the boiler.

She also described Tolkien's chitchat style as "formal," which is perhaps unsurprising considering he learned the language from lyrical texts penned more than eight hundred years earlier. It would be a bit like having light conversation with someone whose entire English education derived from reading Shakespeare. *Good dawning to thee, friend!*

At night Arndis told the children bedtime stories drawn from Icelandic folklore. She told stories of monsters and little trolls with hairy toes, who turned to stone when the light first hit them. Next door, sitting in his study room—"he was always inside the study"—she suspected Tolkien was listening. Whether or not Arndis was the one to introduce Tolkien to certain elements of mythology that later found their way into *The Hobbit*, she knows that "he took lots of ideas from Icelandic folk stories . . . and he really believed that all nature was alive. He lived in a kind of fantasy world."

Life at the house was quiet, and Arndis lamented how little the family did for fun. The only adventures Tolkien had were conducted via his typewriter, as he conjured the fantastical world of Middle Earth. He was clearly inspired by Norse mythology and medieval stories penned by Icelanders during the age of Old Norse. His dwarfs, for example, were skillful with their hands and craftsmanship, just as described in the ancient Icelandic *Eddas*. To top it off, all but one of the hobbits surrounding Bilbo Baggins in Tolkien's epic carry Nordic names.

Colleagues at Oxford presumed Tolkien was producing serious academic papers within his field of philology and linguistics—not "children's books." But Arndis, for her part, was not surprised. She had heard the famous first lines of *The Hobbit*—"In a hole in the ground there lived a hobbit"—in Tolkien's own voice, when he would read the peculiar story to entertain his son Christopher before bedtime.

Arndis left when she "found [herself] thinking in English," but she stayed in touch with the family until World War II. By the end of the war, Reykjavík had grown to the size of Oxford, and she soon settled in Selfoss, the town in the South where today Bobby Fischer is buried. Arndis spoke little about her time as a nanny in England—no one asked—until a neighborhood journalist in Selfoss, a Tolkien fan, heard about her long-gone au pair assignment and interviewed Arndis, by then aged eighty-eight. The interview appeared in *Morgunblaðið*, Iceland's newspaper of record. *The Hobbit*, Arndis affirmed, was still a favorite.

We don't know how significantly Arndis influenced his writing by telling Icelandic stories, or whether she perhaps occasionally helped with translations of folklore. But the reason that Tolkien—a struggling academic at the time—went so far out of his way to hire babysitters was arguably the same reason that ancient kings and modern-day universities have consistently sought Icelandic speakers: they can read stories and scripts written exclusively in Old Norse, a language known today as Icelandic. That very act—reading, writing, and interpreting old scripts—is the oldest profession in Iceland. The monopoly has, for ages, been a lucrative business for the country's educated elite. And we have two men in particular to thank for this—two unlikely heroes, alive centuries apart: thirteenth-century Snorri Sturluson, the man who spent his fortune penning them on calfskin, and the seventeenth-century academic Arni Magnusson, who obsessively hoarded old scripts he'd collected while crossing the country, visiting every farm on the island, traversing epic landscapes like a character in a Tolkien story, only to store them away in a fire-prone tower in Copenhagen.

Without the two bookworms, ruthless in their respective quests, Europe would know less about its own history. Norse mythology—an entire belief system seeking to explain the beginning of time, the purpose of life, the afterlife, and the coming apocalypse—does not exist in conclusive writing outside of Iceland. This Norse ideology of Thor the god of thunder and Odin the god of wisdom—inspiring everything from Richard Wagner operas to Marvel movies—would have died out with the arrival of Christianity had it not been written down, along with Iceland's long list of medieval titles chronicling much of what is known about medieval times in northern Europe.

Icelanders were certainly not the only Europeans who could write in late medieval times. But they wrote more, covering subjects other than Christianity. To begin with, it was to impress the outside world and get on the good side of foreign kings. Then, with the rise of domestic turf wars, it was to impress one another; wealthy Icelanders wrote stories to maintain their status and family power. It was all the result of a political system where no central government held absolute power—only local clansmen competed for influence through stories and foreign support.

❧

Kings, wannabe kings, clansmen, and Christian missionaries were all incredibly busy killing one another in Scandinavia in the medieval age. Small island nations like the Orkney Islands and the Shetland Islands, caught in the cross fire of mainland powerhouses, established large armies to defend their coastlines. Their survival depended on a strong state with high taxes and a large arsenal. The Icelanders, also a small island nation, had no army and, in essence, no government with a monopoly on violence. War in Europe meant peace in remote Iceland. Only during those few moments of cease-fire was Iceland at risk of becoming the obsession of a foreign king, some power-hungry monarch browsing the latest world atlas as if it were a real estate catalog.

Distance was the greatest defense. To discourage ambitious kings even further from pursuing risky missions across the high seas, the country fabricated stories about its mystic risks. This strategy is still depicted on the modern Icelandic krona. On the back of a coin, you'll find the coat of arms, which depicts a bearded giant holding an iron staff in one hand and casually resting the other on a flag shield, looking like the responsible one in a quartet that includes a dragon, an eagle, and a bull.

The drawing is inspired by a tale concerning the tenth-century Danish king Harald Bluetooth, a ruler famous for successfully uniting the tribes of Denmark under Christian rule. Flying high from that victory, he ordered a warlock to go in "some altered form" to check on Iceland. The servant, according to the thirteenth-century book chronicling the story, obediently left Denmark in the shape of a whale (people were more flexible in those days). When he saw the rugged shore of Iceland, things did not look promising: the mountains and hills were full of guardian spirits, "some small, some large." He tried to enter an eastern fjord when a huge dragon rushed down the dale against him with a train of snakes, insects, and toads, all spitting poison at him. He tried again in northern Iceland, but this time he was chased out of the long Eyja Fjord by an enormous eagle with wings that spanned the mountains on either side. The same problem cropped up in the West and the South; a large gray bull ran against him in Breida Fjord; on the southern Reykjanes Peninsula, that tall giant, reaching a head higher than the mountains, chased him out to sea. Just in case this wasn't enough to excuse the warlock's retreat, he adds that "many other giants followed him."

This *alleged* trip—in every meaning of that word—occurred when Iceland's population was somewhere between forty thousand and eighty thousand people. After two centuries of migration, the nation maintained a relatively fixed size, with a population composed of a diverse group of people who had come to seek a new life: wealthy farmers, retired Vikings,

Celtic royalty, mixed-race slaves, and a guy named Geirmundur Heljarskinn (the Black Viking), who said his dad was a Mongolian warlord. The country was a melting pot long before the invention of that culinary-inspired metaphor for a homogeneous society becoming more heterogeneous; travelers from all over came to Iceland to merge into a common culture, one nation. Thanks to its isolation, Iceland evolved on its own terms as the first New World experiment.

For centuries, Iceland did not have a conventionally organized government. Instead, it was a commonwealth ruled by thirty-nine "big men" known as godi (pronounced go-thi). Each godi acted as a miniking—the king of a fjord—with his authority limited to a specific region. But people living within his region did not, by default, owe him any support. The representation was rather a mutual agreement between the godi and a farmer, who in turn spoke for everyone living on his farm.

To be eligible for representation, the farmer had to own at least one cow or six sheep for every resident on his farm. So if a farmer with six people at his house owned, say, two cows and twenty-four sheep, he could cast his support behind the godi representative of his choice. He could even swap and move his support to someone else. The godi would occasionally collect a commission for service he provided, like dividing a will or settling a dispute. He was, in effect, something more like a lawyer; he was first among equals in the region, with little authority to boss people around. The German legend Adam of Bremen put it this way: "The Icelanders have no king except the law."

The godi's help was, for the most part, repaid by the farmer with political support. Each year, around summer solstice, "every ninth man" followed his godi to a beautiful lake-filled region known today as the fields of parliament, or þingvellir (theeng-vehdl-ir). During the two weeks that parliament, or Alþingi (ahl-theeng-i), was in session, attendees set themselves up as if in an outdoor camping festival. People could catch up on the latest news from around the country, congratulate those who had made it to North America and back, buy and sell wares, do a little dance, make a little love, all while carrying out their duties as members of parliament. One of their tasks was to establish what day of the year it was.

This minifestival that sprang up as part of parliamentary activities wasn't simply fun; it created a sense of community. As historian Björn Thorsteinsson puts it, "Icelanders abandoned the role of country dwellers and felt like citizens for those two weeks of the year."

Now the oldest surviving parliament in the world, sessions at the eleventh-century Alþingi were more like a United Nations general assembly than a democratic legislature. All thirty-nine chieftains held equal power, and the balance of power meant that no single chieftain could strong-arm his way to the top. He lobbied for his own interests, or those of his network. Legislation was passed only by virtue of large alliances. The power of each godi was rooted in his personal charisma, and to really flex his parliamentary muscles, he had to show off as a great orator in order to be both heard and remembered. The best ones could be voted in as law speakers, orators whose job it was, before the arrival of the written word, to memorize and proclaim the laws of Iceland out loud. The role of law speaker was of the highest honor, and he was the nation's only paid servant. The job demanded a strong voice; every year he would declaim one third of the existing laws so that others could learn them over a span of three years, the length of his term. His podium was a rock: the Law Rock.

For two hundred years, this relatively anarchic system was held together by the equilibrium of a population that was more or less equally wealthy—or rather, equally poor. The Alþingi continued to govern the nation where law was king for centuries, finding ways to address conflicts without military force. Parliament weathered transformations and tidal shifts that could have torn other nations apart. Christianity was ushered in with a minor spillage of blood. The occasional cat-and-mouse game with a foreign king sometimes threatened peace. But when threats did appear, the country tended to handle them with grace—and even a dash of humor.

When the Alþingi heard that the cheeky Harald Bluetooth had illegally seized the cargo of a shipwrecked Icelandic vessel, it promptly passed a law in response. This law demanded that for "every nose in the country" there would be composed one níðvísa, or slanderous verse, about King Harald. A popular níðvísa, a lyrical insult, had the potential to weaken admiration and loyalty toward the king, essentially serving the same purpose as a scandalous news story. Iceland had enshrined shit talking as official state policy. Unfortunately, the joke went sour when Bluetooth began seizing ships from Iceland and, to add insult to injury, enslaving their crews. Harald couldn't take a joke, and Icelanders backpedaled hard. They not only repealed the law, they made it punishable—by death!—to compose a verse mocking the kings of Denmark, Sweden, or Norway. (There was seldom anything funny about the kings of Norway anyway.)

The slanderous verses didn't take a bite out of Bluetooth's

power, and his reputation as the great unifier of Denmark lives on to this day, with a wireless technology named after him. In fact, the Bluetooth logo—the symbol you press to connect the technology—is made from Harald's runic initials, H and ᛒ.

With only *nice things* now allowed, Iceland had inadvertently launched a new industry. It quickly became the source for propagandists-for-hire for foreign statesmen. Icelanders had the appropriate distance and the Norse language skills required to access the powerful and wealthy in Scandinavia, and perhaps most important, stretching back to the early days of settlement, Icelanders had enjoyed a good reputation as skáld: poets.

The greatest skáld of all was Snorri Sturluson. Snorri had been trained for the role from an early age in the old Oddi school. Writing interested him, but not the frugal, spiritual life that tended to come with it. His plan was to own Iceland, while enjoying a bit of writing on the side. And he almost pulled it off. But Snorri's rapid rise at the dawn of the thirteenth century heralded forty-four years of conflict, still the bloodiest decades in Iceland's history. The war ended with a single warrior left standing, who then signed power over to a Norwegian king, bringing an end to the Icelandic Commonwealth.

❦

Civil wars, in modern academic literature, are explained as meltdowns of greed and grievances. One segment of society, the oppressed and poor, watch other tribes or regions grow richer and richer. The status quo is eventually unbearable for the oppressed group, and when they are so desperate that they finally feel there's nothing to lose, hell breaks loose. The tipping point is unpredictable, but once the lid is off, violence spreads. Fast.

The battle for Iceland was a perfect example of this formula. New money, accumulated by a select few, gradually eroded the godi system. But the events that eventually kicked off a bloodbath took more than a century to unfold, and they started, specifically, when the bishop of Iceland rode his horse to Alþingi in 1096.

Bishop Gissur Ísleifsson knew how to read and write, in a country where most men could not even pee their name in the snow. This was an A for Advantage. Bishop Ísleifsson was also ahead of the curve in mathematics. He figured the church needed revenue streams in order to build places for worship, educate priests, aid the poor, and to make donations to the Vatican. His idea? A nationwide tax, the tithes. Despite its name, the tithes required everyone to give 1 percent of their assets to the church. Taxation of that kind had been met with forceful opposition elsewhere in Europe, where it generally meant 10 percent of income instead of wealth. But the men gathered at Alþingi that day unanimously agreed to do the bishop a favor and install the tax code. What's 1 percent of Iceland's capital anyway? One out of a hundred. Can't be that bad, can it?

The wealth tax changed everything—by making power *fluid*. Before the institution of the tithes, there was not much that farmers and godi chieftains could do to enrich themselves or accumulate wealth. Even slavery, popular elsewhere, wasn't a path to enrichment in Iceland. Agrarian land was limited and the work was seasonal. Slaves, who would have been taken from the British Isles and Norway, didn't ultimately produce more than they cost to keep alive. The feudal system dominated instead: the poor rented property, accumulated debt over the long winter, and paid it off during good summers.

The tithes were meant to fund the church, but who would collect the money in a country without a government and no prior tradition of taxes?

Any godi chieftain who had a relationship with the church—such as those who owned property upon which a church stood—had suddenly hit the jackpot. They would be the conduit through which all the church-bound money flowed. And naturally, these godi urged their friends and enemies to donate their wealth "to the church," especially when they passed away. Best to just give all assets "to the church." Suddenly churches had become the means by which chieftains could accumulate wealth and therefore power. Empowered by this new cash flow, some members of the godi establishment could now afford to intimidate rival chieftains and buy up property in the region, either to expand their own base or place a relative in charge. In the new era, the godi chieftains began to change from purely localized powers to regional ones.

In the midst of this rising plutocracy, one of the nation's most important historians emerged. Born around 1178, Snorri Sturluson grew up in a country that had split in two. The entire region to the South, below the highland glaciers, was controlled by just three families. The rest of the country was still controlled by chieftains from various backgrounds. Snorri's father was a big-time godi until he lost a feud over who would inherit a valuable farm. In return, as a diplomatic gesture, the leader of the southern Oddi family, Jón Loftsson, offered to foster one of his sons. Thus, three-year-old Snorri grew up on Jón's farm at Oddi, one of the wealthiest church estates in the country. Jón was, correspondingly, the wealthiest man. He also ran the oldest school in Iceland, and Snorri set his mind to mastering law and language.

With this kind of tutelage and support, over his lifetime Snorri Sturluson managed to write some of the most important texts of the era: the *Heimskringla*, *The Prose Edda*, and *Egil's Saga*, three canonical works which defined the medieval worldview. His work has been translated into multiple languages, and the different editions' introductions typically make sure to highlight the works' significant contribution to our modern understanding of Western history. Then, as is usual in book introductions, the passage closes with a few words about the author. And that's when things tend to get awkward.

The introduction may announce, for example, that the reader holds a book written by a man who was "extremely crafty and sly, erratic in friendship, disloyal even to his closest relatives, covetous no less than ambitious, as well as being an aggressor and vengeful, erratic and contentious," to quote the early Danish edition of *Heimskringla*. Snorri was, to say the least, a flawed character. This quickly becomes clear in the biography of the Sturlungs family, named *Sturlunga* and written by Snorri's nephew, Sturla Thordarson. Given the way things turned out for the Sturlungs, the nephew was not all that amicable toward Snorri, specifically going out of his way to humiliate his uncle as he relayed his political exploits. The book is not a saga with a capital *S*; those depict Viking settlers, alive two hundred years earlier. With the *Sturlunga* saga, Sturla was trying to explain—perhaps even to himself—how his family, along with all the other Icelandic chieftains, wound up destroying themselves.

When Snorri was twenty, his wealthy foster father, Jón, passed away. It was time to move back home. West Iceland was, by then, the only quarter not ruled by a single-family clan. Snorri turned out to be the right man in the right place at the right time. The regional leaders were eager to gather behind a strongman before some outsider attempted to take over. Snorri quickly took over multiple godi positions and maintained an excellent relationship with the church. He, personally, was not religious at all, judging from his writing, and not a great believer in marriage either: he fathered three children with mistresses before he and his wife, Herdis, divorced.

His only god was power, pure and simple. His old foster family, the Oddi, supported his efforts throughout, assuming that his takeover would benefit them as well. But they were mistaken. Snorri saw them not as family but as opportunity. At the time, the Oddi were linked to the merchants from the (Scottish) Orkney Islands, and competed with Norwegian traders. Snorri saw a game that would make the Norwegians more dependent on him. He ordered the Orkney dealers to be detained, and antagonized the Oddi family into taking action against the Norwegians as a result. The Norwegians in Iceland suddenly needed more protection, and soon enough, a hand tapped Snorri's shoulder and invited him to visit the Norwegian king himself.

That Norwegian king was a small but bright fourteen-year-old, with one year of experience. Snorri, on the other hand, was a savvy, divorced, thirty-nine-year-old playboy. He was the father of four children with four women, embarking on a four-year trip around Norway and Sweden. It was something like a festive sabbatical for the Icelandic charmer; as he traveled, he gathered stories for a forthcoming book about the history of Scandinavian kings. The *Heimskringla*, "The Circle of the World."

The appropriate subtitle for *Heimskringla* (pronounced hayms-khreenglah) would be something like *The World According to Norsemen*. Through stories spanning the beginning of Scandinavian kingdoms, Snorri cast a gallery of kings, their successes and defeats, agents and enemies. In a chronological arrangement, Snorri details how he knows his stuff, either by citing source material or by vetting the credibility of his oral source and his proximity to a particular event—he may have heard from his own father, who in turn had a father with first-hand knowledge.

The epic saga was not only a chronicle of centuries of northern European history, it also had two fundamentally opportunistic goals.

First was the local message, hidden between the lines. Snorri was first and foremost an Icelandic politician—a two-time law speaker who believed in keeping friends close and enemies closer. Ever since the conversion to Christianity, Scandinavian kings had tried to meddle in local politics in pursuit of territory and taxation. Local resistance had not been unanimous: kings were admired, even worshipped reified figures, and some members of parliament (MPs) were eager to fulfill their wishes. Snorri relays one anecdote, set in parliament before his day, wherein the MPs debated a proposition to donate an island, Grímsey, to the Norwegian king.

The law speaker at the time opposed the gift with a persuasive speech about the fallible nature of kings—a good king is fair and peaceful; a bad king is greedy for taxes and vengeance. And because one can never be sure which of the two is next in line, it is best not to be ruled by them. Snorri, for his part, didn't want to be ruled by kings (or anybody), but he knew they were powerful, and he wanted to establish amicable relationships with them.

Second, the ambitious book was a sort of calling card for Iceland, establishing it as the best publishing house out there. At the time, Scandinavian kings were increasingly taking their business to their fellow Christians in southern Europe, commissioning Latin speakers in Venice and elsewhere to document their achievements and praises. By outshining the competition, Snorri aimed to wrest back control of the praise business. In that sense, it was a slam dunk. Soon enough, Norse, not Latin, became the language of choice for Scandinavian texts.

Snorri finished his grand tour back in Bergen, home of the teenage king Hákon. Snorri, however, dealt mostly with the de facto leader, Duke Skule. His blossoming friendship with the duke was, in the end, an unfortunate move; but for the time being, it served to avoid a Norwegian invasion of Iceland. Duke Skule was keen on sending forces to Iceland in response to scattered attacks on Norwegian merchants. Snorri managed to convince Skule that he would make things right, and he even promised to increase Norway's sway over the trade sphere.

In 1220, having assured the duke and Norwegian king that he would vouch for them back in Iceland, Snorri sailed to

Iceland on a brand-new ship, courtesy of the Norwegians. This was the year historians regard as the beginning of the Age of the Sturlungs warfare.

❀

Snorri Sturluson is to Iceland what Aristotle is to Greece and Dante is to Italy: an admired thinker and pioneer of the written word. But without the glowing literary reviews, his legacy would be a lot more problematic. He'd be the man who owned half of Iceland at the dawn of its civil war, counting his money in a glamorous villa, reluctant to share his fortune with his children and relatives. In fact, he tended to treat his children as assets by marrying them into powerful families outside his stronghold, extending his network of godi chieftains. He married a woman named Hallveig Ormsdóttir, conveniently the widow of the nation's second-richest man. They moved to the Steam Valley in western Iceland and embarked on a three-year building extravaganza.

Snorri's estate—named Reykholt—is ground zero for archaeological research in Iceland. Its excavation dates back to 1937, when construction workers, attempting to break ground for a nearby sports hall, stumbled upon hidden underground tunnels, supported by stones.

Over the last three decades, the University of Iceland has been actively unearthing layers of settlement history and has provided an extraordinary picture of Snorri's settlement. So far, we know of a wooden church, most likely made from the oak of an old ship; at least two sleeping cabins and a communal living room; an outdoor iron smelter, erected far from the other buildings in order to prevent fires; a garbage dump, containing traces of barley; and, perhaps most interesting, a channel 122 yards long, which siphoned water from a nearby hot spring into a small house whose purpose is unknown. Studies suggest that the water, running such a long distance in an open stream, would be too cold for the house to be a steam bath. Yet the amount of steam that still would've accumulated inside would have made it difficult to remain in there for any extended period of time. Outside the house, in what appears to be a dump, insects known to live in crops have been discovered. All this suggests that the steamy house may have been used for brewing mead, which can be done at a fairly low temperature, perhaps aided by fire. Snorri, it seems, was so rich he had his own on-site craft brewery.

Much of these findings match the farm's contemporary description from the *Sturlunga*, which also claims the estate was fenced in with a fortlike entrance. And then there were the underground tunnels leading from the main building, through a hill, toward the most famous landmark on the property: the pool of Snorri. The tunnels might have served as an emergency escape route, but more likely they were simply a decadent way to enter the pool by avoiding a walk outside.

The pool still remains. Or at least a *version* of the round-shaped, stone-lined outdoor bath still stands, first described in detail by an eighteenth-century writer. Whether this is really the same pool Snorri bathed in as described in the *Sturlunga* is unclear.

"The actual pool of Snorri was most likely a natural lagoon, heated with runoff water from the nearby hot spring," claims archaeologist Gudrún Sveinbjarnardóttir, author of three books about the Reykholt excavations. In any case, we can be sure that Snorri took baths outdoors somewhere. The area indeed has plenty of hot springs, including Europe's largest, the Deildartunguhver hot spring. And (in my own experience), relaxing in warm water on a cold winter night is the best cure for writer's block, a place where fresh ideas arrive from nowhere. Hence, sometime after moving into his remote poolside mansion, Snorri went on to write one of the most important books in Europe's history: the book of Norse gods.

Iceland's great apostasy in AD 1000, when the Alþingi approved the abandonment of heathen laws and adopted a Christian code, marked the decline of Norse mythology. Christians, aided by the Norwegian king, managed to suppress a majority's religious practice until it dwindled to a secret cult. According to the new laws, worshipping Thor, Odin, Freyr, Baldur, and all the other Norse Gods was indeed still allowed, but only *in secret*. Very clever. Instead of banning the practice altogether and risk a revolt, Christians used a method more similar to an antismoking policy: you can still do it . . . in shame. Alone.

Generations passed, and the church's influence grew stronger. Knowledge of the Viking worldview was passed on in the oral tradition, now detached from any spiritual meaning. The lore was bundled into poems, memorized by each generation. Among the lengthy poems, the most famous is the *Völuspá*, believed to have been authored around the year AD 1000, given its Christian influence. It chronicles the world of Norse gods from the beginning of time, in sixty known stanzas. It's told in the voice of a woman who can see both the beginning of time as well as the future Ragnarök, a cataclysmic event wherein the gods meet in an apocalyptic battle, determining the future of humanity:

Brothers will struggle and slaughter each other,
and sisters' sons spoil kinship's bonds.
It's hard on earth: great whoredom;
axe-age, blade-age, shields are split;
wind-age, wolf-age, before the world crumbles:
no one shall spare another.
        —*Translated by Andy Orchard*

Two hundred years into the age of Christianity, Snorri had an idea that was nothing short of revolutionary: a storybook relaying the oral histories of the Norse gods, gathered from here and there, compiled into a single narrative with twists and turns and a cohesive arc, spanning from the creation of the earth to the looming apocalypse. *The Prose Edda.*

"For someone raised in a society of oral traditions," says medieval scholar Gísli Sigurdsson, "Snorri took an extraordinary leap and basically invented the literary format as we know it."

Nothing in Europe at that time prefigured his style of writing in a narrative form with realistic dialogue, one that relied on source material, intended not for God but the general public, all in a language understood by the masses, rather than the clergy's Latin. He, in other words, was a secular scholar long before such a thing existed in Europe, roughly a century before the Renaissance began in Florence. He's also believed to have pioneered the practice of writing sagas with the narrative form we recognize today: one with a beginning, middle, and end. Without him, Norse mythology would be unknown to the modern man, lost to time like so many other oral myths. You might even say he invented the historical novel.

Snorri actually planned his *Edda* as a textbook framed as a

Christian account of Nordic mythology. He cleverly arranged the stories in such a way as to avoid any criticism that they clashed with Christian orthodoxy. He relays the stories of the Norse gods as though they were real events that, over time, were exaggerated into myth.

The *Edda* has four parts: a prologue, and then three books. The prologue describes the Nordic gods as human Trojan warriors who traveled to northern Europe after the fall of Troy. Odin, the god of wisdom, knew that they'd be glorified up north, so "he made ready to journey out of Turkland." Namely, our most comprehensive account of the origins of Nordic mythology portrays Odin as a Turkish immigrant. Additionally, he and the other gods are depicted as human and living on a place on earth called Midgard, a place surrounded by an "impassable" ocean, guarded by a monstrous sea serpent. Odin and other would-be gods eventually make their way to Asgard, a place protected by a gated bridge, to keep out the giants, monsters, and humans living above and below.

The first book, called *Gylfaginning*, is a more detailed account of the gods and mythology. Again, Snorri has to relay all this within a kind of secondhand framing device to avoid trouble, so the book tells the story of King Gylfi of Sweden. Gylfi tries to travel to Asgard, but he winds up in a huge mysterious palace instead. There he is met by three men: High, Just-as-High, and Third. The three men challenge him to display his wisdom by asking questions, a common trope in Norse sagas. Gylfi proceeds to ask questions about all aspects of Norse mythology and the gods, giants, elves, and dwarfs; the good and bad, the wise and stupid.

Destined for fame as comic book heroes, the Norse gods

used their superpowers to defeat evil beasts. Thor, the eldest son of the all-knowing Odin, creates lightning bolts and thunder as he flies through the sky on a chariot pulled by two goats. While traveling away from the home, he can slaughter the goats at night for a meal and then bring them back to life the next morning by pointing his trademark hammer at their bones. He lives in a palace with 540 rooms. He owns gloves made of iron. At one point, while fighting the Midgard Serpent, he drinks from the ocean to slake his thirst, chugging so much that the seas shrink. Later, the Midgard Serpent turns itself into a giant cat, which Thor, of course, defeats. "No wise man can recount all his achievements," Gylfi is told in *Gylfaginning*.

The second book, *Skáldskaparmál*, is composed of a dialogue between Ægir, a god of the sea, and Bragi, a god of poetry. Their conversation covers both Nordic myth and the nature of poetry, explaining for the reader how poetic language works and how to use more floral, less prosaic language. Bragi especially focuses on the origin of various kennings. Kennings were figures of speech used in Icelandic poetry, a collection of compound words and phrases providing a thesaurus of metaphors. Kennings are a great place to look if you are trying to find the exact intersection of poetry and hyperviolence. Here are a few fine examples: "blood-ember" is the kenning for axe. "Wound-sea" means blood, "feed the eagle" means to kill one's enemies, a "swan of blood" is a raven, the "whale's way" is the sea, and "wave swine" means ship. Mix those together and you're halfway to an Icelandic skáld.

Finally, the *Háttatal* closes the *Edda* by demonstrating various types of verse form using Snorri's own compositions. He plays with the numbers of syllables per line, assonance, consonance, alliteration, and (to some extent) end rhyme. If you wanted to break into the art of writing in the thirteenth century, the *Eddas* were gold for poetry (or to use a couple of kennings, "tears of Freyja" for "Grimnir's lip streams").

Snorri had essentially compiled a theory of poetic verse. His work, however, came at the end of the tradition of praise poetry, and his attempts to revive skaldic verse weren't quite successful. Poetic compositions honoring kings moved from oral traditions to a literary activity, so skaldic poetry was being replaced by the written prose saga. A new genre, the ríma, was emerging as the new means of entertainment. A ríma was a rhyming, alliterative epic poem with two to four lines per stanza. *Ormar's Rímur* details the adventures of Ormar, whose father was slain by giants. Ormar gets a sword from his dead father, chops up one giant, gets himself a beautiful wife as a result, and then goes on to chop up a bunch more people, including slicing his father's killers in half. To put it another way, skaldic verse was replaced by a tradition of saying a couple of short lines and kennings that rhymed, with special attention paid to their rhythm and pleasing sound, to detail a guy's ventures getting revenge, money, and beautiful women. So launched the first rap.

❀

Being the avid politician he was, Snorri neglected his own family. His two brothers, however, wanted a taste of the power associated with the family name, and passed that desire down to their children. Coming of age as a promising, if grossly overconfident, leader, one of the Snorri's nephews, Sturla, began intimidating outside clansmen traveling through his region.

His first move was against a man named Gissur, who becomes important in this story later on. Sturla arrested Gissur and planned to send him abroad. But the plan flopped, and Gissur, angered, allied himself with northern clan leaders against the power-hungry Sturla. Their dramatic and long-awaited confrontation finally took place a year later, at Örlygsstaðir.

As you look over the vast landscape today, with no trees and just a few sheep cropping on yellow grass, it is hard to imagine 1,700 men gathered on their horses for the legendary Örlygsstaðir battle. According to the chronicle, Sturla arrived with a spear that had previously belonged to a famed settler some three hundred years earlier. That is to say, he arrived at the battle of his life with an antique weapon. He fiddled with the weapon and "placed the spear under his feet a few times to straighten it out." The last thing he saw was Gissur's axe, heading straight for his head.

Amid all these growing tensions, Snorri had decided to take a trip abroad to avoid armed confrontation. According to the mythology relayed in the *Edda*, those who die on the battlefield await a good life in Valhalla, the house of the gods. Unfortunately for Snorri, he was not exactly a paragon of traditional masculinity. He was a terrible soldier who sought to expand his power without ever lifting a sword. That aphorism about the pen being mightier did, in the long run, not work well in an era when everyone else was holding a sword (or to use one more kenning, a "wound hoe").

He was in Norway with his friend Duke Skule when he heard about the Örlygsstaðir battle and the death of his nephew. Much of his extended family was now dead, and Snorri, in typical fashion, saw that as an opportunity to reclaim his previously held power. Duke Skule, meanwhile, was plotting a battle of his own to overthrow the king. Norway was emerging as the largest power in Europe, and Duke Skule sought to include Iceland in their ride to the top by making Snorri a duke over Iceland. Snorri thus left Norway unofficially supporting a coup. Unfortunately for him, the coup collapsed, and the king executed Skule in 1240. By then, Snorri had reclaimed much of his domain without making too many enemies. He never imagined that his sideshow in Norwegian politics would catch up with him.

Snorri's last words are something every Icelandic schoolchild memorizes, a favorite subject of elementary quizzes. I remember them from a poster hanging in my elementary school that depicted Snorri dressed in a brown gown, defenseless, holding his hands above his head before a man holding an axe, his mouth gaping from underneath a white beard: "Eigi skal höggva!"—Do not strike! In the picture, Snorri is outside the tunnel to his home, next to the Snorralaug Pool, which became Iceland's first registered archaeological monument. In reality, according to the biography, he was axed to death inside his basement, after a home invasion on a September night. The invader was Gissur, that quiet traveler, now the Norwegian king's contact-man. The king had requested that Gissur bring the traitor to Norway, or else have him killed.

The murder of Snorri Sturluson was the equivalent of the assassination of Abraham Lincoln or Franz Ferdinand. Big men. Big consequences. Hotheads filled the vacuum Snorri's death created, and the civil war erupted to new heights. Regional leaders began traveling around surrounded by small armies of bodyguards. The civil war's first and only naval battle was fought with rocks flying between twenty ships off the northern coast. The violence was senseless and overwhelming: hands and limbs were chopped off the relatives of victims to avoid retaliation. Farms were lit on fire with everyone trapped inside. But despite the escalating chaos, Gissur always got away safely. In one case of arson that killed twenty-five people, including his wife, he escaped death by hiding in a barrel of sour whey, a kind of fridge for a farm's food supplies. He was an antihero, the evil mastermind orchestrating the king's plot to rule over Iceland, and soon the last man standing. He introduced a declaration known as the Old Covenant, which signed the country over to the king.

And with that, the Iceland free state, 350 years of living without a king, ended. Chieftains lost their executive power to agents of the crown. They retained some of their legislative powers at Alþingi, but the legislature merely served to support the king's agenda. The king introduced a new lawbook called *Járnsíða*, banning personal retaliations, and introduced taxes and fines. Laws could not be made without the king's approval. Snorri had predicted all this when he wrote, speaking through the old Arinbjörn Thorirsson in *Egil's Saga*, that "the king's treasury has a wide entrance, but a narrow exit."

Independence took another seven hundred years.

❀

The history of the Middle Ages is a pretty spotty narrative: one day, a ruthless civil war; the next . . . nothing. It's as if the writer of history ran out of vellum and died waiting for the farm's oldest cow to provide the ending. Or the book was passed on, between farms and generations, like a dog-eared library copy with missing pages. There's no rhyme or reason for how some events get documented, and others are lost to the passage of time. Geologists have unearthed ash from massive volcanic eruptions that are never mentioned in writing. Genetic research shows the population of Iceland gradually became more Norwegian, with an unexplained decline among the Celtic quarter. Greenland settlers just suddenly disappeared from the pages.

But it's possible that those events and explanations were all jotted down. Skin is more durable than papyrus fabric, and it can survive the rough and humid storage of cold turf houses, as well as being handled by dirty fingers again and again. But the strength of skin was also its downside—it could be used for other things around the house! Wrap it around a knife and you have an excellent holster to carry around. Poke a hundred holes through the pages and you have a strainer for millet. Done reading? Use the pages as patches for the family's clothing and the knowledge is lost forever, into what the Norse gods called ginnungagap, the bottomless abyss, the empty universe prior to the creation of the cosmos and into which the cosmos will collapse once again during apocalyptic Ragnarök.

About seven hundred vellum manuscripts have survived into the modern age. The golden age of writing peaked after Snorri's death, and when the period ended, Iceland had a library without parallel. Elsewhere in Europe, writing was the exclusive trade of religious scholars and royal servants. The Icelandic library had an authorship far more diverse, and the country's contribution was, to an extent, dramatic in its relative size. Chieftains wrote the sagas to underscore their authority and promote stories of their own relatives.

Entertainment was more important than accuracy to grab attention and knock out rival tales.

All that jockeying for power had led to a lot of writing, but once the king took over, competition among regions and chieftains decreased; hence the pissing contests stopped. Writing simply went out of fashion.

At least that's one theory. Another factor may have been Iceland's radical economic and population decline, beginning with the plague. The bacterial strain known as the black death ravaged northern Europe for fifty years—wiping out two thirds of Norway and half of England—until at last it reached the southern shore of Iceland in the spring of 1402. Isolation, in the end, provided no protection from the spread of the deadliest pandemic recorded in human history.

The plague attacked rich and poor, old and young, altering the distribution of wealth and power far more significantly than political forces. The Norwegian royal family, for starters, pretty much died out. The king married a ten-year-old Danish princess, Margrét. They had a son, Hákon, and through a series of events and inheritance issues Norway merged with Denmark under Danish command. Sweden joined, briefly, creating the Norse-speaking power block some modern politicians still dream of. But soon enough, the Kalmar Union—founded at Kalmar, the Swedish seaside town—collapsed, and Denmark and Sweden were sucked into endless wars.

Icelanders had little to say. Anyway, it made little difference to Iceland whether the orders came down from Norway or Denmark. There was one big order, though, which they ignored at their peril: convert to Lutheranism.

The cataclysmic conversion to Lutheranism was officially taken care of by an executioner in broad daylight on

November 7, 1550, at Skálholt, the episcopal see of the Catholic church and a South Iceland landmark. The attackers, under the wing of the Danish king, captured the last Catholic bishop on his knees and chopped his head off, effectively ending 550 years of Catholic reign.

The Catholic Church, with its own sources of revenue collection, had become a microstate owning much of the most valuable land, a fleet of ships, gold and silver, church bells, weapons, horses, books—all of which now belonged to the Lutheran Church, merged with the Danish kingdom. By grabbing church control, the king took over 17 percent of land properties in one swipe. The government then further tightened its grip by cracking down on what was left of the old heathen culture, including the knowledge of runic letters.

The concept of "runes" does not refer to a single language, but a set of ancient writing systems used in various Germanic languages. They were the dominant writing form until the Christianization of Europe led to the rise of the Latin alphabet, but in Nordic countries, they hung on to runes for a few centuries longer than in continental Europe. The runes are a series of characters, typically carved, with each representing a phoneme (the smallest unit of sound in language). But they were also much more than that.

Unlike characters in the Latin alphabet, runes could represent entire words or even phrases. And each runic symbol represents a different cosmological principle: they are sounds *and* words *and* concepts. When people wrote down runes, they were not simply recording information; they were also *invoking*, calling upon the powers that each rune stood for. Runes were not merely discursive tools; they were potent means of affecting the material world as well. We see this demonstrated in *Egil's Saga*, when Egil uses runes along with a protective spell to shatter a poisoned cup at a feast—runes have a material effect.

Iceland used the runic alphabet known as the Younger Futhark, which is composed of just sixteen runes. If we look at the runes that created Harald Bluetooth's initials and Bluetooth's modern logo, we have ᛒ, meaning "birch," symbolizing fertility and growth (as well as the sound of *B*), while ᚼ meant "hail" and symbolized destruction or chaos (and the sound of *H*). They were, in short, mystic symbols and not the foundation of complicated storytelling (the sagas are penned entirely in Roman letters).

While knowledge of runes disappeared, the clampdown reaching a peak in the witch trials of the 1600s, converting to Lutheranism drastically improved literacy and education. After all, Martin Luther had preached a religion based on unfiltered knowledge of the holy word; people were to read the Bible, not learn the gospel through human figures. The conversion to Lutheranism thus gave rise to increased literacy, education, and a renewed interest in the "antiquarian" studies of old things. Icelanders began examining their own history, and at the dawn of the Renaissance, the first-ever chronological history of Iceland, *Crymogæa* by Arngrimur the Learned, was published, in 1609.

Nothing in Iceland was ever valuable unless it could be traded abroad, for big money, and in this new era of literacy, Icelanders suddenly found themselves in the possession of scripts desired by foreign kings. Precious medieval artifacts recorded on vellum were fast disappearing, doomed by the material's utility.

That is why Iceland's most universally praised national hero is a dry and colorless librarian.

❦

In 1701, Copenhagen was a burgeoning city fortress of sixty thousand, a seaside capital enclosed by canals and high walls with just four gates. The streets were narrow and crowded, lined on each side by cramped, timber-framed buildings, though strewn among the city were architectural jewels. Copenhagen held the Renaissance-style Frederiksborg Palace, symmetrical baroque gardens, and Gothic churches. The University of Copenhagen, the second oldest institute of higher education in Scandinavia, had the Round Tower astronomical observatory, where the speed of light was first quantified. The texts held in the university's library compiled just about everything we knew about the world so far, and somewhere in the bowels of that vast monument to intellectualism was the office of Professor Arni Magnusson.

This particular morning, a letter had arrived for him. From the king.

Arni was a self-made man in Copenhagen, that city of opportunities. He had left his native Iceland at twenty to study divinity. His interest in the gospel stemmed primarily from a love of old scripts rather than religious devotion. He came late to the hobby of manuscript collection. Rival antiquarians had accumulated the largest and most valuable codices, found at churches and official establishments around Europe, and had set up workshops where the copying busywork was delegated to assistants. After completing his education, Arni had the edge of knowing Old Norse, the language that had died out everywhere in Scandinavia except isolated Iceland. Denmark, Sweden, and Norway had evolved regional languages over time, influenced by their global position. The Icelandic that Arni had learned while growing up wasn't the same dialect as the Icelandic spoken by Snorri Sturluson and the saga writers, but the versions were closely enough related for the stories to be readily understood.

Through his roommate at school, Arni was hired as an assistant to the Danish royal antiquarian to transcribe and translate thousands of pages of Icelandic material. The diligent and detailed work he accomplished in his years of apprenticeship alone would have been enough to demarcate him as a great scholar. His practice of transcribing material word for word, including abbreviations and original spellings, was above and beyond the standards of his times.

"And that is the way of the world," he wrote early on, confidently explaining his methods. "Some men put *erroribus* (errors) into circulation, and others afterwards try to eradicate those same *erroribus*. And from this both sorts of men remain busy."

He used multiple copies of the same story to compare them for accuracy, noted where scripts came from, and recorded every peculiar detail about the calligraphy and words written in the margins, whether it was commentary from the writer or notes from previous readers. Two scripts in his collection have childlike stick figures drawn at the bottom by some unknown previous owner, smiling at Arni's "serious and contemplative" manner and his blue eyes, which expressed the "shadow of hidden things in his heart," as one colleague later described him. An apparently melancholy and thoughtful man, his sad face is known as the one-hundred-krona man to every Icelander old enough to have shopped for candy before 1994. His portrait, which was formerly featured on the one-hundred-krona bill, appeared so sad that he was eventually, after a period of inflation, replaced by a fish.

The royal antiquarian passed away suddenly, at a young age, and Arni was left selling his large collection of vellum and manuscripts. The paper copies had value themselves as text ready for print, and Arni kept most of the Icelandic pieces. He proceeded to work for a Danish statesman, Matthias Moth, whose sister was a mistress to the king. This unconventional proximity to the highest power put Arni in a position to influence Icelandic affairs, including trade deals and political positions. In return for his various favors, he asked to be paid in scripts. He traveled to Germany, Norway, and Sweden to gather scripts from local collectors, some for Danish royal libraries, some for himself. After twenty years of charming the Copenhagen elite, he was finally made professor, with his own chair inside a glorious building, those years of unsteady travel and poor income behind him. What could possibly interrupt such a fine life?

Ah. Right. The letter.

In writing, the king requested Arni to set sail "with the first possible ship" to . . . Iceland.

No. No, no, no. Arni loved being Icelandic, but he *hated* Iceland. It was no place for a scholar. Through his political connections, he kept a close eye on Iceland's current affairs and had only a year earlier described, in a letter to a Norwegian friend, how Iceland had "only the worst of news, sheep widely extinct, people passing away, ravaged by famine, in the immense depth of snow." That dire situation had only escalated. Europe was under a cold spell, known now as the Little Ice

Age, which was felt most acutely at the edge of the continent. Fjords and bays were frozen over, and the coastline facing the Arctic Ocean was blocked by drifting icebergs. Fishing was impossible. Ships carrying food could not navigate the ice. Horses were too skinny for travel. Wool was in short supply.

"Even farmers and their children walk around in the frost with much bare skin," a man named Sigurdur Bjornsson relayed in a letter to the Danish authorities, before proceeding to handily blame the entire situation on the homeless. God, he explained, had no other option than to punish the country for all the drifters going around, lying and stealing, unable to hold jobs.

Bombarded with sentimental accounts of Iceland's annus horribilis, King Frederick IV was either touched or frustrated. He had just taken the crown from his father, and his request to Arni entailed a mission never before undertaken: count the number of people who live in Iceland, and note everything about them—their names, sex, where they live and what they do (particularly if they don't do anything). Then, the king commanded, write another book assessing the scale of properties in Iceland, with suggestions on how abandoned land could be put back into use. Assess possible sulfur mining areas, and the state of harbors and trends in tax collection. Audit administrative and legal practices. And count the cows and all the sheep.

He was to receive a stipend and an assistant for this task, predicted to take two years. It took thirteen.

Understandably, one of the first things Arni did in Iceland while gearing up for the task ahead was to order more coffee from Denmark. It failed to arrive with the bimonthly ship. In a letter found by historians, one lawmaker at Alþingi, apologizing for the lack of good service, offers to send him a quarter pound, regretting how little he had and noting his distaste for the drink. Coffee and tea was for Danish officials, if anyone. And so, as a native, Arni may have been "Iceland's first caffeine addict," suggests history professor Már Jónsson, author of the most extensive biography of Arni.

He was also the first man in the world to conduct a complete census of an entire country. Nearly exhausting the nation's paper supply, district commissioners summoned people for head counts and completed the assignment within seven months, before the annual Alþingi gathering. Every region sent its officials with the results of the census to Þingvellir for official delivery to Arni and his assistant. Parliament's agenda that session, as noted in Alþingi books, began with a trial over a woman accused of killing a baby (found guilty and executed by drowning) and three men accused of theft (found guilty and executed by hanging). Third item: after tallying the census results, Alþingi revealed that the people of Iceland totaled 50,358. Minus, er, the four criminals that parliament had just executed. And the 497 that were accidentally counted twice, as discovered two centuries later when historians pored over the files, then collecting dust in Copenhagen, having been totally ignored upon their release. Further frustrating this epic exercise in bureaucracy, the population was hit by a great smallpox epidemic three years later and the population plunged to 30,000 people.

"After the outbreak there was at least enough food to go around," noted one history book, in the kind of outrageous optimism extreme circumstances can foster.

Arni did not catch the disease, a remarkable stroke of luck given that he spent the deadliest years embarking on the epic "land register," going from one farm to the next. The prominent scholar of Old Norse clearly did not shake hands with many people. His assistant noted how locals were suspicious of "them questions," assuming that the king was collecting the data for tax purposes. But the register was meant to reform a stagnant economy based on agricultural methods that had not changed much since the invention of agriculture. Arni was detached from his native rural Iceland—"smelling of perfume instead of alcohol"—but his actions suggest he genuinely cared about the goals of the mission. He stayed years beyond what was expected of him and took a rare stance against administrative and legal corruption, making so many powerful enemies that he eventually had no option but to leave.

One of Arni's greatest achievements as a script collector was his dedication to preserving the small stuff; the single pages and obscure findings that didn't have immediate value compared with complete skin books. He was like a hoarder, sniffing about and filling his pockets with tired-looking curios. In the 1943 novel *Iceland's Bell*, Nobel Prize–winning author Halldór Laxness depicts Arni Magnusson (re-named Arnas Arnæus) as an obsessive character, discovering vellum leaflets under the bed of an old woman:

"The things our dear old ladies hoard," the character muses over the priceless find.

The land register was completed in 1712 and remains a remarkable documentation of eighteenth-century Iceland. Without the insights provided by the register, books like *Iceland's Bell* would not have had the historical material required. But it did not lead to reform as initially intended. It wasn't even translated into Danish. Arni left the country during a time of war between Denmark and Sweden.

Denmark, with England's support, had attacked Sweden, which was weak from a war with Peter the Great and the Russian Empire. So Arni packed up the manuscripts he had accumulated, along with the detailed land register, into fifty-five wooden boxes. He decided to wait to ship them until after the Danes had pushed back the Swedish military ships. Eight years later, a convoy of thirty horses traveled from the Skálholt church (near Geysir) to Hafnarfjörður (near Reykjavík) carrying one of the most precious cargoes in the history of a country that so often struggled to make anything other nations would want.

❁

And so the precious cargo sat, tucked away in Arni's house in Copenhagen, until a day in 1728 that would change the face of the city forever.

On a windy Wednesday evening, October 20, a seven-year-old boy accidentally knocked over a candle. After a warm, dry summer, in the face of strong gusts, the flames quickly caught and spread from house to neighboring house, raging larger and larger. Firefighters had conducted a drill earlier in the day to test hoses; many of them had topped off the exercise with a few pints and now were drunk. They struggled to bring pumps to the fire through winding streets full of panicked civilians. To make it worse, the water supply in that part of the city was cut off due to construction. When orders came down to fetch water from the canals surrounding the city, the city's panicked military commander ordered the city gate closed, fearing desertion. The fire raged all night, and by Thursday morning, the fire chief was so exhausted and overwhelmed that he . . . got drunk. In short, bungled responses turned the accident from a small fire into absolute devastation.

By morning, Arni was beginning to see that the fire was not under control. He went to work, trying to rescue his precious library. Elsewhere, the unfortunate fire brigade started firing cannon at already-burning houses to make them collapse; when that didn't work, they started trying to blow them up with gunpowder. This (perhaps predictably) back-fired when the gunpowder exploded early, killing people and igniting more nearby buildings, including a church where people had stored their property to keep it safe. By then it was the largest fire in the history of Copenhagen. Arni, racing against time, was piling his precious books into a horse-drawn carriage with the help of servants and two friends. The fire was spreading to city hall, destroying the city archives; at the same time, new fires were breaking out, started by embers carried by the wind. One after another, the buildings of the University of Copenhagen went up in flames: the community building, the head building, the anatomy theater. At last the fire reached the university library, housed in the attic of a church. The entire library—thirty-five thousand volumes—lay there. They included archival documents from Niels Krag and Tycho Brahe; some of the first printed versions of Aristotle's works; scientific works dating from the fifteenth century; precious volumes about medieval history (with only a single existing copy). The ceiling gave way. Every single volume tumbled into the flames, gone forever—save a few (illegally lent) works that happened to be checked out. Next were the houses of the university professors: all their notes, their man-uscripts, the personal collections, gone.

One can only suppose what Arni was feeling. Imagine the

air acrid with smoke; the screams of people fleeing, trying to save their houses; the crash of buildings collapsing in the distance. Surrounded by precious ancient volumes that he knew could never, ever be replaced, he hurriedly filled the horse carts. In the distance, the Round Tower was engulfed in flames, destroying Tycho Brahe's celestial globe, made in 1570 and the first in history. Church bells sang out Thomas Kingo's *Turn Your Anger, Lord, by Mercy*, before that church too caught fire, sending the bells clanging into the fire below. The fire brigade tried setting off charges again, this time accidentally burning down the vice mayor's house.

Arni managed to rescue three or four loads of his books, struggling through the crowd to a friend's house. At last the fire spread too close for him to rescue any more. His own home burned down at around four that afternoon.

The fire raged until October 23. In the end, nearly half the medieval section was destroyed, totaling about a third of the city. A full fifth of the residents of Copenhagen had been left homeless. This was awful, but the cultural destruction was truly staggering: virtually all of the books of Copenhagen had been destroyed. The University of Copenhagen had lost everything; at Borchs Kollegium, 3,150 volumes burned; the city archives were lost. Arni had managed to save an impressive amount of his own collection, considering. He rescued most of his books of sagas, including most of the oldest and most valuable core of the collection, the ancient vellum books. But he lost his own work, his notes and writing, and most of the printed books, including the last known copy of the *Breviaria* of 1534, the first book printed in Iceland.

"Almost all the books in Copenhagen were incinerated. But many of the Icelandic handwritten manuscripts were saved because Arni Magnusson . . . managed to get the manuscripts out in time," attests Professor Morten Fink-Jensen, a researcher and University of Copenhagen historian. This did little to console the now-homeless Arni. In the harsh winter that followed the fire, Arni had to move three times, all the while wrestling with his own losses, the extent of which he couldn't even measure because he'd never taken a full inventory. By the following Christmas Eve, he had fallen ill. Upon his death, he bequeathed his remaining collection—nearly 1,600 Icelandic manuscripts—to the university. Today the most important ones are collected in the Arnamagnæan Institute, located both in Copenhagen and Reykjavík. There, Icelanders are once again employed in reading, writing, and interpreting old scripts. Like Tolkien babysitters, they're watching over the country's most precious cultural contribution.

3

Iceland Triggers a Climate Crisis

Iceland from 1750 to 1809

The population of Iceland is 1,000 times
smaller than that of the United States. We do
not hide behind our apparent lack of
superpower status. What we lack in
manpower, we make up in volcanoes. But we
are still figuring out how to aim them.

—PRIME MINISTER SIGURDUR INGI
JOHANNSSON, SPEAKING AT A WHITE
HOUSE DINNER FOR NORDIC LEADERS.

Ice in the Gulf of Mexico. A withering, dried-up Nile. Missing monsoons in India. An acid fog that chokes Europe. Horses that have "lost all their flesh," so that "the skin began to rot off along the spines." These may sound like biblical plagues, or the storyline of the latest climate apocalypse action movie, but in fact they all happened in a single year—the Year of Awe—when events in Iceland rippled out in ways that weren't understood for centuries. It began with heat.

That summer, blistering weather smothered the workers of Europe. Days and weeks passed as temperatures rocketed from hot to hotter. But in late June the air turned, and the sun faded to a dim shadow overhead. Summer was suddenly over. The climate would not be the same for years.

Observing the shifting weather from southern England, British naturalist Gilbert White wrote how a thick "peculiar haze or smokey fog" blanketed the atmosphere on June 22, 1783. "The sun," White observed, "looked as blank as a clouded moon."

1783

In eastern England, ships were stuck at port, unable to navigate through the haze. Smog from coal-fueled industrial plants blended with the murky sky. The fog was "unlike anything known within the memory of man," and the strange cloud drifted over the western continent, raising thunderstorms whose intensity was unknown in living memory.

In Paris, the US ambassador was familiar with thunderstorms but curious about the mysterious fog. That ambassador was Benjamin Franklin, a legendary polymath remembered today as one of America's Founding Fathers, who had already made history by flying a kite in a storm to prove the electrical nature of lightning (he was more careful than it sounds!). While in France, Franklin apparently conducted another experiment to demonstrate how the rays of the sun barely broke through the "dry fog" covering the city. When he focused the sun's rays through a burning glass, he wrote, they would "scarce kindle brown paper." From the exercise, Franklin predicted that winter would be "early frozen."

He was correct. As early as June, according to letters from the Netherlands, leaves began falling from trees, with forests looking as though it were already late autumn. The following winter was the coldest in 250 years. Western Europe's average temperature that January, minus 0.6°C, was more than 3°

below the 30-year average. Toward the end of 1783, Europeans dubbed this eerie time as Annus Mirabilis, the Year of Awe. In the newborn nation of the United States, ice sealed the harbor of Baltimore from January to March, temperatures in Connecticut fell to minus 11°F, and trees in Alaska hardly grew at all.

Amid the thick haze and blood-colored sun, many anticipated the arrival of Judgment Day. The secular Benjamin Franklin was more sober in his analysis. In a lecture delivered in the United States a year later, he suggested that the "universal fog" came from Iceland, and more precisely, the notorious Mount Hekla volcano, which he knew had erupted back in 1766. He was close, but not quite on the mark. Just forty-five miles from Hekla, the earth had cracked open in the largest explosion in a thousand years. For eight months, 130 craters stretching some fifteen miles along a volcanic fissure spewed magma and toxic gas over the Northern Hemisphere, and possibly beyond.

The results were so widespread, so disparate, and so extreme that it begs disbelief. In England, a dry sulfurous fog choked workers and led to tens of thousands of deaths. Calamitous summer thunderstorms dropped hailstones reported to "measure near five inches in circumference," so large they killed cattle, according to the *Newcastle Courant*. Noxious dews and frosts damaged crops. Snow fell in Poland even though it was June. The effects spread: by July, the haze was noticed in China. Japan experienced widespread failure of the rice harvest and the most severe famine in the nation's history. Inuit oral histories refer to "a summer that did not come." Cool temperatures in Eurasia and Africa weakened the African and Indian monsoons, and without the rains, severe drought occurred in India and regions of China. Weak monsoons led to record low water levels in the Nile River; a low Nile meant famine. The next year, Egypt lost roughly one sixth of its population.

As the months stretched on, the effects were even more keenly felt. Back in Franklin's homeland, the winter average temperature on the US East Coast was 8.6°F below average. The Mississippi River froze at New Orleans, and ice floes were reported in the Gulf of Mexico. Record freezes of the Chesapeake Bay delayed congressmen who were coming to Annapolis to vote for the Treaty of Paris and end the American Revolutionary War.

Iceland—the country that had never invaded anyone, had never proselytized a religion, had never had any economic impact—was, for the first time, on everyone's mind and lips.

that's cool!

With one major difference, Iceland is basically Hawaii upside down.

Both areas rest on top of exceptionally active "hot spots" where molten rock (magma) streams continuously from the center of the earth (the mantle) into chambers (volcanoes) underneath the crust. But unlike Hawaii, Iceland is located on a plate boundary sitting atop the fissure separating the Eurasian and the North American tectonic plates. These plate boundaries are constantly moving apart—2.5 centimeters per year—which causes volcanic activity *in addition* to the hot spot. Hence, Iceland is six times the size of Hawaii, with five times the number of active volcanoes.

There are other islands sitting atop the same mid-Atlantic

Ridge, such as the Azores and the Canary Islands. But there, without the boost of a hot spot, eruptions occur centuries apart.

Iceland has, on average, an eruption every four to five years. After the island was discovered and settled, it didn't take long for Europeans to recognize it as the place of "fire and ice." That three-word label is pretty much as old as the invention of the controlled use of fire (give or take four hundred thousand years), and has been used to sum up the island's features on book covers new and old; in advertising for volcano snowmobile tours; in the first lines of Led Zeppelin's "Immigrant Song"; on labels for local overpriced Vodka; and in Jules Verne's classic *Journey to the Center of the Earth*, which takes the reader down through a volcanic crater underneath the Snæfellsjökull Glacier. First translated into Icelandic in 1944, the book's title was simply *The Secrets of Snæfellsjökull (Leyndardómar Snæfellsjökuls)*. And long before it appeared in marketing and popular culture, the contrast was used by the earliest tourists and travel writers to magnify their own bravery. Volcanic Iceland was, according to them, the gateway to hell.

To be specific, the door to hell was located inside the crater of the infamous Mount Hekla, the much-maligned volcano that Benjamin Franklin guessed was responsible for the deadly haze over Europe.

Hekla (pronounced hekk-lah) has erupted twenty-three times in the last thousand years, making it Iceland's third most active volcano. Unlike the top two—Katla and Grímsvötn, buried underneath glaciers—the Hekla mountain *looks* like a volcano as it looms over the populated southern flatlands. And it has the ability to spew ash high into the troposphere, where northerly winds blow it down the globe, into the lungs and living rooms of unsuspecting Europeans. Hekla's two most powerful eruptions, those of 1104 and 1300, brought a cloud of ash flying over northern Europe like a guerrilla marketing campaign for doomsday: *Hell is real!* So you'd better come to church.

With every eruption, stories of Hekla became as fractured and layered as the ground beneath it. One English poem dubbed it the "eternal prison of Judas," and early maps of Iceland marked its location with depictions of massive flames. Icelandic folklore told of ravenlike birds attacking visitors with their iron beaks, protecting a summit of boiling mud pits and geysers. But the visitors were as mythical as the birds. For centuries, no one dared to summit Hekla and see the peak for themselves.

So in June 1750, residents of Selsund, the farm nearest to the mountain's base, were baffled by the question posed by two young men in tailored Danish clothes: Which way up?

The two travelers were twenty-four-year-old Eggert Ólafsson and thirty-one-year-old Bjarni Pálsson. Both had been born and raised on Iceland farms, and they later met at the University of Copenhagen, where they held Arni Magnusson scholarships, set up to promote the education of book smart Icelanders. Eggert was greatly interested in natural history, and Bjarni was on track to become Iceland's first physician, when the Royal Danish Academy of Sciences and Letters approached them with an epic dispatch: deliver to the king a guide to the natural wonders of Iceland and the local population's way of life. It was to be "proper knowledge" of a place where "vague and imperfect ideas had hitherto prevailed," as it says in the English translation of the final *Travels in Iceland*, a seminal work for the age of the Enlightenment.

Bjarni and Eggert, on a mission from the king, were undeterred by the villagers' skepticism. They reached the summit

of Hekla at midnight on June 20, the time of year known today as the summer solstice. On this, the longest day of the
year, standing 4,892 feet above sea level, they looked around
at the peak and saw "nothing but snow and ice. No waterfalls,
boiling hot springs, fire or smoke." The revelation was somewhat awkward for their guide from the Selsund farm who had
quit midway, lamenting a "headache," clearly afraid to cross
Satan's alleged doorstep.

Eggert and Bjarni were at the height of their career as the
greatest myth busters of their generation, at the dawn of the
natural sciences.

Earlier expedition leaders had skimmed the landscape in
comparison, and taken a degree of liberty with their recollec-
tions, recounting tales of crossing bridges made of whalebone
and meeting locals who lived to be 150 years old. Facts did not
get in their way. Their goal was to feed a market hungry for
historical and geographical publications, the most common
category of nonreligious books since the invention of the
printing press. Iceland was the exotic North, and there was
hardly anyone around to correct false claims. Rarely was
there documented proof that an author had ever actually *visited* the country, and typically each publication was influenced by previously printed books, the myths repeated again
and again. Icelanders living in Denmark tried to dispel the
rumors, but the most popular "facts" came back like zombies:
two books published fifty years apart by Dithmar Blefken (in
Dutch) and Olaus Magnus (in Swedish) claim, respectively,
that Icelanders live for up to 150 to 300 years—because of the
pure climate, of course. Which I'd say is fair reasoning: the
human body is organic, and we all know that vegetables and
other organic things last longer in the fridge.

These "travelers" describe locals who live in underground houses together with their livestock and wash their face with urine every morning. They marvel that Icelanders show more affection for their dogs than their children (what's wrong with that?), dress so similarly that it is hard to tell women from men (again, why not?), and offer to sell foreign merchants the blowing wind, to name just a few stereotypes.

In fact, Icelanders *did* live underground, in a sense. For nearly all of recorded history, from the ninth to the nineteenth century, the Icelandic home had been a house primarily constructed from grass, stone, and mud. Turf houses typically exhibited a rectangular shape, but like any architectural tradition, they evolved over the centuries, according to the era's climate and the availability of imported timber. The first settlers arrived during a time of warm climate and plentiful trees. They built longhouses (langhús) with turf laid over a long wooden frame, similar to houses built in northern Europe and Greenland at the time. Today's visitors can find a reconstructed example of a longhouse at the Stöng farm in southern Iceland, whose original was destroyed in the Hekla eruption of 1104.

After the medieval warm period, houses became smaller and more energy efficient, adapting to a one-room baðstofa layout where people lived and slept in a single space. The houses typically had a stone foundation and wooden roof panels—imported wood, driftwood, or even whalebone—layered with turf and soil. The natural material provided more efficient insulation than wood or brick houses and better protection from earthquakes. To keep the heat from escaping, there was a long pathway between the living room and the door. People slept naked inside the baðstofa living space, packed at least two to a bed (standards of privacy were a bit different then—more in line with the lifestyle of a 1960s commune, where you might wake up to a couple having sex next to you).

Grass houses can still be found in the countryside; humble in height and size, most have a wooden facade and structure, representing the final nineteenth-century style of turf houses influenced by Danish architecture and hygiene standards. The basic peasant farmhouse was, in the words of John Stanley, an eighteenth-century English snob traveling around the country, like "a molehill on the outside and a cave on the inside."

Respectable guests like Eggert and Bjarni did not sleep inside with their hosts, but in tents on the property. They arrived during those four to five months of the year when traveling and camping is possible. The rest of the year, the weather patterns on the island are unpredictable and change fast. Even over the summer a lot could go wrong on a trip when one is crossing territory with no roads and rivers with no bridges. They did, at least, have the advantage of cartography. By that time, maps of Iceland had taken on a fairly accurate shape. The peninsular West Fjord region, in the northwestern corner of the country, extended from the mainland like a head. The Snæfellsnes Peninsula extended west like an arm, and in the Southwest lay the shoe-shaped Reykjanes Peninsula. Off the coast lay the Westmann Islands in the South and Grímsey Island in the high North. The East Fjords were marked with the vague lines of guesswork; the East is to this day the least visited and most isolated part of the country.

Bjarni and Eggert's book, *Travels in Iceland*, was written in Danish and published for readers in Denmark, the country where the most famous "mountain" is a 482-foot hill nicknamed the Sky Mountain. The unfamiliarity of Iceland's landscape and geothermal wonders gave Bjarni and Eggert a lot to work with. They avoided the hyperbolic and romantic descriptions that defined travel logs before and after. Their observant and detailed writing reads like an encyclopedia, describing the habits of birds and the spiral shapes of shells. The modern-day reader, however, will find more value in their descriptions of people and ways of life on farms and at fishing ports. "The most noble pastime of Icelanders, is undoubtedly, to read publicly the Sagas," they wrote of the old tradition of baðstofulestur, the act of someone reading aloud in the living room baðstofa, to pass time and keep others awake during knitting work.

They were unafraid to make sweeping generalizations about the character of each region. The people of the southern Flói "spoke little" but were "no fools," while those in the port village of Eyrarbakki appeared "filthy," with poor and foreign-influenced manners. The farther they traveled from the harbor villages, the more positively they wrote about the region, for different reasons. Bjarni was interested in people's health and was pleased to see how the isolated farms were free of contagious disease. He noted actions against the spread of most common illnesses, down to STDs, and at one point discusses problems women can face during menstruation. Eggert, on the other hand, praised the farm life for its cultural purity. "From foreign merchants, people learn more bad habits than good," is a quote in Eggert's spirit. He lamented how the public used foreign slang, like Danish and Latin, "without even knowing what it meant." And in the past twenty years, the book notes, people in port towns have taken up the fashion of drinking imported red wine, with terrible lack of sophistication.

On the farms, people typically ate skyr morning and evening, snacking on dried fish (harðfiskur) with butter for lunch.

Lamb, usually smoked, was for festivities, and wealthier farms had rye flatbread (flatkaka) and butter with their dried fish.

Skyr is technically a cheese, but today it is sold as "protein-rich" yogurt. The traditional recipe is to heat milk, mix in old skyr for the right kind of bacteria, and then allow it to ferment for a few hours. The practice is believed to have been forgotten elsewhere in Scandinavia, and today one of the wealthiest Icelanders alive is a skyr mogul called Siggi. Harðfiskur (pronounced harth-fisk-ur), a kind of fish jerky, is another part of the Icelandic diet popular since the age of settlement. Light and long lasting, one kilo of harðfiskur (costing about seventy dollars today) is made from ten kilos of fresh fish fillets. Farms afforded their harðfiskur by sending men to work in fishing ports over the winter, when the farm offered little action besides knitting and keeping the livestock from dying. The farmworkers returned home with all the money that they hadn't spent on booze, and, more often than not, a mild case of scurvy.

Scurvy is a deadly disease caused by a deficiency of vitamin C, an essential nutrient mostly found in fruits and vegetables. Eggert and Bjarni described the symptoms as appearing "similar to leprosy," as it presents with hair loss, rotten teeth, and bleached skin after just one month without any vitamin C. The image of the toothless pirate has long signified the condition in popular culture, but for centuries it was a real problem for people living on frozen ground in the high North. Greenlanders got their dose from eating raw meat and fish, and Icelandic farmers inland drank milk, which has low levels of vitamin C. Meanwhile, along the coast, dulse (Söl) or "sea lettuce flakes" were long consumed for their health benefits, but overall, coastal communities suffered the worst rates of scurvy.

Eggert and Bjarni were puzzled as to why Icelanders did

not heed the king's call to grow vegetables. Why not harvest nutritious food for the harsh winters? The Danish king had implemented various incentives and, in 1758, even awarded a medal to the farmer who harvested the first "Icelandic" potato. Still, it took decades of famines for the jarðepli, or "earth apples," to be widely grown and accepted as food. Once farmers did begin to plant their own vegetable gardens, the "Danish" potato competed with the turnip in popularity. Turnips are more resilient, and their roots are hardy enough to weather a freeze, unlike potato plants, whose entire crop can die on a cold summer night. The yellow turnip is also much richer in vitamin C (though farmers may not have known this at the time), giving it the nickname the orange of the North. As with many Icelandic dishes, the turnip is eaten boiled with butter and salt, a dish called *rófustappa*.

❀

Salt was also on Bjarni's and Eggert's minds when they conducted an unusual experiment by placing a pot of seawater over a hot spring in western Iceland. The act reflected the Enlightenment's conceptualization of nature, as a resource waiting to be transformed into an object of value that served man. "Beautiful" landscapes at that time meant land with the potential for exploration and harvest. Beauty lay in the utilitarian. Land was a means to an end. Moss-grown lava fields, which covered almost 10 percent of the country, were by no means an interesting landscape. Gullfoss, a stunning waterfall in the South, had to wait for the Romantic era to be acknowledged for its beauty.

With their minds devoted to science and utility, Eggert and

Bjarni focused their mission on geothermal areas, making an effort to visit hot springs both big and small. Thus they spent little time in the West Fjords and the East, geographically the oldest and coldest parts of the country.

The salt-making experiment failed as a consequence of the size of pot they had laid over the hot spring. But they concluded that with a specially made boiler, it would be a sound production method. The only problem remaining, which they did not address, is that hot springs are rarely near the ocean. Most border the Highlands area, almost a hundred miles inland, either in volcanic "high-tempered" mud pot areas (Lake Mývatn, Kerlingarfjöll) or areas with steaming spring water, such as Hveravellir and, most famously, Geysir in the southern Haukadalur region. Once Bjarni and Eggert arrived in the remote farmland of Haukadalur, they were delighted to see the hot springs near Geysir used to boil meat and milk (for making skyr). It's a sight still common today, as locals bury rye bread in the hot ground for overnight baking. Geysir's ability to live up to its name, however, is long extinct.

In many Western languages, including English, the word for a periodically erupting hot spring is *geyser*, derived from the days Europeans first saw drawings of the one and only Geysir in southern Iceland. In Icelandic, the word for erupting hot springs is *goshver* and the word *Geysir* is only written with a capital G when it refers to that particular place. The Geysir has been in a state of hibernation since 1915, literally too cool to perform for the two million annual visitors to the area. Instead, a few yards away, the smaller Strokkur (Icelandic for "churn") blows into the air. How much bigger was Geysir in its prime? We can bring that question over to Bjarni and Eggert, who took the first documented measurement of its height. This was not, by any means, a precise measurement. They first measured the nearby mountain, and then eyeballed Geysir's column as slightly lower, putting their guesstimate at 360 feet. Modern estimates tone it down to 230 feet, still incredibly high considering that the nearby and still impressive Strokkur shoots 50 to a 100 feet into the air. Eggert and Bjarni measured the depth as well and, incidentally, noted that Geysir became more active the more rocks they threw in! That still holds true: Geysir can be forced to blow by increasing the pressure in the natural underground pipelines fueling the eruption. In fact, up until the 1990s, the owner of Geysir made it blow on special occasions by pouring a wheelbarrow of soap into the water. As a child, on National Day once, I got to see it erupt when I was traveling with my grandparents. They lived in the countryside nearby, where they, like any good Enlightenment thinkers, put the land to use and made a living growing flowers inside geothermally heated greenhouses.

Eggert and Bjarni made a distinction between natural baths (laugar) and hot springs (hverir). Laugar are the naturally heated reservoirs where people, now and then, unwind after a day of travel or work. In the Highlands region, it was a known technique for travelers to sleep on the banks of warm pools with their feet in the hot water so that the warmth could circulate through the rest of their bodies. Eggert and Bjarni urged for the establishment of public baths, with facilities to change clothes so that the sick and old did not have to walk long distances from the bath to nearby houses—which was, they noted, a challenging practice put in place for young men to demonstrate their strength. Snorralaug, the pool allegedly built by Snorri Sturluson, amazed them as the only medieval monument. And by Lake Mývatn, they witnessed how locals built "dry baths" with rock plates placed over a steaming hot spring, an invention that really pleased their practical minds.

But Iceland, they warned, was not all idyllic. Among the risks of the landscape? Hot tub accidents. People who bathed alone in the middle of nowhere had, on occasion, fainted and died. That is, remarkably, one of the few hazards still relevant in modern life, as seen after the 2014 Holuhraun eruption. When the fissure eruption stopped, magma reaching temperatures of 1,180°C (2,156°F) had spread "like honey" over six months across the landscape north of the Vatnajökull Glacier, covering an area the size of Manhattan. People trekked to see the largest field of lava in 231 years (since the Laki eruption) and after a long day of hiking, they would jump into a naturally heated lagoon where the lava had trapped a cold river. Local rangers found that their job began to resemble that of lifeguards, as they had to prevent people from standing up too quickly in the steaming water.

Another experiment, romantic in nature but carried out via dry scientific methods, was Eggert's measurement of the Northern Lights. He logged the places and times he saw the auroras, noting that they occurred on cold winter nights, which is only partially true. The Northern Lights occur when a magnetic solar wind slams into the earth's magnetic field and causes atoms in the upper atmosphere to glow. It happens year-round, but summer nights are too bright for them to break through. Contrary to the name, the Northern Lights do not grow stronger the nearer you get to the North Pole. There is an optimum point, called the aurora belt, shaped like a doughnut around the Arctic Circle and reaching several hundred miles below and above. Evidence suggests the belt moves in response to changes in the earth's magnetic field. That would mean that the auroras were visible only to Inuits in North Greenland during medieval times—and would explain why their first descriptions from Iceland date back to seventeenth-century visitors from Denmark. The saga writers do not mention the spectacular streaks of color. All things considered, natural phenomena were never the topic of medieval writers. Silence on the auroras does not prove nonexistence. For all we know, the Northern Lights danced above the static observers, waiting hundreds of years for someone to invent Instagram.

In their respective notes, Bjarni tends to exhibit an interest in the many ways Iceland kills people; whereas Eggert was more of a traditional romantic, not only in the sense that he was interested in the glow of the Northern Lights, he was also dedicated to preserving Icelandic culture. He wrote poetry that portrayed Iceland in glowing terms, and wanted Icelanders to speak Icelandic, not Danish. He aimed to preserve the language and proposed rules for spelling that drew from the sagas' syntax instead of Danish linguistics.

Tragically, before the 1772 publication of *Travels in Iceland*, Eggert died in an accident with his wife, Ingibjörg Gudmundsdóttir, just after their marriage. Near her home in the Breida Fjord region, they were rowing a small boat in bad weather. It either capsized or the waves washed them overboard. Back then, few people knew how to swim. His untimely death in the fjord cemented his position as a romantic symbol for later generations of Icelandic patriots. One hundred years later, when Icelanders began campaigning for their independence, they found patriotic zeal in his poetry, and in his ideas of a "pure" and unique mother tongue.

Bjarni went on to become Iceland's first director of health.

By the time he passed away, he had trained a number of Icelanders in the basic practice of medicine at the Hólaskóli school, an elite institution at the time. One trainee was Jón Steingrímsson, whom he met under intense circumstances at the principal's office after a theft on campus. Jón was under suspicion after a stolen key was found in his belongings. By his own account, the faculty had been trying to torture a confession out of him. Bjarni walked in and saw straight off that the boy was telling the truth. Jón later wrote that his "loyal friend . . . had a pure affection for people in need."

His admiration for Bjarni may have also bolstered his own ambition to write. Years after Bjarni died, Jón published an autobiography, simply titled *The Biography*, which is today considered a milestone description of one of the largest volcanic eruptions in modern times. This was the massive 1783 eruption that threw the Northern Hemisphere's climate into chaos for years. Jón was so naive, sincere, and fatalistic that he stayed at his farm under the shadow of the spewing volcano from start to finish, while most others fled or died. He described what happened in honest diary entries, convinced in his heart that it was all because people of the area used tobacco and drank so heavily.

❈

When historians today say that the Laki eruption began on June 8, 1783, what they really mean is that in Jón Steingrímsson's diary, June 8 is the day when "dust" first fell from the sky, as if someone were burning charcoal nearby. The following night, his bed shook from small earthquakes. Soon it was raining sand. Then the water turned black. The very air grew opaque. "The dark-gray and bluish fog blocks the visibility of your own hands," Jón wrote.

Jón lived near today's Klaustur, a sleepy village of three hundred people located about thirty miles from the Laki craters—still a two-hour drive on a dirt road. Before June 1783, the area looked like any other desolated field in the Highlands. Flat. Peaceful. And 130 craters weren't pockmarking an area of fifteen square miles—until the earth ripped open in a fissure eruption. The area had erupted before, but for the past thousand years the magma had made its way through the crust dozens of miles away at the "subglacial" volcano of Grímsvötn, located under the Vatnajökull Glacier, covering about 8 percent of Iceland. Eruptions were always fused by meltwater from the glacier. At Laki nothing held back the fire, beyond surface water. There were ten major eruptions in the first few months. Each began with an earthquake, then the opening of a new fissure, a short explosive eruption, and then fire-fountaining and lava flows. Towering pillars of ash and noxious fumes reached as high as eight miles into the sky.

The Laki eruption ultimately spewed 220 square miles of lava, enough to pave the entire city of Chicago in basalt about three feet deep. Most of that emerged in the first seven weeks of the eruption, and it moved at a rate of roughly nine miles per day. Icelanders call the Laki eruption Skaftáreldar, after the Skaftá River that became a channel for the running lava. After forty-three days, the lava was coming down the river roughly a mile from Jón's church in the Klaustur farm.

Iceland's Highlands region bordering the South—from Hella to Skaftafell, if these geographical landmarks tell you anything—is the volcanic part of Iceland. Eruptions can occur elsewhere—namely, on the Reykjanes Peninsula, Snæfellsnes

Peninsula, and the Askja region—but the risk is hypothetical. The South, on the other hand, regularly issues warnings of possible activity. Sneeze next to the Katla volcano, goes the local joke, and a seismologist in Reykjavík will analyze the disturbance. The imminent threat from an eruption is due to widespread flooding from subglacial eruptions. Within hours, a stream of meltwater can wash cars and bridges toward shore. In 2010, one rather small subglacial volcano added a completely different dimension to its disruption scale by halting air traffic for weeks. Eyjafjallajökull—pronounced "Hey, I forgot your yogurt" if spoken fast—rumbled from a two-hundred-year sleep underneath an ice cap on the southern coast with an explosive eruption that threw volcanic ash several miles into the atmosphere and onward with northerly winds to the mainland, affecting Europe's airspace as far as Bulgaria. Some five million people were stranded for at least a week. In retrospect, the flight ban was a panic reaction due to the novelty of the event. But overreaction or not, another, more powerful, volcano is bound to erupt near the southern coast and upend travel plans near and far. Because, as the mayor of a nearby village once told me, every day we move closer to the next eruption.

Jón had witnessed a volcanic eruption before, on a trip to Reykjavík in 1755. A massive stroke of ash came from the crater of Katla some hundred miles from Jón's home. Buried underneath glacial ice, hundreds of yards thick, Jón encountered only the smog, not running lava. But eleven days into the Laki eruption, he witnessed molten lava . . . coming toward the town, and he knew exactly what to do! Gather inside the church. He called on the people to come for mass, and he addressed a scared crowd that was "shaking from the threat above." Do not be afraid, he urged from the podium, resorting to the self-help creed of telling people to accept their fates with "an open heart." The people prayed. The river steamed. And, conveniently for the memoir, "God was called upon" during mass, and the lava changed direction in the middle of the river (likely from the cooling of the water), saving the church and houses from destruction.

Unfortunately, the rest of Iceland was still pretty much doomed. The eruption continued for another seven months, bringing about the darkest days in Iceland's history, known as the Mist Hardship (Móðuharðindin). Black ash covered the country like a blanket covering the deceased. Acid rain burned holes through leaves and killed trees. Sheep were struck with fluorosis due to the millions of tons of fluorine released into the air and grass. The condition affected their bones, so they were unable to open their mouths to eat the last withered grasses. "There was hardly a part of them free of swellings, especially their jaws, so large that they protruded through the skin," recalls Jón. "Both bones and gristle were as soft as if they had been chewed." Roughly 80 percent of the sheep in Iceland died, contributing to the onset of famine.

Of the ten thousand people who died in Iceland—nearly a quarter of the population—none were killed by lava or direct contact with the volcano. They were victims of a famine that lasted for two frozen years. After the first winter, some 70 percent of livestock were already dead due to the lack of hay. Many farmers died trying to travel toward the nearest port to obtain fish, and those who made it were too famished for their body to consume fresh fish. After the first year, one shocked Danish eyewitness reported that even priests and landowners were weak from malnourishment. People did not have the energy to bury the dead, instead resorting to mass graves. The population, once again, plunged to thirty-eight thousand people.

⊛

Five months after the eruption began, Denmark tried to send a ship with emergency supplies. According to one account, shipmates on board the vessel saw smoke over the country from miles away. But they had to turn around twice due to foul weather, and then spent the winter in northern Norway. Officials in Denmark had taken action too late, interpreting the initial reports as a routine eruption with limited regional effects, rather than seeing it for what it was: a global catastrophe.

As Laki spewed ash and lava, it also shot 1.7 million tons of sulfuric dioxide per day into the atmosphere. Up there, it formed 200 megatons of sulfuric acid aerosols, which were swept on the jet stream toward the rest of the Northern Hemisphere. Over Europe, high pressure brought it down to the ground, creating a choking, hellish-smelling fog.

Inhaled, the sulfurous fog caused headaches, burning eyes, tingling lips, sicknesses like bronchitis, and breathing difficulties. New studies of burial records in England and France suggest Laki's toll may have been much higher than previously guessed: into the tens of thousands. Professor John Grattan of Aberystwyth University, Wales, estimates that Laki's cloud killed twenty-three thousand Britons, making it the greatest natural disaster in modern British history. People would work outside in the fields from dawn to dusk, breathing the toxic air, and "then they keeled over," says Grattan. Volcanologists at the University of Cambridge combed records and found even more dire consequences—they reported that there were thirty thousand extra deaths that year, despite the absence of famine, plague, or war. In the months of August and September, rates of death were up 40 percent. In Bedfordshire, September was "the worst month in the whole of the 18th century," according to volcanologist Claire Witham.

The particles in the air also reflected sunlight, leading to an extraordinarily cold winter. The freeze was so complete that Vienna began to run out of firewood because the Danube was frozen. The entire lemon harvest of northern Italy was destroyed by frost. And then, after the extreme winter, the spring thaw caused severe flood damage in Germany and central Europe; Seville and Cádiz were described as being "under water."

Over the years, the Laki catastrophe has often winkingly been framed as a contributor to the French Revolution. But the revolution happened six years after the eruption, and the atmospheric changes from Laki lasted less than three years. So did it really have an impact?

Before the eruption, in the late seventeenth century, French cities were growing rapidly and, more and more, working-class townspeople were dependent on agricultural trade for survival. The discovery of gold mines in Brazil led to a better economy, and peasants now owned land and had a higher standard of living and education. The mortality rate also decreased, so France's population soared, leaving it the most populous country in Europe. But by the autumn of 1783, the cooling caused by the Laki craters on top of two decades of poor harvest and rising bread prices had kindled unrest.

France's involvement in the American Revolution and King Louis XVI's reckless spending had brought the country near bankruptcy, and to make up for this insolvency, the regime imposed heavy taxes without offering anything in return to ease the burden on workers. It also began to tax nobles and clergy for the first time. Meanwhile, the rise of wealthy commoners meant that merchants and manufacturers wanted their share of political power. Up to then, the working class had benefited alongside the bourgeois elite surrounding King Louis XVI; the two classes were living nearer to each other than ever before. Empowered by years of success, the poor did not accept going to bed hungry. Peasants, armed with that new higher standard of education, wanted full rights. Philosophers like Voltaire and Rousseau were advancing ideas of social reform, and the ideas of the Enlightenment were reaching every corner. This meant (unfortunately for the monarchy) that peasants were fully aware of their dire situation, and even able to articulate alternatives. The philosophies had been read more widely in France than anywhere else. People no longer saw the monarchy as divinely ordained. They wanted change.

In short, the Laki chaos accelerated the desperation of peasants, but Louis XVI and Marie Antoinette had had it coming for a long time.

The French Revolution ended long decades of peace in Europe. Leading the French army was the Corsican-born Napoléon Bonaparte, riding his white horse to victory over much of the mainland. Britain, guarded by its watery borders and large arsenal, was for a while considered the only power that could stand against his forces. Denmark tried to stay neutral, as a beneficiary of trade with both factions, but got caught in the middle. Britain, knowing that the French navy had been paralyzed since the 1805 Battle of Trafalgar, feared Denmark's powerful sailing fleet might fall into the wrong hands.

The best thing to do, the British concluded, was to invade Copenhagen and burn the glorious wooden fleet to ashes. They succeeded in 1807, destroying three fourths of the city and killing thousands.

Denmark and Britain were officially at war for years to come, but without much open conflict. Denmark was weak without a navy and Britain was busy on the continental front. The main confrontation was out at sea, as Britain blocked the sea routes of Danish merchant and navy ships in the North Atlantic, leaving Iceland the hardest-hit victim of the Anglo-Danish faction of the widespread Napoleonic Wars. Imports stopped and the coastline was vulnerable to pirates. Currency either collected dust, because there was nothing to buy, or changed hands at gunpoint in the famous Gilpin robbery, named after the British pirate Gilpin, who got away with stealing the country's silver coin treasury (he considered the paper money worthless).

The standstill was a setback particularly for Reykjavík, a city then emerging as the nation's capital. Wool factories had begun to spring up in town, opening the door to industrialization. The devastation of the Laki eruption had driven the country to reform its economy and seek better trade deals with Denmark. Survivors of the Mist Hardship came out of the haze scrambling for new survival strategies, leading them to embrace ideas that had been proposed by Eggert and Bjarni decades earlier. Farmers planted vegetables, and the feudal-like system of land ownership was broken up. Fishermen invested in larger ships, pushing up wages in the competition for labor. Seasons passed. Iceland staggered to its feet.

The lack of Danish imports wasn't easy, but people survived. For an entire year, no one on the island even *knew* about the French Revolution busily laying the groundwork for modern democracy, equal rights, and freedom of speech. The revolutionary spirit was completely foreign to the nation until the summer of 1809, when a band of British soap traders sailed ashore and declared the country independent from Denmark. Iceland would be a republic, like the United States and the First French Republic. This stint in rebellion lasted just six weeks—but its spirit of freedom lived on.

4

Nationalism

Iceland from 1809 to 1918

They can eat seaweed.

—FREDERIK TRAMPE, THE DANISH GOVERNOR
OVER ICELAND, COMMENTING ON (ALLEGED!)
FOOD SHORTAGE IN REYKJAVÍK DURING THE
NAPOLEONIC WARS.

Scrape the rocks for moss and eat it.

—MAGNUS STEPHENSEN, A COLLEAGUE OF
TRAMPE'S, OFFERING ANOTHER SPLENDID
CULINARY ADVISEMENT TO THE FAMISHED.

Let them eat cake.

—QUEEN MARIE ANTOINETTE MAKING A
RATHER FRIENDLY INVITATION TO THE
PEOPLE OF FRANCE, ALL THINGS CONSIDERED.

On a June afternoon like any other, in 1809, a flag bearing a white Scandinavian cross over a red background fluttered high over the cool stone buildings of Reykjavík. This was the Danish Dannebrog, the oldest continually used national flag, flying over the most Danish community of Iceland.

Meanwhile, out on Faxa Bay, wind filled the sails of the armed barque *Margaret & Anne* as it approached from the horizon. Soon, as they drew closer to shore, the crew would lower their sails, drop anchor, and prepare the ship's dinghy for landing. And then, under the command of soap mogul Samuel Phelps, they would become revolutionaries and tear down the flag that flew over Reykjavík.

They launched their uprising at what appeared to be an opportune time. Reykjavík was, like the rest of the nation, two years into a food shortage caused by the Napoleonic Wars. The food shortage could largely be attributed to Britain, which was tormenting Denmark in retribution for siding primarily with Napoléon's allies. Britain had blocked the little that remained of Denmark's sailing fleet from accessing major Atlantic routes, including Iceland's. To cope with the desperate times, Reykjavík's elite class of Danish administrators and Copenhagen-educated Icelanders had decided to permit residence only for those townspeople who were physically healthy and able to provide for themselves. The rest (the poor and weak) were sent "home"—thanks for trying, no dice!—reducing the capital's population from 446 to 369 people. Officials considered sending prisoners home too, but decided instead to keep them alive on horsemeat. The local priest was most likely against that diet still associated with heathen worship.

But at last a ship had arrived, stocked with food. The *Margaret & Anne*'s cargo held tobacco, potatoes, wheat, millet, timber, nails, and other items that farmers could trade for suet and tallow in order to make soap. There was just one problem: only Danes were allowed to trade with locals, and businessman Samuel Phelps was British.

Phelps had anticipated this issue, and thought he'd resolved it. He had come to Iceland earlier that year and been granted an exception to the Danish monopoly. Thus he came to shore assuming that his permits were sorted. But the Danish governor, Frederik Trampe, had been away when the permit was originally granted and, upon return, was not keen to approve any exceptions. To the contrary, he made it punishable "by death" to do business with British travelers, no doubt to protect his own import business.

And so, rather than filling their bowls with moss and slime, the people of Reykjavík got their very first revolution. That Sunday, Phelps and the ship's captain and men from the crew of the *Margaret & Anne* armed themselves. They grabbed machetes and muzzle-loaded guns—awfully big firearms to carry around a village with just two policemen—and marched from the harbor, storming Governor Trampe's house. This goon squad of British sailors, led by a soap mogul, arrested the governor at gunpoint and then hauled their captive to a cabin inside their ship. And that was it. The revolution was over in just a few hours, without spilling a drop of blood or meeting any real resistance. One hundred years of Danish reign ended just like that, while most people were busy attending Sunday mass.

Phelps had successfully arranged a (profitable) revolution. But in order for the gears of business to turn, someone would need to step in and fill the power vacuum left by the now furious Governor Trampe. The native Icelanders couldn't be trusted, and Phelps knew he couldn't rule on behalf of England without England's knowledge. Instead, he invited one of his crewmen to be in charge of the country. The new ruler's name was Jørgen Jørgensen, a twenty-nine-year-old Danish sailor who had joined the mission as a translator. He accepted the new role with perhaps a bit too much enthusiasm. As it turned out, Jørgensen was not one to maintain the status quo. He took up residency in the governor's house and hung outside, on public display, a poster with the proclamation that Iceland was now "free and loose from Danish Rule." He made several proclamations in the revolutionary spirit: Danes could no longer collect heavy taxes and fix the prices of imports; instead, Iceland would decide its own future. The Alþingi was to be reestablished as a democratic assembly. Iceland was an independent country. Meanwhile, Jørgensen would take up the role of "protector."

He confiscated weapons from Danish officials and ordered the release of all inmates locked inside the newly built prison that today houses the prime minister's office. His acts as protector went beyond mere liberation: Danish residents were put under curfew. In case of riots, he would hire many of the inmates as bodyguards, who followed him around dressed in green suits. Escorted by a personal army of four to eight men, he patrolled the town wearing a long navy-blue coat. To secure the capital from invasion, his men built a barrier along the beach, set to be lined with cannon facing the primary landing spot for Reykjavík. When the wall was tall enough to support a flag pole, Jørgensen considered the construction a success and promptly took it upon himself to draft the first national flag for Iceland: three white cods in the upper-left corner of an ocean-blue background (his design was inspired by a sixteenth-century coat of arms, which features stockfish, or flat cod, under a crown). Governor Trampe, still locked inside the ship, watched these events unfold through a porthole. He later said that the worst part—mental torture, really—was having to see that flag every time he looked outside. Three free cod, blowing in the wind.

But their protector had a secret. Jørgensen had not told his shipmates that he was himself a prisoner of war, having joined the Iceland expedition in order to flee parole. He had been arrested on a Danish battleship years earlier and taken to

London, where he met Samuel Phelps while on patrol. The idea of sailing to Iceland had been his idea, although he did not know much about the country. Despite being a Danish citizen, he held the British view that Iceland was oppressed by Denmark. Of course, the Brits may have only clucked their tongues about oppression because they hadn't gotten there first. Around the time of the uprising, Britain had considered taking over Iceland, but was unconvinced of its usefulness. An internal government report suggested turning the island into a prison, with inmates manning a labor-intensive fishing industry. But in the end, they decided that grabbing Iceland wasn't worth the trouble, because British sailors and whalers could already move around the northern seas freely.

Denmark, meanwhile, had its own set of justifications. It considered its monopoly on trade with Iceland a necessary form of taxation. How else would the country pay for its governance and contribute to their beloved king? For many years, Danish merchant ships had to pay the government for a trade license, issued in limited batches, which allowed the government to dictate prices for locals who had nowhere else to shop. After the Mist Hardship, the last official famine in Iceland's history, the Danish government eased up on the monopoly, which had been somewhat to blame for the lack of food. So when Jørgensen arrived, trade was free between Danish merchants, still in position to easily collaborate on price fixing. But the new protector of Iceland had done away with all that. Jørgensen had turned Reykjavík upside down in just two and a half weeks, and was now eager to change the country and end Denmark's greedy stranglehold.

So he jumped on a horse and took his revolution to northern Iceland.

To fully paint the picture here, you should know that Iceland has a special breed of horse. Long a point of national pride, the Icelandic horse has five gaits, as opposed to the standard horse's three (walk, trot, gallop). But despite the sophisticated skill set, the Icelandic horse often suffers a lack of respect due to its size, somewhere between a pony and a regular horse. The short-statured horse doesn't really convey the dignitas you'd expect of a statesman riding to free a small island nation from six hundred years of foreign rule. This was not quite Napoléon's famous Marengo, rearing up over the heads of the enemy. And one other thing setting Jørgensen apart from Napoléon was the timing: he was not the right man at the right time.

On his way to the northern capital of Akureyri, Jørgensen confronted Danish merchants wherever he found them and accused them of swindling the local population with outrageous prices and fake competition. He aimed his gun at one and got into a fistfight with another. In theory, the local population could have used this opportunity to force real change, opening up the country to free trade and reinstituting the Alþingi. But . . . nobody really grasped what he was talking about. Independence? Self-rule? Jørgensen had skipped the grassroots part of the grassroots revolution. What excited people more than his political ideas was his promise to erase personal debt with the Danish king—most people's priorities were more in line with Samuel Phelps's, who had viewed the revolution as a business opportunity.

Today, Jørgensen is unfairly mocked in Iceland's historical canon. He is nicknamed the Dog Day king, after the dog days of summer, which last from mid-June to mid-August, when the Sirius star rises, reflecting his brief two-month tenure as the king of Iceland (though to be fair, he never called himself king).

When Jørgensen returned to Reykjavík after a mildly successful trip north, Phelps had turned the revolution to hypocrisy by paying local farmers in items they did not want—wineglasses, among other things—and stocking the ship with "seized" Danish assets. Jørgensen was not happy. Meanwhile, the British navy ship *Talbot*, while making a stop in another part of Iceland, got wind of what was going on in Reykjavík. Upon approaching Reykjavík, the navy officer on board *Talbot* saw a foreign flag not recognized by any state. He then received a smuggled letter from the captive Danish governor wherein he explained what had happened.

And so in the end, it was Britain, not Denmark, that put an end to the revolution. Jørgensen and Phelps were both arrested and put on a ship to London.

Jørgensen was swiftly thrown behind bars for having jumped parole. There he became infamous among the guards and inmates for his obsessive gambling habits. He was eventually locked up—twice—for unpaid gambling debts in Britain, but in the meantime, he talked his way into the British intelligence service as a spy. He roamed war-torn France and Germany and witnessed the Battle of Waterloo. One biographer has called him the "19th-century Forrest Gump," given how often he was close to the action. After his second spate of gambling trouble, the British authorities put him on a ship to Australia, where he worked his way up from being a prisoner to an assistant to the ship's medic. He arrived in Tasmania, a small island nation south of the continent, and was later appointed to the position of policeman in the capital, Hobart. He became something of a local legend, and upon his death at the age of sixty-one, roughly thirty years after his adventure in Iceland, he left behind a big collection of memoirs, reports, and books. It took the better half of his lifetime for Icelanders to realize what he had been offering: statehood.

❀

Let's say you're a farmer in the Balkans in the early nineteenth century. On your way home from the fields, someone flags you down and asks you what you are—Macedonian? Greek? Serbian? It's likely that you'd shrug, confused by the question, and answer simply, "I'm a Slav."

Conceiving of the French identity around the time of the French Revolution seems easy; people in France who were ethnically French and spoke French. Right? But in fact, identifying as a particular nationality is a relatively new development in much of Europe. In the late eighteenth century, only about half of the people in "France" could speak French. Languages and borders didn't match up. Neither did ethnicity, of course. Most people were mainly loyal to their city or province or religion or language, rather than the idea of a nation-state.

But then in the mid-1800s, nationalism really kicked off. People were moving from the countryside into the city, so they needed to share a language in order to communicate. Trains and newspapers were also making people feel more interconnected. And thanks in part to the Enlightenment and the French Revolution, people began to place their faith in governments rather than religion. Suddenly power came not from God or from the king but from the people.

Intellectuals across Europe were also drawn to the Napoleonic Code, which strongly influenced the laws of many countries that formed during and after the Napoleonic Wars, and upheld the ideological goals of nationalism and democracy.

Serbia was the first to move, revolting against the Ottoman Empire with the idea of an independent nation in mind. Next came Greece, also shrugging off the Ottomans to become an independent state. Belgium broke off from the Netherlands, Poland tried to ditch Russia, and Hungary led a national revolt against Austria, even though they benefited from being part of the Habsburg monarchy. Norway got away from Sweden, and Ireland struggled (and failed) once more toward autonomy. But this wasn't all simply about independence: this was about the new, larger idea of a national identity. People started to have the idea that language, ethnicity, and borders should all align and add up to one nation-state.

This movement for independence and national unity was not a default position for small nations like Iceland. The people of the Faroe Islands, an archipelago between Iceland and Denmark, who also had a unique language and population, did not break away from the Danish realm. And over in England, the people of Wales were content to send representatives to London instead of seeking independence, while the Frieslanders of Holland became Dutch, to name just a few examples around Europe. They did not want full sovereignty—just more control over their own affairs.

Thus nationalism traveled a full circle around Europe, eventually reaching Iceland via a college dorm.

In Copenhagen, the acclaimed student of natural sciences Jónas Hallgrímsson wrote the first lines to the poem *Ísland*:

> Iceland, fortunate isle! Our beautiful, bountiful mother!
> Where are thine ancient renown, freedom and valorous
>   deeds?
> All in the world is fleeting: the time of thy courtliest
>   splendor
> flashes like lightning at night, afar from a bygone age.
> *—Translated by Gudmundur Gíslason*

He was writing romantic poetry about the Icelandic landscape for the magazine he and his friends had founded: *Fjölnir* (Fjeul-nir). The four University of Copenhagen students launched *Fjölnir* to begin to make the case for Iceland's self-rule.

Their case was strengthened by the fact that it was exceptionally easy to conceive of Iceland as a separate nation, far easier than it was for most other states in Europe. The population was largely homogeneous, spoke a unique language, and lived within borders clearly defined by the sea. Furthermore, the nation had a history of self-rule, only giving up its long-held independence to end a civil war. And finally, it was ruled by a king stationed seven hundred miles away, who had never in the past six hundred years so much as visited. It was thus easy to make the case that a local assembly would be better at deciding what was best for Iceland.

That was the argument, clean and simple. One might expect the students would articulate their patriotic case along these lines, rousing the population to come together as one united nation. Perhaps many men, roused by the nationalistic fervor, would ride their horses over the hinterlands toward the Danish-controlled port towns. Midway to their destination, someone would deliver a speech, Braveheart-style, ending with a chant; maybe they'd perform something similar to the "Viking clap," which Iceland's soccer fans have become famous for. Chilled to the bone by this fierce display of unity, and convinced of those compelling arguments, the Danish officials would rush to their ships. As they sailed away, the deposed rulers would watch the beautiful coastal landscape recede, their hearts heavy with remorse.

But of course that's not what happened. Instead of deploying razor-sharp rationale, the cosmopolitan founders of *Fjölnir* magazine addressed their countrymen in the style of motivational speakers. Iceland—which, it's worth mentioning, is written *Ísland* in the Icelandic language—was a beautiful country worthy of independence because of its rich cultural past, they said. In a fit of stereotypical nationalist nostalgia, they claimed that the country's "Golden Age" was when Alþingi parliamentarians rode on horseback to Þingvellir during the summer and penned the acclaimed sagas during the winter. The publication spent more ink on romantic descriptions of the landscape than any practical structural vision of an improved government. Snorri Sturluson, according to the students, was a hero of the modern age, and the Icelandic language, preserved in the work of Snorri and others, was being badly contaminated with Danish.

From one farm to the next, workers came in from the fields and sat down to scratch their heads at these romantic poems about fjords. Iceland was still a largely conservative agrarian society, and to them, praising long-gone history and rugged landscapes in flowery romantic language was, at best, an academic exercise. "The wisdom from books can't be put in an askur," they would say, askurs being wooden bowl-like vessels from which they'd eat their meals. But interestingly, what bothered people perhaps even more than the message was the medium—the new style of poetry. It was full of foreign meter! It lacked the traditional phrases! Lyrical narratives should rhyme! That's how conservative the community was. So while the movement for independence grew bigger, the farmers never forgave the *Fjölnir* pioneers for their style. For the time being, the independence movement was without a clear leader.

❀

Jónas Hallgrímsson's career as a poet was cut short when he fell down the stairs to his apartment upon arriving home from Hviids Vinstue, one of the oldest pubs in Copenhagen. He broke his leg and died from blood poisoning, aged thirty-seven. His was not an unusual case: controversial and misunderstood, the earliest Icelandic nationalists struggled to stay sober and, alas, alive. The father of the movement, Baldvin Einarsson, passed out next to a burning candle and died at the age of thirty-two when his bed caught fire. Two other early nationalists, Jóhann Halldórsson and Skafti Stefánsson, drunkenly stumbled into a canal and drowned.

In short, the movement was led by drunk, drunker, drunkest.

At last a serious young man from the West Fjords sailed to port in Copenhagen, the city he and others no longer wanted as the capital of Iceland. Just like the early founder of America's Jamestown colony, his name was John Smith. Sort of. His first name, Jón, is a variation on John and the most common name in Iceland's history; in the 1703 census conducted by Arni

Magnusson, 24 percent of the male population was named Jón. The second most common was his father's name, Sigurður. Thus his name, Jón Sigurðsson (pronounced John Sikh-urths-son) is the Icelandic version of John Smith.

Jón was tall and classically handsome, with high cheek-bones and long sideburns. From his photo it's difficult to imagine his being anything other than a statesman. He certainly could have wound up as a professor instead. Like Arni Magnusson a century before him, he climbed the academic ladder by reading and copying old scripts in his elegant hand-writing. Compared with the creative and party-happy Ice-landers living in the city, Jón's student life was as dull as his name, to the point of being dreadfully annoying; his room-mate at school admitted he preferred chatting with Jón in Danish because he was always correcting his grammar in Ice-landic. But his nitpicking freed Iceland.

Jón made gradual political steps, writing his first articles under the pseudonym 8 + 1 in Danish newspapers. Although the rationale behind his pseudonym is mysterious, his very rationality stood at odds with the romantic thinkers who had come before him. He did his homework and delivered a practi-cal case for Iceland's independence that defined the cause for decades to come. To foster support, in 1841 he founded the annual magazine *Ný félagsrit*, and to foster admiration, he had his photograph taken all the time at Copenhagen's new portrait studios. Thanks to a trove of preserved papers and photos, his intelligence and charisma are still admired to-day; indeed, he's a national hero, and his birthday, June 17, is National Day. His actions and ideas have also held up in the face of modern standards and scrutiny. In the more than four thousand private letters written by Jón to his allies at the time, preserved at the National Archives, he is but rarely chauvinistic, bigoted, or vulgar.

His private life is shadowed by just one awkward fact, something school textbooks do not highlight. It's a small thing, really, not so uncommon, and related to the love of his life, whom he married—Ingibjörg Einarsdóttir, his first cousin. Jón met the sweet-natured Ingibjörg when he briefly lived in Reykjavík before departing for Copenhagen. There he worked for her father, Uncle Einar. They became engaged, with their marriage set to take place when Jón completed his studies. It was a strange arrangement, and perhaps Icelanders will find it stranger than others. It's long been fairly common, even encouraged, in various societies to marry one's cousin. It keeps wealth and land in the family, and in more conservative times, a cousin may have been the only person of the opposite sex a person really got to see. Queen Victoria, like many members of the royal family, married her cousin; so did US president John Adams, Edgar Allan Poe, Charles Darwin, Albert Einstein, and others. Even today, worldwide, more than 10 percent of marriages are between cousins.

While it's only been taboo relatively recently in much of the Western world, marrying one's (albeit distant) relative is a more serious problem in Iceland. On a small island nation settled a mere 1,200 years ago, most people are at least distantly related. It's also something Icelanders are simply more aware of because, thanks to people like Ari, Icelanders have a special familiarity with genealogy and can trace their roots far back quite easily. Today a comprehensive database with the family records of every Icelander who has ever lived is available online. Reykjavík-based pharmaceutical company deCODE built the platform to trace genealogical diseases and made it available to everyone in it. That means I can type the name of another Icelander to see to what degree we share the same ancestry. Just recently I have learned that Snorri Sturluson is my twenty-third paternal ancestor, and Arni Magnusson is my eleventh cousin. The singer Björk is a very, very distant relative—our family trees are apart until 1740, when a mutual forefather named Jón Jónsson, whom I know nothing about, made a mutual connection.

See how this can become awkward? The local market of lovers has roughly fifty thousand people of each sex aged twenty to forty years old. There is an actual chance of accidentally hooking up with a distant relative. The odds are about one in a thousand, according to a calculation I once did for an article that ran in a local newspaper ahead of *Þjóðhátíð*, the largest camping festival in the country. But there is an app for that. The *ÍslendingaAPP* claims to "prevent awkward moments at family reunions" with a spin on deCODE's database. Two potential lovers can simply "bump the app before bumping in bed." When the app was introduced, one newspaper called it "the lifeguard at the gene pool" and revealed a widely erroneous claim about incest. Despite our modern aversion, relation by blood is, as it turns out, good for fertility. According to a recent study examining 160,000 Icelandic couples from 1800 to 1965, third and fourth cousins have the best chance of increasing their fertility, suggesting that some distance is good.

In any case, Jón and Ingibjörg never had children. Jón's biographer, Gudjón (a variation of the name Jón) Fridriksson, thinks Jón may have been infertile after catching syphilis (another hiccup the textbooks overlook) at the age of twenty-nine, while their relationship was long distance. In fact, they were engaged but long distance for twelve years, long beyond Jón's years as a student. He never, in the end, completed his degree; he had time for neither school nor love. Iceland's liberation consumed him.

❀

Jón was determined. But Denmark, though just half the size of Iceland, had ruled over Iceland for centuries. It took them another hundred years to let go completely.

The label "oppressor" is easy to throw around, but to pinpoint what exactly that oppression entailed is a bit harder. Denmark did not force Icelanders to speak Danish, nor did it draft the population for battle. Neither did Denmark extract natural resources, nor build the streets of Copenhagen on the backs of Icelanders. It did indeed enforce strict laws, unfair judicial procedures, and radical change—beheading our last Catholic bishop was definitely not very nice. Yet the treatment was not much different from what the Danish population themselves, and most Europeans for that matter, had to put up with.

Denmark's administrative control over Iceland was weak, creating a vacuum for strong informal networks that acted according to their own interests. For hundreds of years, for example, poor people had had to seek permission from "their" municipality to change jobs, marry, or settle in another region, a system that kept down the price of labor and hindered a transition from agriculture to fishing. Officially, the idea was to prevent people from marrying without access to land and thus the means to raise children. The practice was abolished only after pressure from Denmark, which was concerned, apparently, with equal rights. So in fact, this elite class of wealthy farmers, with their tactics of oppression, were the proponents of the strongest argument for Danish rule. Wealthy Icelanders had been taking advantage of poor Icelanders through the Danish law that had protected them.

Mostly the Danes engaged in a bit of trade: Danish merchant ships sailed to Iceland with what the country needed, and they left with hand-knitted clothes (socks and gloves mostly) that the locals had spent the winter making. Iceland also sold some dried fish and lamb meat, but back in the ports of Denmark, people hardly came running toward the harbor waving money.

In fact, among Danes, Iceland was considered a charity case of sorts, one that cost more than it could contribute. The country was rarely featured in the Danish press, and few people knew much about this "dependent territory," as its status was officially known. Few countries in Europe were as poor and as backward, lacking industry and modern infrastructure. And that was exactly what formed the core of Jón's argument: Danish neglect. A government, under local command, could drive change, sweeping Iceland along into industry and progress.

Unsurprisingly, the Danes ignored little Iceland when it came knocking with the idea. The timing was terrible. In Denmark's southern Schleswig-Holstein region, German-speaking rebels were fighting to break away and join neighboring Prussia. Any laxity toward Iceland could set a bad example at a time when the realm could not afford any risks. Denmark had also recently lost Norway, its partner in kingship, to Sweden in the Napoleonic Wars, and warfare had left the state essentially bankrupt. At the same time, wealthy Danish businessmen and professionals were advocating for French-inspired ideas of a constitutional state with branches of government to replace the monarchy's absolute power. They had to wait until 1848, when Fredrick VII put on the crown and abolished absolutism.

Under the new ruling order, Iceland's place was suddenly in flux. Our hero Jón looked up from the history books with a solid legal argument.

Iceland was never really a part of Denmark, he argued. Rather, it had been the property of the Danish-Norwegian king. The country had initially sworn loyalty to the Norwegian king—not the Norwegian state—and then renewed their vows as subjects under Danish absolutism. Now absolutism was gone, and Iceland should also get its own constitution and advisory assembly. In other words, it was time to restore the Alþingi. What's more, Jón added, trade should be free because of the inefficiency of buying, for instance, British timber via Danish wholesale. And finally, he added, Iceland was never a burden, and here he pulled from his hat an elaborate calculation of exactly how much Iceland was owed for overpaying for their imports.

Incredibly, Denmark was swayed. Iceland did not quite get full sovereignty, but in 1845 the Alþingi was restored. In an old classroom, for the first time in hundreds of years, the Alþingi assembled once again. It had been imbued with very little power, but still, Iceland had a parliament again. Allies of Jón's managed to establish the new assembly in Reykjavík, rather than Þingvellir, even though the romantic nationalists, as well as the king himself, favored the original Þingvellir location. Over the decades to come, largely thanks to this particular decision, Reykjavík transformed from a Danish shopping street to an Icelandic capital. The town became industrialized with trawlers and trade unions. The brain drain to Copenhagen slowed, with better schools and professional training finally available at home.

Independence took generations, as each milestone was slowly achieved: a constitution in 1874, home rule in 1904, sovereignty status in 1918, a republic in 1944. The largest achievement yet would be to bring the idea to life. The next movement would be to mobilize the population and build a political class.

In retrospect, it was fortuitous that Iceland started the fight early, as they dodged the risk of being used as a token in Denmark's dwindling global enterprise. The establishment of the Alþingi protected Iceland in unforeseen ways. Had Iceland's autonomy been nonexistent, like that of most other colonies, Denmark could have invited in their allies for political favors.

The piecemeal distribution of Iceland likely would have begun with France in 1856, when the superpower respectfully asked to purchase a remote fjord in the West Fjords region, the Dýrafjörður, in order to establish a base for their North Atlantic fishing fleet, along with a fish-processing center housing four thousand to five thousand people, five times the size of Reykjavík. Iceland's parliament rejected the proposal, and Denmark did not dare override the decision. Next, the United States came poking around, operating under the principles of the Monroe Doctrine, seeking to drive European influence out of the Americas with money as much as force. They made various bids for land, including offering Russia $7.2 million for Alaska in 1867, and another bid that same year for the Virgin Islands, Denmark's only colony in the region (the offer was accepted decades later). In the lead up to the Danish negotiations, the US secretary of state, William H. Seward, had the Department of State prepare a report on the feasibility of purchasing Iceland and Greenland, titled "A Report on the Resources of Iceland and Greenland." The offer was never put to a vote.

And just as well for the Americans, because in the end, the United States got to borrow Iceland for free, and all it took was World War II.

5

World War II

Iceland from 1918 to 1945

I always said it. Hitler should not be trusted.
Had people just taken my advice, this mess
[World War II] would never have happened.

—A SHEEP FARMER IN NORTHERN ICELAND
LECTURING HIS WORKERS DURING A
COFFEE BREAK, ACCORDING TO *NÚ ER
HLÁTUR NÝVAKINN*, A COLLECTION OF
ANECDOTES FROM THE REGION.

Some of the oldest color film footage ever taken of Iceland was shot aboard a cruise ship sailing around the Westmann Islands. The archipelago of fifteen dome-shaped islands sits on a volcanic hot spot just ten miles off the southern coast. The largest island, Heimaey, is inhabited by a community referred to as the Eyjamenn—the island people—by "continental" Icelanders. The journey as the ship enters Heimaey's harbor is stunning. It sails through a narrow inlet, passing sheer black-green cliffs that plunge into the sea, crossed by the flight of fulmars and skuas. The old film footage is silent. All it reveals, so far, is a voyage in an astounding landscape. End of shot.

Next cut: the camera is on solid ground, pointed at some of the quaint houses that once dotted Heimaey (in 1973, the town would have to be rebuilt after a volcanic eruption). The sequence moves quickly, reflecting the price of color film, but the cameraperson lingers for a few seconds on the sight of clean laundry luffing on a clothesline in the ocean breeze. Green gardens suggest the peak of summer. The idyllic motifs continue as the filmmaker's eye is drawn to children. One girl stands with her fist gripping the neck of a dead puffin, a local delicacy. She poses with two friends. The camera then cuts to a blond boy, probably around eight years old, and stays on him long enough to capture a shy smile toward the camera. The clip suggests an eye drawn toward the innocent, the gentle and pure. In context, it's bone-chilling.

Holding the camera was Eva Braun. Eva Braun, Adolf Hitler's girlfriend and partner in suicide: a woman who stayed with him for a decade, through the entire Holocaust; the only woman who could call der Führer by his first name, Adolf, dear.

Braun was in Iceland in the summer of 1939, the year World War II began, traveling on board the *Milwaukee*, a cruise liner from the Nazi state-operated leisure organization Kraft durch Freude. The ship's manifest lists her real name, next to her mother's and her older sister's, Gretl. Only they know about the life she leads back home; the relationship with Hitler was a secret for fourteen years, based on Hitler's idea that a bachelor status would lure female followers.

After the Westmann Islands, the ship docked in Reykjavík and rented out the entire local taxi fleet in order to view the hot springs in nearby Hveragerði. From there the ship's course was set for the Northwest and Northeast, docking at the regional capitals of Ísafjörður and Akureyri. According to a pamphlet about the voyage, the *Milwaukee* returned to Travemünde, Germany, on August 3, less than a month before

Germany kicked off the most devastating war in history by invading Poland.

At the ship's stern flew the Nazi flag, bearing the swastika. The symbol was in fact already familiar in Iceland: its left-facing form (卍) was known as Thor's hammer and was featured in the logo of the nation's largest shipping company. Germany's version, with its rightward tilt, prompted curiosity at first. But by then, the presence of Germans had become familiar, and no one bothered the wealthy visitors with questions on style.

Months before Eva Braun's visit, Germany had bought a prominent villa in downtown Reykjavík, one designed by the legendary Gudjón Samúelsson, the creator of the National Theater and the Hallgrímskirkja Church. The three-floor Túngata 18 was set to host an incoming consultant and Nazi party favorite: the retired physician Dr. Werner Gerlach. For debt-burdened Germany, he had a startlingly large budget to spend on a tiny island nation still under the rule of the Danish king.

The full scale of Germany's prewar operations remains unclear due to the sheer volume of documents the Nazi regime destroyed during the course of its collapse. We do know that after the Weimar Republic's end in 1933, state-sponsored German "scientists" were arriving in Iceland in ever-growing numbers, with vague objectives. We also know that the German flag carrier Lufthansa sent corporate agents to lobby for a transatlantic base that could function as a layover between Germany and the United States. The political objective of Dr. Gerlach has come to light only in recent decades, thanks to local historian Thor Whitehead's study of private letters and diaries. Dr. Gerlach, documents show, was a puppet for

Heinrich Himmler, leader of the Nazi death squad Schutz-staffel, better known by its runic letters ⚡⚡. Himmler, the evil architect of the Holocaust, was a firm believer in the concept of the Thousand-Year Reich—a "pure" German empire set to last for a millennium—and he was considering Iceland as the site for a long-term fort in the North Atlantic.

Winston Churchill, summarizing an observation made by one of his generals, said during the war: "Whoever possesses Iceland holds a pistol firmly pointed at England, America and Canada." Iceland's location in the middle of the North Atlantic turned out to be crucial during the war years. But neither side knew just how important Iceland was going to get. Early on, the Nazis' interest in Iceland was as ideological as it was militaristic. Iceland, with its homogeneous populace and violent history, complemented the Nazi conception of "Aryan heritage." Bizarrely, they viewed the isolated nation as harboring a kind of "original" Aryan race, one rooted in heroic sagas and all-knowing gods like Odin and Thor.

Reality of life in Iceland would later disappoint the dispatched agents. But among Nazi leaders who never actually visited Iceland, the crush was real. And extremely dangerous, as the dream of conquering Iceland filtered up to the Nazi Party's highest ranks.

Himmler did not succeed. But the specter of a Nazi invasion changed the fate of Iceland forever.

❀

In 1929, the United States plunged into the Great Depression. Investors lost faith in Wall Street and pulled out vast sums of money in a panic. Meanwhile, on Main Street in Reykjavík, optimism and excitement saturated the national atmosphere. The biggest celebration in the nation's history was on the horizon: the one-thousand-year anniversary of the Alþingi. Everyone (everyone!) was invited for a multiday celebration at the original Law Rock in Þingvellir. Remember the Tolkien nanny Arndís, from earlier? She left England at the start of that summer primarily so she wouldn't miss out on this epic party.

Iceland was a sovereign state, reaching its teenage years after Denmark had finally signed the emancipation papers, in 1918. The king of Denmark would still be Iceland's head of state, according to the treaty, but the commitment was set to expire twenty-six years later, when it would put Iceland's future into its own hands: it could remain under the protection of the Danish king, or it could become a republic with its own leader and foreign ties.

Inconveniently, Denmark had approved the breakup in the midst of the coldest winter in living memory (and on record, still). The Spanish flu had also ravaged Reykjavík just months prior, claiming the lives of some five hundred people, many of them at their prime (older people had immunity from an earlier, milder outbreak). And on top of that, the Katla volcano—the mother of all volcanoes—sent southern Icelanders fleeing a V-4 eruption.

Icelanders, in short, barely had the energy to wave the Danes goodbye. Cold, ill, and fleeing lava, many wondered if standing on their own was such a good idea after all.

The flu, frost, and ash eventually passed. Come 1930, there was a serious need for a morale boost. The free nation could finally address its Alþingi founders with dignity and show the world where "the oldest still-running" parliament was founded.* In my humble opinion, no nation is better at humble bragging than Iceland (no offense, Sweden). For example, memorizing the stats of "per capita" achievements is a common adult interest and, per capita, this 1930 celebration outdid any national festival the world had seen thus far. Some forty thousand people, a third of the population, arrived with tents and an extra pair of clean socks.

The Danish king Christian IV bestowed the honor of his visit on the festival, arriving on a royal vessel. Instead of carrying flowers, he had his butlers unload a large piece of lumber. "Here," it is said he shouted: "I've brought you the old Valþjófsstaða door!" The wooden church door, with its thirteenth-century carvings, had been rescued from destruction during the Laki eruptions—or stolen by the Danes, depending on who's talking—and is today considered the most valuable non-book item in the National Museum, together with the famous Eyrarland statue, a millennium-old bronze statue of Thor.

The ceremony began with Þingvellir (now a UNESCO World Heritage site) being declared a national park, and a sacred place in the nation's history. For two days, a program of national pep talks ran from morning to evening. Those assembled burst into song with more frequency than a Bollywood film and, naturally, the melody of Icelandic patriotism is best delivered by choir. Organizers had, in fact, formed an

* Alþingi did assemble when the country was under Danish-Norwegian kings for all but forty-four years, but it served more like a local court and municipality. Its location remained at Þingvellir from AD 930 until Reykjavík emerged as the de facto capital. During the transition period, it was between housing arrangements for a while and was, for some years officially registered in the living room of its richest member.

elite Þingvellir choir just for the event, selecting the best voices from the hundreds of choirs across the country. There was also a two-hundred-person gymnastic show (none of it filmed!), and every evening from nine to eleven, a tournament of glíma (glee-ma), the old Viking sport similar to judo that, much like the recipe for skyr, had died out everywhere else.

The king watched the speeches. What did he think? To Denmark, Iceland was like some strange cousin who always had money troubles. Was he melancholic about its newly won independence? Happy? It was impossible to tell. At some point, their behavior begged the question: are they just . . . drunk?

Alcohol was forbidden at the celebration (wink, wink), just as it was officially illegal throughout the entire country. Prohibition passed in a 1915 referendum, but it didn't hold water for long. Spain tipped the scales seven years later by refusing to buy salted cod (bacalao) unless Iceland imported its red wine. Fine! Our hands were tied.

Thereafter, anyone caught drinking moonshine could simply blame a wine tasting gone bad. Prohibition was repealed in another national referendum in 1933. But the majority vote was tight and, to appease a powerful temperance movement, Iceland's parliament decided beer would remain illegal. The ban held for seventy-four years, while all other booze was completely legal. Meanwhile, red wine was too expensive for binge drinking. Thus the Icelandic drink of choice became a 50 proof caraway-infused unsweetened schnapps named Brennivín (literally, "burning wine"), sold in green bottles resembling those used to hold medicine, meant to make the drink look unappealing and sold at the state-run liquor stores with grumpy staff.*

"I don't recall falling asleep sober that summer," wrote an older Reykjavík resident in his memoir (as recounted by author Jakob F. Ásgeirsson). Worn out from two straight days of inspiring speeches, rousing gymnastics, and perhaps a touch of drink, people packed their tents and headed home. For more partying.

It was good that the locals had gotten their fun in all summer, because reality set in brutally at the start of fall. The collapse of American finance meant US banks could no longer lend money to Germany and Austria, the two nations still licking their wounds from the Great War. European banks' cashflow ran dry, and national economies across the continent swiftly shut their doors, imposing tariffs and restrictions on the flow of money into and out of the country. Demand for Iceland's fish took a big hit, while the price of imports increased. Suddenly it seemed that the more globalized your economy, the more vulnerable you were.

And foreign trade was the lifeblood of Iceland's economy. So much of what people used simply could not be manufactured domestically. Out of fear that the krona would lose too much of its value and set off hyperinflation, the government imposed a strict form of capital controls. All "nonessential" spending of precious foreign currency was monitored by bureaucrats. Need to buy paint? Fill out this form. Travel abroad? Fill out a form listing the details of your entire budget. People

---

* With alcoholism still widespread, most Icelanders favor strict government restrictions on alcohol sales. Apart from bars, alcohol—beer included—is only sold at government-run monopoly stores, with limited opening hours and high taxes.

needed permission and paperwork for every import, down to a single book. Fruit was limited to a Christmas luxury and, for a while, was considered nonessential for everyone but the sick and old—and they had to show a doctor's note at the grocery store. Unemployment soared, and people careened from a joyful summer party into a depressed autumn.

Amid the economic suffering, a group of Reykjavík brainiacs with mariners' caps and mustaches began to assemble for a different kind of party: the Communist Party.

The Icelandic Communist Party was part of the Comintern, the Lenin-founded organization advocating world domination through union-led revolutions. The leader was a charismatic Trotsky look-alike who headed the Icelandic herring monopoly (herring, the "silver of the sea," was fished by multinational ships in Icelandic waters, and this monopoly was meant to prevent them from elbowing out local enterprises). Early members included the two most respected Icelandic writers, Halldór Laxness and Þórbergur Þórdarson, who became magnets for support.

Soon enough, Reykjavík saw its first-ever riot. The Gutto fight took place when workers clashed with police outside a city hall assembly—or, depending on who tells the story, policemen with white batons attacked unarmed proletarians using their civil rights to protest.

Meanwhile, a group of right-wingers thought the authorities were too soft. "Hit 'em harder!" they said, and soon enough, they had established their own political movement: the Icelandic Nazi Party (officially named the Nationalist Party).

The Nazis were led by a man named Gísli Sigurbjörnsson, nicknamed Gitler, on the streets of Reykjavík. Membership was largely composed of frustrated middle-class university students who got scared as they saw their privilege chipped away by the recession. The same was true of fascist movements elsewhere. In 1930, when Hitler was still a fringe figure, some 5 to 10 percent of all German university students were members of the Nazi Party. Academics were also early supporters of fascist ideologies because the agenda embraced research and rarified the past.

The Reykjavík Nazis kept busy by dressing up in uniforms and posing for photographs in public, while the Communists wrote songs and poems and catchy slogans—an outdoor-indoor divide. The groups only rarely clashed, and the excitement raised by swastika flags and smart uniforms can only last so long without any serious action or widespread support. Years later, Gitler and his clean-cut friends lost momentum after some embarrassing election results, never exceeding 2.8 percent of votes in local elections. Their last public march was in 1938.

So in the spring of 1939, when the uptight Dr. Gerlach arrived in the world's northernmost capital, he struggled to make friends with anyone other than German nationals living in Iceland and a few long-standing German allies. Gerlach was described as one of the best pathologists in Europe, but his devotion to the Nazi Party got him fired from his university in Switzerland. In return, his promotion within the Nazi Party was swift. He was invited to serve the Third Reich in Iceland, a place of "high culture." What an honor! Imagine the anticipation of a Nazi who'd been promised he could work with "pure" Aryans. His voyage was like that of a kid heading to an actual unicorn ranch, only to be stabbed by a horn.

The people of Iceland were filthy, and their so-called capital was a complete shithole. Literally.

This was a town with open sewers and no paved streets; it was no place for a man who wore tight, spotless uniforms and high boots. At the edge of town, sheep roamed freely. Gerlach's house was near the harbor (the Old Harbor), and rowdy drunks kept him and his family awake at night. Workers were unreliable and greedy for foreign cash. The newspapers mocked Hitler day after day, and despite Gerlach's repeated grievances, the prime minister refused to censor the press. Theaters performed plays written by Jews. The retail store where he planned to buy a dress for his wife had just two items on sale, and they were both the same size. People ate pickled sheep testicles (hrútspungar), burned sheep's head (svið), and held forks in their right hands like shovels. There were no apples in the store.

"The Jews," Gerlach wrote, "will never creep into local businesses. The Icelanders are simply worse swindlers." Wow! In just a few months, the Icelanders had trashed their own reputation. But Gerlach kept these frustrations private. As was typical in Nazi Germany, he was afraid to speak his mind when reporting back to higher-ranking officials like Himmler. These officials regarded Iceland with general admiration, and tarnishing that image would potentially ruin his own funding. So he focused his ambitions on people with German roots of some kind: German nationals living in Iceland and local elites who had studied in Germany. His family—his wife and daughter— even founded a Hitler Youth movement for the children of German nationals (Icelandic laws forbid weapons, so the camp was part Boy Scout activities, part brainwashing).

Whitehead believes that Gerlach's fundamental orders

were in fact meant to establish a "fifth army" of rebels who would aid the German military when it descended on the country. It was still unclear whether the Nazis would invade Iceland in the near future; the plan, for now, was mostly in service to Himmler's obsession with Nordic culture as the "lost relatives" of the Aryan race. Himmler had personally founded an entire institution in Germany called the Forefather Legacy to study the Nordic legacy and sought to revive old Norse celebrations like the ones around the winter solstice to replace Christian rituals, considered "too Jewish." No wonder the Third Reich had sponsored a team of glíma to attend the 1936 Olympics in Berlin. The wrestlers competed in an unofficial tournament, and some reports claim that Hitler was briefly among the spectators.

Gerlach, according to his notes, did admire one thing in Reykjavík: the local pool. Built the year he arrived, the Sundhöll Reykjavíkur swim hall is another work of Gudjón Samúelsson and part of a national push to fight the nation's enemy number one: the ocean. In an era when fully half of the men worked at sea for some length of time, and on ever-larger vessels, a sudden storm could devastate whole villages, even regions, overnight. The death counts of seamen were reported regularly over public radio, much like the loss of foot soldiers during wartime. A listener would hear the announcer read a name, along with the victim's home address, marital status, and number of children. When a small dinghy capsized near Akranes, some three hundred breaststrokes away from land—and six children lost their fathers—the country had had enough of bad maritime news, so the government passed a law mandating swimming lessons for students in grades one through ten. Soon every community—large and small, rich and poor—had a public pool with children going back and forth from morning to afternoon. It seemed like a logical response. Yet for decades to come, Icelanders would continue to listen to the radio with a sigh and murmur, Hafið gefur, hafið tekur—the ocean gives, the ocean takes away. Whether or not you've learned to swim the backstroke, the freezing ocean is a difficult place to escape.

Because the country had no military, to join a boat crew meant you were enrolling in Iceland's single most dangerous profession. And despite the alarming news of another war brewing in continental Europe, Iceland remained fixated on safety at sea—not national defense. No army = no enemies. That was the logic. The other Nordic nations practiced the same strategy, but with armed neutrality, much as Switzerland did. Being small and neutral and nonthreatening had served the nation well during the First World War. Sailors and fishmongers waved the white flag and sold their catch across battle lines, even prompting a bidding war between Germany and the United States. As the various forces on the mainland assembled to blow one another to smithereens, again, the government of Iceland said, again: We'll take care of the fish. How much do you need?

But as it turned out, World War II was not simply a rerun of the Great War. German forces had much greater ambitions than reclaiming what was previously lost. Hitler had been ramping up the military for years, until it reached an unprecedented strength. He wanted to own Europe. He would settle for nothing less. The invasion of Poland was his first move; the next was even more surprising: the occupation of Denmark and Norway. Germany needed iron ore to keep up military production and sought to force its way toward mineral-rich northern Sweden via Denmark and Norway. Control over Norway, furthermore, gave Germany access to the North Atlantic, the sea route vital to Britain's supply chain.

From a military standpoint, the next smart move would be to grab a peaceful mid-Atlantic island and turn it into a base camp.

Whoever gets there first, wins.

To Iceland!

❀

For anyone who is enduring a winter within the Arctic Circle, one thing is important to keep in mind: the sun pays back its debt in full. The annual hours of sunlight total the same, everywhere on earth. At the extreme end, the North Pole has six straight months of night, followed by six months of day. Iceland is a version of that, tuned down by 25° latitude.

The darkest day of the year is December 21. From then on, the days slowly get longer again. By February, the day is extending by seven minutes per day. Come March, bank robbers have just enough time to do their thing in broad daylight. By April, the Northern Lights fade into the ever-bright evenings, and birds arrive from their winter whereabouts. And May provides no place to hide—no darkness.

The British army invaded Reykjavík at five a.m. on a Friday in May. The mission, dubbed Operation Fork, was meant to surprise the people of Iceland, arriving as it did with the ship lights shut off. But when the four warships sailed into harbor, a massive crowd of onlookers stood there watching. They'd seen them miles away.

The convoy had first passed the Reykjanes Peninsula, the

boot-shaped corner that stretches out of Reykjavík, with fish-ermen in Keflavík noticing the unusual convoy. But it was the middle of the night, and they didn't see a reason to notify the authorities because Iceland had nothing to do with the war—those guys must be headed somewhere else. Britain, for its part, had not taken into consideration that the ships would arrive on a public holiday and a payday for fishermen, when a good number were awake in the middle of the night, drinking and dancing. Police and taxi drivers on drunkard duty were the first to spot ships on the horizon. One, two, three, four . . . gray . . . warships. Were they British or German? No one knew.

The British cabinet had decided not to notify Icelandic au-thorities ahead of their arrival and instead jumped straight to an actual invasion. Their reasoning was that despite unoffi-cially leaning toward Britain in the war, the Icelandic govern-ment would likely reject any suggestion of military protection due to their "neutrality." If they'd first been given the oppor-tunity to reject the Brits, the forthcoming invasion might be met with more hostility. Plus, if word got out, Germany had their fleet in northern Norway and could get there faster than the British.

The only two people in Reykjavík certain about the nation-ality of the approaching ships were the British consul (thanks to a radio telegram) and the German consul (thanks to the process of elimination). Dr. Gerlach had long since sensed that the Icelandic public, as well as Icelandic politicians, fa-vored the British in the war. "Iceland: a British country under a Danish crown," he wrote in one of his secret files—the very documents he'd intended to burn before British forces arrived. "Bring the files! Light the boiler!" he'd ordered, realizing no one at the residence knew how to light the coal heater. "Get me Moris!"

Alvin Hermann Ernst Moris was an older man of German origin who worked as a janitor at the consul. He lived at the other end of town. And he had chronic back pain. To leave the house, he needed to put on a corset-shaped support frame, and he couldn't do it by himself, as he explained to the consul maid who was sent running to his house. Being a polite man, Moris didn't want to wake up the lady who usually helped him. The maid, therefore, had to make several fumbling attempts to get him dressed. Historians owe a lot to these two slow consul staffers, because all the while, Gerlach's files awaited the flames.

The harbor crowd grew bigger, and then significantly less anxious as soon as the ship's flag was visible. The British consul arrived with his suitcase, a clear indicator of the nationality of the incoming troops. Britain was hoping for a peaceful operation—though the mariners were ordered to load their guns just in case. But as the ship got closer, it was easy to read the crowd: everybody was standing completely still, even the police.

The consul, according to witnesses, tapped the shoulder of a policeman standing in the middle of the crowd and asked, "Would you mind getting the crowd to stand back a bit so that the soldiers can get off the destroyer?"

The policeman, whose job description likely did not require him to help foreign invaders, just nodded: "Certainly."

Britain, the empire that has invaded all but twenty-two countries in the world (by an estimate defining the term broadly; others claim all but sixty-three nations have been invaded), could check Iceland off as a smooth operation.

At six a.m., the first regiment of soldiers stood lining the harbor, at ease. A noticeably drunk man walked through the crowd and raised his fist, shaking it in the direction of one soldier. Another ashed his cigarette into the barrel of a rifle. Then they, along with the rest of the crowd, wandered off. That was it: the resistance.

Some historians have argued that Icelanders actually could have fended off the invaders using hunting rifles, pitchforks, and fish cutters. Such was the disastrous shape of things on board the warships: the arsenal was more or less a junkyard dating from the First World War, and the soldiers were seasick and utterly untrained shooters. From a strategic point, the operation was totally haphazard; much of the planning was conducted en route and the force was supplied with few maps, most of poor quality, with one of them having been drawn from memory. Civil engineers on board, according to some sources, included a railway expert despite zero need for such expertise in a country without train tracks. No member of the expedition was fully fluent in the Icelandic language.

"It was all a bluff," the mariner Berd Ward recalled in an interview years later. "The Germans would have rolled over us had it come to a battle." But Germany was busy elsewhere; that very same day it shocked the Allies with a lightning invasion of the Low Countries—Belgium, Luxembourg, and the Netherlands—starting the six-week battle for France. And around lunchtime, the prime minister of Britain, Neville Chamberlain, resigned, to be replaced by Winston Churchill. Gisli Jökull Gislason, author of *Iceland in World War II*, calls May 10, 1940, "one of the most dramatic days in the history of the world."

The British forces—a bunch of twentysomethings in uniforms that were, as a rule, either too baggy or too short—split up to seize the town. One unit set up roadblocks at the city's only exit to make sure German residents would not attempt escape. Another went farther from town, under orders to occupy every flat piece of ground, anything that could be a potential landing strip for the Germans—an ambitious task in the flat South. British commander R. G. Sturges, in a statement issued via flyer, apologized sincerely for the "inconvenience." The goal, he said, was to "save Iceland from the fate that Denmark and Norway have suffered." The British manner of "polite but firm" very much characterized the entire operation: while seizing telecommunications, the soldiers made sure to knock before they broke down a few doors. The building's janitor was then showered with apologies and a promise to pay for the damages.

Dr. Gerlach, meanwhile, was not keeping it cool. He had been let down by everyone, even his crippled janitor. *Knock, knock!* The British forces had arrived at the local Nazi's neat cream-colored house set behind the mowed lawn. They stood outside dangling cuffs. Dr. Gerlach tried to stall them by yelling through the door, "You can't come in here! Iceland is a neutral nation!"

A British officer on the other side of the door replied in deadpan Oxford English: "You mean neutral like Denmark?"

Suddenly a soldier noticed smoke coming out of the back window, and the forces rushed inside. Gerlach's wife and daughter were burning the classified documents in the upstairs bathroom, still in their pajamas. A mariner grabbed a bed sheet and stifled the fire. Fearing the house had booby traps, the Brits forced Gerlach to walk first into every room. And then onto a ship bound for London. He was extradited in a prisoner swap months later and continued to serve the SS, stationed in Paris, among other places.

The documents that escaped the fire shed light on how a supposedly rational physician got consumed by a Nazi cult. Signed pictures of Himmler and Hermann Göring, the supreme commander of the Luftwaffe, were found in the family's possession, as well as two paintings of Hitler and a portrait statue, surrounded by candles. "Very strange scene," one British officer wrote. A receipt from the downtown store Flowers & Fruits for one French hydrangea, bought on Hitler's birthday (April 20), was among the files recovered.

Over the next several weeks, British forces sought to establish control over the entire country. Locals still did not seem quite clear on where they'd come from. A British soldier recalled meeting a man yelling, "I like you! I like you!" in English, but then adding, just in case, "And Heil Hitler!"

Germany's blitzkrieg—a shock strategy of striking without notice and moving fast across the front lines—got them France. Withdrawing from the fight, British forces got trapped in the French coastal town of Dunkirk. Roughly 320,000 troops managed to flee German airstrikes on rescue boats that took them to safety in England. Charles de Gaulle, the leader of France, fled to London. Churchill addressed his nation: "The Battle of France is over. The Battle of Britain is about to begin."

The Allies—Britain and France—had been ousted from Europe, and the Nazis controlled the entire coastline from Spain to Norway. The only thing standing in the way of a Nazi invasion of the UK were twenty-one nautical miles, the width of the English Channel at its narrowest point. Knowing the German Kriegsmarine could not get past the Royal Navy, Hitler decided to use his sea forces strategically. Instead of attacking

Britain directly, the plan was to strangle its cargo routes, depriving the island nation of everything from food and clothing to oil and iron.

Control of Iceland would help. Hitler—a villain who spent his political career yelling so much that he needed polyps removed from his vocal cords, twice—ordered his generals to put together a plan to snatch the northern fort. Forming a plan was better than arguing with Hitler, so, knowing that Germany lacked the resources, German generals drafted a wishful plan dubbed Fall of Icarus.

During the first eighteen months of the war, Germany destroyed some 40 percent of Britain's merchant ships. Their strategy was working tremendously well. Britain tried to guard its cargo by embedding it with battleships, which met only mild success. Because Germans only needed their fleet to attack—not transport—they could focus production on submarines called U-boats, an English abbreviation of Unterseeboot. One by one, the U-boats scouted the main sea routes. Once a target was spotted, the U-boats would gather in a "wolfpack." The surprise attacks decimated the convoys. For a while, it looked as if the U-boats alone might win Hitler the battle for Britain, which would have allowed him to focus entirely on the invasion of the Soviet Union, secretly his ultimate goal in the war. German submarine crews saw it as just a matter of time before Britain surrendered. They later referred to these first two years in the Atlantic as "the Happy Time."

In the United States, President Roosevelt realized that Hitler's ambition and the rise of fascist political powers could not be ignored much longer and started seeking a stronger alliance with Britain and France—the Allies. His problem, however, was to convince the American public. Opinion polls, a relatively new political phenomenon, showed 84 percent against "sending Army and Navy to fight Germans," according to a 1939 Gallup poll. Roosevelt's administration took careful but gradual steps toward increased military spending, first strictly in the form of military aid to Britain. Under the Lend-Lease Act, as the aid was known, Britain could order war supplies, food, and clothing, regardless of their ability to pay.

Roosevelt's second move was to extend the so-called Pan-American Security Zone to Iceland, moving the defense line beyond its North American boundaries in Greenland. Following the move, US diplomats asked Icelandic officials to "ask" the United States for protection during the war. The idea was to assist Britain by taking over its tasks in Iceland without officially entering the war, allowing Britain to send the twenty-five thousand troops stationed in Iceland on to direct combat. Iceland went ahead with a formal "request," which the United States was "obliged" to approve under the new defense line.

After one year of British occupation, the Americans arrived in Reykjavík. Local restaurants changed their menus from fish and chips to hot dogs and meatloaf.

⊛

At its peak, the occupation of Iceland would include the equivalent, statistically speaking, of 55 million foreign troops occupying the United States based on 1940 populations. There were nearly fifty thousand men and dozens of female nurses, equaling about 40 percent of Icelanders. And they were all speaking a language few locals understood. But even if they could have a chat, what was there to talk about? The Americans didn't know the rules in soccer, had never read *Njál's Saga*, and they thought capelin was a type of cigarette (it's a fish). They walked around with chewing gum and a smile, exhibiting exceptional dental health, and shopped for more gum in Carl's Yankee Doodle Inn, one of many new commercial openings. Compared with the early British mariners, they looked "war-reared like thoroughbred horses," in spotless uniforms with rifles attached to the shoulder. Always with the rifle, they were no fun to sit next to in the movie theater, the barrel either blocking the view or sticking up the nostrils "constantly." But the single most annoying thing about them (according to some, at least) was the fact that Icelandic women saw them as great guys.

"The first time I saw a man 'seat' a woman by pulling out the chair behind her was an American," said Sigridur Bjornsdóttir, a hotel receptionist for many years, interviewed in old age for a television documentary. "We had no idea this kind of gentleman existed!"

Throughout the occupation, no issue sparked more animosity than the love affairs between Icelandic women and American soldiers. Young women were eager to mingle with boys their age who could introduce them to new music, share drinks of club soda with imported lime, and teach them dances they'd seen in the movies. Anyone with even mild levels of curiosity and rebellion would be, right? Had fifty thousand young women invaded, would the Icelandic men have told one another to hold back on the partying in order to save the nation from moral decay that would mark the end of Nordic culture as we know it and cause them and everyone they know to live in regret and shame and disgust? Probably not. Probably they, too, would have tied on their dancing shoes and not come home until the next day. Newspapers at the time—surprise—did not see the "problem" in this light. "The Situation," as the issue was known, called for sensational media stories about prostitution and the beginning of an American takeover by blood. The government even established the "Situation Committee" in order to investigate and advise on the matter and temporarily locked up juvenile girls accused of streetwalking. Men hovered outside American nightclubs to write down the names of women attending, and more than once a local newspaper published their names.

Despite the bad blood, Icelandic men had to get along with the occupation forces during the day, at least. They either worked for the military or wanted to work for the military. To host tens of thousands of newcomers, the country needed houses, with pipes and plumbing. And, of course, an entire defense infrastructure: airports, harbors, warehouses for weaponry, bunkers, and sand blocks. Laundry services alone, needed to wash the uniforms and sweaty outfits of thousands of military personnel, created its own labor market for women at the hot springs in the Laugar valley, the site of Reykjavík's largest outdoor pool. Men fretted over the interaction leading to "laundry love," but they were, for the most part, too busy to act. A famous tale from a hiring agency in Reykjavík describes a farmer arriving in search of a worker for the lambing season. No way, he was told—everyone was too busy building barracks. "Rats," the man replied, "this means I have to quit the military work myself!"

Thousands of farmers permanently abandoned their bucolic lifestyle over the booming years, and the rural population dropped from 35 percent to 27 percent of the nation over a span of just six years, beginning a trend of urbanization that in other Western countries had occurred much earlier. In the words of Indridi Thorsteinsson, who was a teenager when the war broke out: "We used to pester our parents for money to buy movie tickets with friends. But after the soldiers arrived, we were spending money on taxis without going anywhere, just for the pleasure of driving around." Indridi later wrote *Cab 79*, an era-defining novel featuring a farmer who moves to Reykjavík to work as a taxi driver during the war. (His son, by the way, is the crime author Arnaldur Indridason, whose best-selling Nordic noir, *Silence of the Grave*, is set in occupied Reykjavík.)

All that work was paid in precious dollars. From 1940 to 1946, the purchasing power of unskilled workers (meaning just about everyone) grew a whopping 86 percent, an insane rate of economic success at a time when most other capital cities in Europe were in rubble. With bank vaults full of foreign cash, the government still didn't relax the capital controls on "nonessential" items like gifts. Blank printing paper was easy to import, for example, but not the actual printed books. So the nation's writers, painters, and sculptors had to roll up their sleeves too, and make stuff that people wanted to buy. Books were the easiest to mass-produce and were soon seen as generous Christmas gifts. The tradition is still alive, in fact: the Book Flood is when publishers release most of their titles, ahead of the Christmas season. The influence of the original Book Flood, which created a wider and more consumer-focused selection than the country had ever before seen, is evident by the publishing date of various translated children's books—many of them first entered the market in the 1940s to meet a rise in demand for children's literature. Other emerging genres died out, such as the one of writing creatively shocking accounts of women who were "seduced" by the soldiers, with priceless titles like *The Underworlds of Reykjavík* and *After Midnight at Hotel Borg*, with a gripping cover blurb:

> What can happen when a young, inexperienced, sensitive girl first comes to the capital and takes her first steps into the nightlife.
>
> The street lights are off. The music of the cafés is silenced. Then . . .
>
> Read the true story, told by the girl herself!

My favorite is *Love in the Backseat*, a vivid tell-all by a taxi driver named Gudlaugur Gudmundsson with chapters titled "Both Were Butt Naked," "What a Long Day That Was," and "Sit Down! Sit Down!" In a range of stories, published after the war, Gudlaugur is unapologetic about his tendency to prey on his clients. In his own telling, his passengers are very happy to get him involved. Together the stories show the many forms of relationship between local women and foreign soldiers, each as complicated as love itself. One couple pays him to drive them to a quiet location a few times each week and then leave the car for ninety minutes so they can spend time together in secret. Another soldier seeks Gudlaugur's advice when he is being transferred to the mainland but lacks courage to tell his Icelandic girlfriend that he is in fact married with kids back in America, and he does not plan to keep in touch. "Is she pregnant?" Gudlaugur asks, and the soldier confirms she's not. With that Gudlaugur offers to tell the girl the man has died in combat, to shield her from "unnecessary" heartbreak. The gallery of passengers continues, each consumed by love and a social dilemma. A married woman in her fifties makes love to a lieutenant half her age in Gudlaugur's backseat. At night he picks up passengers outside the Borg Hotel and witnesses prostration, exploitation, and violence. A soldier who gets in the car with a seventeen-year-old girl gets aggressive with her. Gudlaugur stops the car. The man turns around, furious:

> When he's halfway out the car door, I give him a decent smack in the face so he collapses and falls backwards between the seats. The girl sobs, shaking with fear, her cloths ripped. . . . I tell her: "Stop crying. Hold him down with your feet and let me know if he wakes up."

These conflicts reflected a completely different wartime experience from that of other countries. The sounds of bombs and machine guns would occasionally erupt far on the horizon. Germany lacked long-distance airplanes and used them primarily to attack ships; flying over land was deemed too risky and unlikely to do much serious damage. This meant that the American soldiers stood scouting the air and sea in wind, rain, sun, and snow without ever coming across any action. But be careful what you wish for. First-time soldiers in Iceland were typically promoted to combat later on, often shipped to another part of the world they knew very little about.

❁

World War II was truly a global war. While World War I saw thirty national forces take part, during World War II the fight was among eighty-one nations that declared war against either the Allies or the Axis. Some nations resisted. For the first six months in Iceland, American troops were strictly a defense force, not actors in the Battle of the Atlantic. But days after Japan's surprise attack in the Pacific, Hitler addressed the German parliament urging for a war against the Americans. He claimed that American forces had already entered the "German fighting zone" by occupying Iceland six months earlier, and their presence on the island was in order "to make the German U-boat warfare as ineffective as it was in 1915–1916." Hitler's list of grievances against the Americans went on, in an incredibly long and incoherent speech; the decision itself is widely regarded as the "most puzzling" move in World War II. America had twice the population of Germany and a massive production infrastructure at a time when the German war machine was stretched out fighting Stalin's Red Army.

Britain agreed to help the Soviet Union against the Nazis with military supplies delivered over the Arctic via Iceland. Iceland was officially a transatlantic cog in a global war machine, a stopover for Allied gear and personnel on their way to the battlefields, from London to Moscow.

To understand how much of warfare was a matter of logistics, consider the rate at which equipment was lost in the war: 11,000 small arms, 68 tanks, 30 aircrafts destroyed, on average, *every day* for 2,194 days running. By this estimate, about 150,000 tanks moved around the globe to destroy and be destroyed. To operate those weapons, about 70 million soldiers fought on behalf of their countries. Some 20 million military personnel died, or roughly 9,000 each day.

The Battle of the Atlantic, a name Churchill claims to have coined, was the longest continuous battle in the war. A series of technological breakthroughs turned the tables for the Allies. First they developed a shortwave radar to detect surfaced U-boats, one small enough to fit into an aircraft; then the introduction of the Leigh light, a massive searchlight for antisubmarine airplanes, allowed them to patrol at night.

The planes, for the most part, took off from Iceland, a country-turned-landing-ship. British forces, to begin with, made a permanent mark on Reykjavík by building a massive airport on its outskirts, known today as the domestic airport and loathed by city planners for occupying prime real estate. The Americans went on to build an even bigger airport on the desolated Reykjanes Peninsula: the Keflavík International Airport, originally named Moss Airport after a pilot who died in a storm. Iceland also gave the Allies exclusive access to weather stations in the middle of the North Atlantic. To know the weather is to know when to strike.

That focus on geography disregards the significance and sacrifice of the Icelandic people, which I'd argue was considerable. Britain, early in the war, turned half its trawler fleet into warships, about six hundred ships. The move was considered vital to keep the upper hand in the Atlantic, but the government worried that a shortage of cheap fish would wreck the national diet of fish and chips. That, as noted by officials, would grossly "upset" the working class, and subsequently affect morale and military production. So Iceland, on orders from London, could sell its entire catch to idle fish factories in England.

But that meant sailing through a war zone, at half the speed of German submarines.

Icelandic sailors demanded a 150 to 200 percent risk fee for crossing the Atlantic. At first, the demand was considered ridiculous. The route wasn't that hazardous! But a year later no one questioned their sacrifices anymore. Armed or not, the U-boats were ordered to weaken the British supply chain by any means available. From sea or air, sailors could expect an attack at any time, each attack a story of defeat. In Skjálfandi Bay, northern Iceland, a cargo vessel was sunk by two German planes that appeared out of nowhere and disappeared just as swiftly, the attackers' identity never known. Another small fishing vessel, the *Holmsteinn*, happened to sail upon a U-boat that had surfaced to meet with a nearby supply ship. The U-boat, in order not to waste a torpedo, shot the boat with a machine gun at close range. Otherwise, the sailors might reveal the U-boat's location, and in a brutal war the next battle matters. Surviving that day, and the next, was all that mattered. Not the fact that Icelandic sailors had a history of helping German seafarers in the past: as recently as 1940, a German crew arriving from Brazil was rescued and brought to harbor in Reykjavík, saving sixty men and two cats.

After the war, Icelandic sailors continued to suffer. Deepsea mines littered the ocean, numbering hundreds of thousands. The Germans and British had laid the traps across charted territory, the longest "fence" reaching from the Shetlands to eastern Iceland via the Faroe Islands. But the mines' location depended on a single anchor chain. Detached from anchor, the floating metal balls, half the size of a Mini Cooper, would drift off and explode against a rock, or a beach, or a passing ship. Even today, fishermen can expect their nets to haul the occasional mine, one that is fortunately unlikely to explode after eighty years in the ocean.

American president Dwight Eisenhower, the five-star general in the war who lead the Normandy invasion, said in his memoir that Iceland's strategic location made a difference on both the western front and eastern front. He, understandably, didn't go so far as to thank Iceland for the Free World's prevailing, but the statement makes a strong point about the speed and duration of the war that claimed the lives of 1,000 people every hour. That means 24,000 lives a day, ongoing for six years and a day, by the lowest estimate. It is, of course, impossible to quantify by how much Iceland-led operations may have shortened the war's duration. A single month? That's 720,000 lives, 60 percent of them civilians.

❀

At age thirty-three, Eva Braun married Hitler. Forty hours later, the couple committed suicide by taking a capsule of cyanide; Hitler then shot himself in the head, while Eva died from the poison.

Braun, or Ms. Hitler, had attempted suicide twice already during their relationship, one that began when she was nineteen and worked as a photography assistant to his personal documentarian. We know little about their relationship besides testimonies from Hitler's inner circle, the only people who knew about it. Braun herself did not keep a diary, but she took pictures, both movies and stills. Her film footage from Iceland was discovered in her private possessions, along with photographs of der Führer engaged in leisurely activities, like reading the paper at their summer residence the Eagle's Nest.

According to *Hitler and Film*, a book by Bill Niven, the couple spent countless evenings satisfying Hitler's strong passion for moving pictures. The screenings took place after supper, often in the company of his closest circle, who described him as having "incredible stamina" to binge movies past midnight—favoring American westerns despite officially banning Hollywood films. He watched all kinds of films, even those starring Jewish actors, at least early on. Braun's Iceland film may well have made his screening party at some point.

If it did, Hitler and his guests watched a world gone by. Beer was still banned, but just about everything else was different—over a six-year period, the country had gone from Europe's poorest to richest. And it kept growing. Iceland qualified for Marshall Plan aid after the war despite having gained two airports, hundreds of barracks to house the urban poor, and multiple bridges precisely because of the war. The Americans were, to many, a delightful alternative to Danish influence in the country, and in 1944 the country voted for complete independence. Voter turnout was 98.4 percent overall, reaching 100 percent in two districts. One man, allegedly, woke up from a coma just to vote yes for an Icelandic republic. Only 377 people, a fractional percentage, voted in favor of remaining in the Danish kingdom.

Americans, who had promised to leave immediately after the war, patted Icelanders on the back. "Freedom! That's the spirit."

About 2 percent of Icelandic women, aged eighteen to thirty-four, left as brides with American soldiers. Another 450 to 500 children, fathered by Americans, were left behind. They made up for the lives lost in the war: 300 locals, mostly sailors. That number may seem relatively low, but considering the total population, it was, in fact, comparable to the US loss of 300,000 people; each country lost 0.2 percent of its population. (The United States, of course, was never invaded beyond Pearl Harbor, so its human toll was low in light of the 70 million overall casualties).

The main lesson for Iceland was that neutrality did not offer protection. The Republic of Iceland took its first steps on the world stage at a time when the world was headed for reconciliation and international cooperation. But who would they work with now? While the Icelandic Nazi Party was history, the Communists were only growing in strength. When parliament voted to join NATO, the western defense alliance, "commies" clashed with police on Austurvöllur Square. Police used teargas and brutally chased protesters with batons, a shocking scene that tainted politics for years to come.

Entering the United Nations was much less controversial, an honor even. But in retrospect, the UN membership was much more fateful, for the world at least: the first Icelandic delegate found himself the kingmaker on a committee tasked with discussing a proposal to establish a Jewish nation in the land of Palestine. Ears open. Clock ticking. What to do, Mr. Iceland?

Peace . . . out.

The Birth of Israel

Iceland from 1944 to 1965

You are God's chosen people. We are God's
frozen people.

—PRIME MINISTER DAVÍÐ ODDSSON TO HIS
ISRAELI COLLEAGUE SHIMON PERES AT
ÞINGVELLIR, ACCORDING TO *KJARNI*
MÁLSINS BY HANNES H. GISSURARSON.

Washington, DC, was experiencing a housing crisis when Thor Thors arrived to establish an Icelandic embassy west of the Atlantic. Past him strutted women in Rita Hayworth curls, men in snappy fedoras, children swinging sticks they pretended were rifles, harried families heading to pick up ration books. It was 1941. The United States had just joined World War II, and the workforce was busy building bombs and learning the names and alliances of some far-flung nations: Malta, Cyprus, Iceland.

Ambassador Thors did not have the government allowance needed to buy a house for the Icelandic embassy, and finding a rental proved impossible. His own pockets, however, suffered no such limits, and after a week in the city he bought a house near Massachusetts Avenue, a private villa with a large garage. That garage was chosen as the site of Iceland's first embassy in the States. Jokes about the Thors family now rang true: Thor Thors was indeed Iceland's landlord.

Thor conducted his new ambassadorial business: welcoming delegates, opening and closing the garage's door. As the war economy cooled, the ambassador moved into a more suitable office building and hired an assistant—his niece. He occasionally reported to the Icelandic authorities, but more often, he delivered news via private correspondence with the prime minister—his brother.

His life as garage ambassador seems to have been a comfortable one. "If you wish to leave the political squabble and become a free man," Thor writes on one occasion to his pen pal kin and Iceland's longest-serving prime minister, Ólafur, "consider becoming an ambassador in, say, Copenhagen." When comparing the difference between hectic politics and unmonitored diplomacy, Thor spoke with experience, having served as a member of Iceland's parliament before moving west.

Iceland's foremost political actors were apparently casual in their communications, ready to blur the line between political and personal. One can imagine "free man" Thor sitting back in his breezy garage embassy, opening letters from his big brother, Prime Minister Ólafur, as the streetcars of 1940s DC clanged by in the distance. His new little embassy was free from scrutiny, unlike, say, the grand and palatial embassies of France or Germany, with their elegant arched doorways and position in the headlines.

Meanwhile, the Thors brothers casually doled out exclusive state secrets to each other. "You better protect them," warned Ólafur, "like the pupil of your eye." Such was their close and casual correspondence that a *Morgunblaðið* (Mork-un-blath-ith) reporter, on a visit to DC, noted with some surprise that

Thors had more insights into current affairs in Iceland "than someone like me who has just left the country."

The Icelandic word for nepotism—*frændhygli*—did not exist until 1995. It was the regular way of life. Success was a lottery determined by birth. The Thors family was the grand prize winner.

In 1945, this family of around 250 members led the largest political party, largest private company, largest shipping enterprise, largest construction company, largest bank, and largest oil supplier. In essence, a Thors family reunion had the potential to arrange deals and decisions affecting the entire nation while cousins shared a plate of lamb chops. No other family clan matched their influence in the postwar economy, when Iceland was suddenly the land of opportunities.

❦

The Thors family legacy began with Thor Philip Axel Jensen. Born and raised in Denmark, Thor Jensen set sail for Iceland in 1878, at the age of fourteen, to work as an apprentice for a Danish trade company. The voyage aboard the *Juno* took fifteen days. He passed the time by playing tunes on the accordion for the crew. The ship sailed around Iceland's northern coast in strong headwinds, and young Thor Jensen saw tall icebergs "blow forward with the wind and currents." Struck by the fantastic scenery, it dawned on him that he knew virtually nothing about the country he was about to live in. It was too late to turn back now. He was set to stay on the unfamiliar island for at least two trading seasons.

He would wind up the richest man in Iceland.

At the time, Danish was so widely spoken in Iceland that

Danish businessmen operating there did not bother learning Icelandic. Thor Jensen, however, was a driven autodidact. Raised among eleven siblings by a single mother, he went to a boarding school for orphans and went straight from school to his apprenticeship in northern Iceland. There he used every opportunity to better understand his Icelandic customers until he felt a kinship with them. The shop where he worked sold newspapers, and he set himself to work learning one word at a time, starting with the headlines. He was a quick study, and soon began picking up more and more Icelandic. While this seems natural, it was a truly entrepreneurial approach at the time. Danish businessmen had never before bothered asking regular Icelanders what they might need. After the first year, Thor learned one of the common needs of the region: they were short on blank notebooks. They needed empty pages on which to pen official information—thus Thor proceeded to learn the basics of bookbinding.

As he studied and worked at the shop, Thor met a local girl named Margrét. They married and moved to Reykjavík, together raising twelve children.

While today Thor Jensen's accomplishments may read like a standard approach for a business mogul, Thor's methods were nothing short of revolutionary at the time. He streamlined production methods and cut out all middlemen. With the backing of his former Danish employer, he established cargo routes to the mainland, exporting fish and importing merchants. He bought his own longline steamer to catch cod and processed the catch into bacalao at his own fish factory, bypassing hundreds of farmers who owned the market before him; he industrialized dairy farming and produced up to two hundred thousand gallons of milk annually, outpacing the capacity of more than eighty regular Icelandic farmers. He sold cheap imports in large quantities—barrels and boxes—way ahead of Costco, the American bulk-size store, today operating one of its busiest warehouses in a Reykjavík suburb.

Thor's success was mixed. As in any business, there were good years and bad. Very bad indeed. His first shipping and fishing enterprise, nicknamed the Million Krona Company, went bankrupt in just seven years. But regardless of the balance sheet, his became the ultimate story of an immigrant pioneer. Here was a man who hailed from the country of Iceland's controllers, a foreigner who was so haughty that he claimed his business's wealth would soon equal Iceland's entire state budget (which it nearly did). He was generous with his employees, but on his own terms; he pushed hard against unions and their first-ever collective demand for the milestone Vökulög, laws which granted sailors a minimum of six hours rest for every eighteen hours of continuous work. His persona dominated as much as his enterprise. When the Spanish flu blazed through Reykjavík in 1918, infecting more than half the residents, he opened a massive soup kitchen to feed everybody.

Meanwhile, along with the wealth of controversial cod mogul Thor Jensen, rumors grew.

The most prominent and malicious gossip circulating about Jensen claimed that the Dane was also a Jew. This was a serious accusation to level at someone in the isolated country at the start of the nineteenth century. Back then, island states like Iceland and Japan were some of the only nation-states left in the world who still had a corresponding ethnic identity in their homogenous and indigenous population. There existed an unspoken political agreement to maintain the nation's homogeneity. During World War II, about ninety Jews made their way to Iceland and sought refuge. Only thirteen of them were granted asylum, despite awareness of the situation they were fleeing.

This lack of hospitality wasn't based on Nazi slurs about the "inferiority" of Jews, but was instead a general and overarching xenophobia. The Nazi ideology never became mainstream in Iceland's politics, largely because Nazi sympathizers had no minority around to persecute. However, it was this very scarcity of targets that led to "Jew branding," suggests Jewish historian Vilhjálmur Vilhjálmsson, referring to the act of labeling "Jewish-looking" people as foreign without any further evidence. And the Thors family ticked all the boxes: foreign, dark-featured, long-nosed, founders of a syndicate. Thor Jensen's mysterious origins aided these rumors (while in reality his Danish forefathers were simply undocumented proletarians). According to Kjartan Thors, a great-grandchild of Thor Jensen, the leader of the so-called Progressive Party allegedly went so far as to send an agent to Europe's mainland to dig up dirt concerning Jensen's alleged Semitic roots.

The agent came up empty-handed: Thor's phenomenal success at industrializing fishing and farming made him the founder of a dynasty, but not a diaspora. These accusations may, however, have played a role in Jensen's children's reinventing themselves.

Ambassador Thor Thors's original name was identical to his father's, Thor Jensen. According to Gudmundur Magnússon, the Thors family biographer, Thors's siblings sought to change the name after one of his brothers traveled to Denmark and found out how common the name was (it is, in fact, the most common surname of Denmark). Back then, it was legal to adopt new family names—author Halldór Gudjónsson, born one year before Thor Thors, changed his name to Halldór Laxness—and thus, in 1915, the Thors siblings all changed their name. A letter sent to authorities requesting the motion doesn't articulate why the change and why this name. Most likely, they just considered Thors to be more authentic, and the aesthetics of it resembled "good" Icelandic family names like Thorarensen and Thorsteinsson. After 1925, Iceland stopped allowing new family names, in order to protect the tradition of patronymic surnames.*

In retrospect, these failed slanders, the Progressive Party's spy on the mainland, and the brand-new name drawn up from scratch are almost poignant in light of the support Jensen's son, Ambassador Thor Thors, would eventually lend the Jewish nation at its most crucial moment.

❀

The surname wasn't the only thing setting the father and son apart. Thor Thors stayed away from industrial farming; he wore suits all his life and was animated by political machinations—and the limelight that came with them. Four years into his position as an ambassador, he briefly described his duties for a reporter: "Some days include a diplomatic lunch at one place, a

---

* In 2020, the government began reversing the century-old ban on family names, allowing parents to adopt new ones for their children. The effect remains unclear, but critics say the patronymic traditions will die out within three generations, citing examples from other Nordic nations. Iceland is the only European nation still using patronymic and matronymic last names.

visit to 2-3 places for cocktail hour, and, finally, a dinner with yet another crowd." As one columnist noted, by that account he attended about 1,825 parties a year.

During World War II, Thor's duties as an ambassador involved making sure important cargo reached Iceland, establishing business connections for companies like Icelandair, and lobbying for the international recognition of the Republic of Iceland. The country had almost no experience creating an independent foreign policy, and the skills Thor gained in Washington paralleled no other Icelandic résumé. When Iceland's foreign minister had to pick an ambassador for Canada, Argentina, and Brazil he appointed Thor—for all three! Daily operations were left in the hands of local consuls, and Thor remained in DC as a kind of American ambassador in chief.

Thor believed international partnership would best establish the country as an independent republic and pressed the government to partake in the conferences that led to the founding of the United Nations. It was a significant commitment for an economy the size of an average US state, with only a few jobs to spare in foreign service. Fortunately, Thor's appetite for work and parties continued to grow. When the United Nations Charter was signed in San Francisco in June 1945, Thor described the mood of the conference to be like a "silver moon's courtship" (the expression makes no sense in Icelandic either). Iceland did not join the United Nations until a year later, as the founding members were required to declare war on Japan in order to create pressure to end the war. Iceland, despite being an "associate power" with the Allies in the battle for the North Atlantic, still sought to be neutral in warfare. But when the time came, Thor was quick to recommend himself as Iceland's representative.

During his time as representative, he gave the General Assembly two lasting things: a gavel resembling the hammer of Thor, and an argument for the birth of Israel—creating a use for the gavel to this very day.

❀

The question of Palestine and Israel would become a touchstone for the UN General Assembly. Jewish nationalists, known as Zionists, sought to reestablish the land of Israel, promised to descendants of Abraham in the Bible and described in the Torah as "a land flowing with milk and honey." The return to Israel had survived as a religious notion, but the idea of a homeland was never considered a viable political ideology until the nineteenth century, when it began to gain traction in opposition to anti-Semitism and certain nationalist movements in Europe. Early ideas were batted around—including one proposition, seriously debated for about two years, to establish a Jewish homeland in modern-day Uganda—but with a measly sixty-seven-word document called the Balfour Declaration, Palestine became the final focus. With that single sentence, Britain waded neck deep into the Palestinian question and stayed there for three decades until it dropped the issue into the lap of the United Nations.

During the First World War, an Arab uprising and other forces had driven the Ottomans out of the Levant. British and French officials set to work decolonizing (or recolonizing) the rest of the Middle East—which was, apparently, an indoor task requiring only a map and a ruler. Although Britain had previously agreed to honor Arab independence if they kicked out the Ottomans, they each interpreted "independence" somewhat differently, and after the Turks' retreat, the Brits drew up the infamous Sykes-Picot Agreement. This secret treaty eventually left the Palestine region, then known as Mandatory Palestine, under British control.

Key to the establishment of Mandatory Palestine was the Balfour Declaration. Issued in 1917, this was a statement supporting the establishment of a "national home for the Jewish people" in Palestine. Crucially, this was the first time a major political power had officially supported Zionism. Suddenly the movement was mainstream, with the backing of a heavyweight, though the nature of that backing wasn't entirely clear—the term "national home" was vague and had no precedent or agreed definition. Over the next twenty-five years, more than four hundred thousand Jews immigrated to Palestine.

As one might imagine, the next few decades were troubled in Mandatory Palestine. Arab Palestinians went on strike, revolted, boycotted, and conducted armed insurgencies. Zionists carried out bombings against the British administration, assassinated a UN mediator, broke its members out of prison with TNT, and kidnapped and hanged British sergeants. These last acts were key, finally, to Britain's throwing up its hands and declaring that it wanted to end its mandate and withdraw, asking the UN to untie the knot it had created in the Levant.

The man for the job? The Icelander in the pinstripe suits. Thor Thors was tapped for the role of rapporteur on the new Ad Hoc Committee on the Palestinian Question. The United Nations at the time had just 57 members (there are 193 today), and the idea was to select "neutral" nations to lead the efforts in the Middle East—that is, no Arab nations, no Muslim nations, no Mediterranean neighbors, no Eurocentric nations who called it the Near East because it was near them, no anti-Semitic nations, not the Big Five, and definitely not Britain. Every nation, neutral or not, would of course vote on a potential solution at the General Assembly. But for the time being, the policy legwork rested in the hands of Guatemala, Sweden, Peru, Canada, Australia, Iran (yes, Iran), and so on.

The Palestinian question had gained new urgency after World War II, once the truth of the Holocaust, with its shocking stories and images of genocide, had begun to proliferate around the globe. The number burned into every citizen's brain was 6 million. Over the course of World War II, the Nazis had executed 6 million Jews under Europe's very nose. Fleeing persecution, the Jewish population of Palestine grew to 33 percent of the total population. Some Zionists believed they were bringing "people without a land to a land without people," but others knew that, in the words of a rabbi sent to examine Palestine, "the bride is lovely but married to another man." In 1946, Palestine was home to 1.3 million Arabs.

Prior to the Ad Hoc Committee in 1947, the UN had operated a summer-long investigative body named the Special Committee on Palestine. This committee of eleven delegates had traveled to Mandatory Palestine to meet with Jews and Arabs and make recommendations to the United Nations based on the insight they'd gained. On the mission, they learned the Hebrew greeting shalom, but not the Arab equivalent: Palestinian leaders, outraged by the visit and its agenda, made next to no effort to lobby the committee. In fact, this wasn't just a lack of effort; the nonparticipation was a deliberate move to reflect the illegitimacy of the committee. Arab residents, both Christian and Muslim, were instructed to ignore the committee. Typically bustling souqs stood empty when the delegation walked through. Local reporters were told to ignore the story, and during a visit to a Palestinian school in the Negev Desert, pupils acted as if the delegates weren't present. Unfortunately for the Arabic Palestinians, the strategy ultimately benefited the Jewish Agency, the diplomatic body of the Zionist movement. Smiles, flowers, fresh oranges, friendly flags, and warm handshakes welcomed the delegation in every corner of the Jewish-controlled sections of Palestine. The mayor of Tel Aviv declared a public holiday upon their arrival. Streets were spotlessly clean, with shining windows. The Jewish Agency made sure events were attended by local Jews who spoke the native language of delegation members—be it Swedish or Spanish or Farsi—to more effectively relay the vision for a Jewish state.

Committee members returned home, presumably humming the melody of "Hatikvah" (the Israeli national anthem). Later that summer, part of the committee traveled to the Allied-controlled regions of Germany and Austria to speak with Holocaust survivors at displacement camps. For an entire week, the committee gathered testimonies from people expressing a "strong desire" for a Jewish homeland.

Give them what they want, the committee concluded, in a proposal with two options. Option A, favored by the Jewish Agency, was a two-state solution with an economic union, meaning a single currency and free trade. Option B, a minority proposal within the committee, was a version of a one-state solution with a "federal" state overseeing the Jewish and Arab regions, with Jerusalem as its capital. Palestinians rejected both. Their charge was that the Western world was paying its own debt to the Jewish people with someone else's land. They never developed a negotiation strategy, other than choosing not to negotiate.

The Ad Hoc Committee, composed of representatives from all fifty-seven member states, was tasked with finding a political path for the investigative proposals; it would develop a proposition that the General Assembly would eventually vote to pass or reject. Nothing suggests that Thor particularly sought to take an active role in the committee, which is, perhaps, why he was appointed to lead on such a sensitive issue. His role as rapporteur was internal in nature; the rapporteur coordinated subcommittees and delivered updates. He had authority over the written proposal and, in the rare absence of a committee chair, he would deliver the concluding remarks. The rapporteur, in essence, was a diplomat among diplomats.

Another thing that set Thor apart from other representatives and made it easier for him to maneuver opposing views was the fact that Iceland's UN policy was, well, his. His brother (the prime minister), the foreign secretary (an old political comrade), and the minister of foreign affairs wrote in a cable telegraph: "[We] grant you the authority to decide in accordance with your opinion." Instead of articulating his opinion, Thor mostly lamented the long meetings in New York, when the Arab Higher Committee and the Jewish Agency would present their case in detail over the course of the committee's approximately thirty meetings.

"The Arabs," he wrote, vaguely revealing his stance, "consider the land theirs alone."

❦

The Jewish diplomat Abba Eban wrote in his biography, "History, after all, is the story of opportunities; once they are lost they are unlikely to recur."

The United Nations made a "decision" about Israel, not an "agreement," and the timing made all the difference. In 1947, Stalin was still one year away from lashing out against Russian Jews as "traitors," and the Middle East was still a decade away from Cold War proxy wars. At this sweet spot in history, the Soviet Union and the United States actually agreed on dividing Mandatory Palestine. Had the case dragged on, if the UN debate had ended in a deadlock, it is unlikely that the British, with their massive armies, would have walked out and left a power vacuum, while the Cold War would have determined the course of any future negotiations.

Abba Eban was not going to allow that to happen. The Jewish diplomat spent his working life in smoke-filled rooms near United Nations Plaza in New York. His autobiography chronicles countless visits to private hotel rooms and includes lines such as: "A consensus means that everyone agrees to say collectively what no one believes individually."

The *Ad Hoc Committee Report* became known as the *United Nations Partition Plan for Palestine* when it was presented to the General Assembly in November, less than six months after the UN took action on the question. It was a two-state solution that would give Jews vast amounts of Arab land. No Western nation was eager to make a decision; for one, a vote for the motion would damage relations with the oil rich Middle East.

Support for a two-state solution, based on Eban's insights, had a tight margin; the General Assembly requires a two-thirds majority for approval, and to complicate the vote, many countries in Asia and Latin America were planning on nonvoting abstentions. More important, the partition might not come to a vote at all. Unless the case was presented with urgency, with a firm stance against any vague solution, delaying tactics might sabotage the plan.

Eban had presumed that H. V. Evatt of Australia would be the chairman of the Ad Hoc Committee, but he was frantically preparing to leave town—precisely to avoid his spokesman's role because he feared it could damage his bid for the presidency of the General Assembly (which he won the following year). Next in line was the Thai vice chairman, who said he was needed back home as soon as he saw that the Ad Hoc Committee was headed toward a firm partition plan.

"He prudently departed for Bangkok on the *Queen Mary*, ostensibly on the grounds that a revolutionary situation existed in his country, but actually in order to avoid having to cast a vote against the partition," Eban wrote. The turn of events left "the key to this turning point [. . .] in the hands of a small island country in the middle of the Atlantic Ocean with a population of less than 175,000." Don't panic, Thor. No pressure.

Eban found the address of Thor's hotel, the Barclay, and knocked on the door of room 211. The man who opened held the fate of the Jewish nation in his hands. Thor. He seemed completely unprepared.

"If we succeed, we will realize a millennial dream," Eban told Thor, frankly adding: "If we fail, that dream might be extinguished for generations to come." Reading between the lines of Eban's biography, one can deduce that Thor responded with a long, sentimental ramble about the likeness of Iceland and Israel: both cultures deeply imbued with biblical and mythical memories; both nations determined to be themselves, sharing their language and literature with no other nation; both fighting for sovereignty. Eban left with nothing of substance.

Later that day, Thor stood in front of the General Assembly in a black pinstripe suit against the green marble background of the main podium. His speech chronicled how the Palestinian question had bounced from one committee to another, and what the two colliding parties, the Arabs and Jews, had to say on each side. Any further efforts to negotiate an agreement were "doomed to failure" due to "the vast gap between the contending parties." He, instead, pressed for a "firm decision" that would "face the facts." Only then could the next phase, that of reconciliation, begin.

"Thors [. . .] was magnificent," wrote Eban in delight. "From that moment on, the debate went inexorably our way." The motion was approved, 33 to 13 (with 11 abstentions).

The official partition mandate was to come into effect when British rule expired on May 14, 1948. At four p.m., when the day came, as the last British troops departed from Haifa, David Ben-Gurion delivered a speech at the Tel Aviv Museum of Art declaring the "establishment of the Jewish State in Palestine, to be called Medinath Israel." At midnight, the State of Israel formally came into being. Palestinian citizens were no longer British protected persons, and any British forces still there were suddenly considered occupiers of foreign territory. At eight a.m. the next day, all neighboring countries responded with war. Egypt, Transjordan, Syria, and forces from Iraq entered Palestine. But within ten months, they were beaten back, and Israel controlled not only its own purported state but also nearly 60 percent of the proposed Arab state. The war resulted in the displacement of nearly seven hundred thousand Palestinian Arabs, an expulsion known as

Al-Nakba (literally "the catastrophe"), many of whose descendants remain in refugee camps today. Since then the area has, on average, turned into a battlefield every seven years.

Israel sought membership in the United Nations within a year after its founding—ahead of Spain, Finland, and Indonesia, to name a few—and was accepted with a vote from Iceland, whereas Denmark and Sweden abstained. Abba Eban became Israel's foreign minister and made an honorary visit to Iceland during his first year in office. In fact, the two nations enjoyed friendly relations for years—they were, after all, two small nations founded within four years of each other, and Iceland could claim a hand in Israel's creation. David Ben-Gurion, Israel's first prime minister, made a courtesy visit to Iceland as well. Golda Meir, another iconic prime minister, visited as foreign minister and admired the "peaceful" landscape. In return, Iceland's president Ásgeir Ásgeirsson became the first foreign head of state to address Israel's Knesset (parliament). During Ásgeir's visit, he cut a ribbon opening a suburban street in burgeoning Jerusalem—a road named Iceland Street.

❀

Despite the Middle East being thrown into turmoil, the creation of Israel was considered a job well done for the lone diplomat from Iceland. His legacy was secured, for better or for worse.

The following summer, Thor went on holiday. With his wife and three children—two boys and a girl, Margrét—in tow, they drove from DC up to Hyannis Port, in Massachusetts. The seaside village is an affluent summer community on

Cape Cod, boasting a premier golf course and yacht club. Even today, the Cape and nearby islands of Nantucket and Martha's Vineyard are popular vacation spots for US presidents. Back then, the concentration of elite power in a village of less than two hundred housing units was practically unparalleled. And the company grew ever more prestigious the closer you moved toward the Kennedy compound, a waterfront property housing businessman Joseph P. Kennedy, father of John F. Kennedy and his eight siblings.

JFK was thirty-one at the time, ten years older than Margrét, Thor's daughter. Both of them were admired for their good looks and charm—and at some point, their paths crossed in the little town of Hyannis Port. This was a classic tale of boy meets girl. Or rather, a tale of dynasty meets dynasty: the Real Kennedy meeting the Icelandic Kennedy. He invited her on "a few dates," according to Gudmundur Magnússon's interviews with family members.

We'll never know the details of Margrét's relationship with the future US president. At the age of twenty-six, Margrét died when a sleeping pill got stuck in her throat, leading to suffocation. In all likelihood, though, their relationship didn't last beyond the summer holiday. About four years later, John met his spouse, Jackie. And had he not been assassinated three years into his presidency, JFK would have met Thor Thors in the White House, in 1964. That was the year he accompanied the Icelandic prime minister (a position no longer held by his brother Ólafur) to a meeting with President Lyndon B. Johnson. There Thor's grandiose style was fully on display, as well as his tendency to blur the line between the individual and the state he represented, this time via his gift giving. His gift, Thor had decided, could not imitate any previous presents to the US president; it must be unique. So he asked the Icelandic government to donate a special edition of the Gudbrand's Bible, an elegant replica of the first Icelandic translation of the Bible. This decorated edition was published in a limited run a decade earlier, and had become a valuable contemporary item in the Icelandic book trade.

President Johnson, Prime Minister Benediktsson, and Ambassador Thors walked around the White House Rose Garden and spent twenty minutes in the Oval Office. In return for the book, the leader of the free world gave the two pals a box of things he seemed to have grabbed on his way out of the Oval Office: a signed portrait of himself (size 8 by 10), a golden tray in which to store maps (naturally everybody should have one), a book with transcripts of his speeches (just topping one hundred pages, after a little over a year in office), and the latest images from the Ranger space missions.

These images turned out to be an especially appropriate gift for the Icelanders. The Ranger program was a series of unmanned space probes sent into orbit to photograph the moon in the early 1960s. These probes provided exclusive, if blurry, images of the moon's surface, from which NASA was able to make scientific projections. It seemed to scientists that the moon was covered with basaltic rocks, especially so-called palagonite tuff. With this (mis)information, NASA added to its astronaut curriculum a trip to the place on earth that most resembled the lunar landscape. The Apollo team was set to travel to the center of Iceland.

The Moon Landing

Iceland from 1965 to 1969

An Icelander can only name two species of
tree; the Christmas tree and that other tree.

—HELGI HÁLFDANARSON, A PROLIFIC
TRANSLATOR OF FOREIGN CLASSICS WHO
TURNED SHAKESPEARE AND THE QURAN INTO
ICELANDIC, IN A NEWSPAPER ARTICLE ON THE
GENERAL LACK OF VOCABULARY FOR TREES
AND FLOWERS.

Two years before making history with one small step onto
the moon, Neil Armstrong went salmon fishing in northern Iceland. A picture of him, standing by a river, is exhibited
in a regional museum, but the image is so small that at first
you might assume it's just a regular snapshot of recreational
life in the 1960s. Smiling faintly as he holds a fishing rod, the
thirty-six-year-old Armstrong could pass for a local—until
you notice his baseball cap and fancy aviator shades. And, of
course, his four layers of clothing.

Armstrong was just one of the prospective spacemen
around Iceland that summer, all living in NASA training
camps in the interior. The constant daylight of long summer
days obscured their ultimate destination. They were there because in the middle of Iceland's Highlands, NASA had found a
landscape that paralleled the lunar: no vegetation, no life, no

colors, no landmarks. The entire area was essentially a natural gravel field.

"If you want to go to a place on earth that looks like the Moon," wrote Dr. Elbert King, a geologist from the University of Houston who trained Apollo astronauts, "Central Iceland should be high on your list, as it beautifully displays volcanic geology with virtually no vegetation cover." The would-be astronauts took advantage of the bare ground by splitting into teams and playing soccer to unwind after training days, using rocks to mark the goalposts. A walk to the nearest tree would have taken the men days. They would've had to cross the Hóla-sandur, the black sand desert, and head toward the northeastern coast. Even then, the tree, weather-beaten like everything else on the eroded North Atlantic island, wasn't much taller than Armstrong's fishing rod.

The term "lunar landscape" is a phrase often used to describe the boundless Icelandic deserts, shaped by volcanic eruptions and covered in different shades of lava. The volcanic regions of Iceland are great training fields "owing to their desiccation, low nutrient availability, and temperature extremes, in addition to the advantages of geological youth and isolation from sources of anthropogenic contamination," according to a 2018 NASA document.

Thus their very barrenness is an asset. But lately, creeping about these deserts is a peculiar purple alien: the Alaskan lupine. This plant arrived on the scene not long after the astronauts, and it was at first embraced as an efficient cover for eroded land. But the experiment blew up in Iceland's face and left a permanent purple mark. Now the lupine is considered an invasive plant, as it threatens not only the existing flora but also the barren volcanic interior, a place of "magnificent desolation," the words Buzz Aldrin once used to describe the moon.

The rolling black sands of Hólasandur where the astronauts once traveled is today a purple field. As the climate changes, the lupine spreads into places previously protected from the plant by cold temperatures and low rainfall. Some Icelanders welcome the Alaskan flower; some decry its invasion. It's a highly contentious issue, as the fight for Iceland's color has spurred a new form of identity politics.

❀

Lupinus nootkatensis—known in its native Alaska and British Columbia as the Nootka lupine—is a member of the pea family. In gardening parlance, it's a nitrogen fixer: it hosts bacteria that gather nitrogen from the air and then transfer the gas to the plant's roots. If you plow under lupines (or peas for that matter), the nitrogen is released into the soil, providing nourishment for the plants that follow. It's a pretty and elegant solution for nurturing exhausted soil.

The Alaskan lupine arrived in Iceland in 1945 in a suitcase. But the story of its deliberate introduction began some thousand years before its arrival.

When the first settlers disembarked from Viking ships in the ninth century, two thirds of the island was covered in greenery, and it had only one terrestrial mammal, the Arctic fox. The island's first humans settled in with a shipload of livestock and began to pursue the same agrarian lifestyle they were used to, cutting down trees and burning the wood, totally oblivious to the damage they were doing. Iceland's soil forms more slowly and erodes much more quickly than mainland Europe's.

By the time the Icelandic government formed the national forest service in 1908, the early settlers would have hardly recognized the stark coastline. By then, Iceland was ecologically "the most heavily damaged country in Europe," to quote celebrity polymath and author Jared Diamond. Wind erosion was, grain by grain, blowing the country out to sea.

The destruction continued unabated. By the mid-twentieth century, when other European nations were rebuilding after the Second World War, the Icelandic Forest Service was pondering human-induced destruction of a different kind. Icelanders had so heavily exploited their island home by logging the native birch forests and overgrazing the land that only 25 percent of the country's original green cover remained.

The agency sought solutions abroad. They sent their director, Hákon Bjarnason, on a three-month mission to Alaska. His task was to gather plants and trees he liked and those he thought could thrive in Iceland. The return stamp in his passport, November 3, 1945, marks the birth of our lupine saga.

For the first three decades, the plant lived in green spaces near Reykjavík. Arni Bragason, director of the Soil Conservation Service of Iceland, told me that it wasn't until 1976 that the lupine's seeds were actively collected and released into the wild, tasked with bolstering the country's feeble soil. Lupines performed admirably and acted like fertilizer factories, purpling the landscape at almost no cost and without the need for special training: seeds could be collected by anyone, tossed into a hole no larger than a shoe's heel and—abracadabra—the scenery eventually changed. Maybe forever.

In 2006, I was standing at the entrance of a grocery store in Selfoss, waiting to snag passersby for "The Question of the Day." Environmental questions were always tough; no sane person visits the grocery store to discuss the death of our planet. But this day I struck a chord with what seemed like a pretty lightweight query: What do you think about the Alaskan lupine?

Everyone had an opinion. The people at the grocery store fell, as a rule, into either pro- or antilupine camps; there was no ambivalence. Most answers were long and emotional, not dispassionately scientific.

The first two people told me anecdotes about lupine magic: how it prevented erosion and blowing sand and made it possible to plant trees. The third said the lupine had destroyed the view from his summer cottage. The fourth claimed to destroy lupine lands in his free time, but was hesitant to state this publicly. Almost everyone predicted two different futures: there was one with lupine, and one without lupine. And the fifth person gave a lengthy rant that I, due to space considerations, trimmed down to a single question: "Lupine, everywhere! How did this happen?"

Many of the people I questioned had witnessed lupine's invasion in real time. If you drive the Ring Road in early summer, it's like barreling down a road paved straight through an endless succession of lupine fields, as though the flowers came first, and it's we who are the invaders. But they didn't. The magnificent desolation has been replaced by waves of purple blue, a sight that has thrilled tourists for decades along the popular southern coastline. While covering the issue for

The New York Times, I met a couple from Texas posing for an engagement photo against a field of blossoms near the Skógar waterfall. Dressed elegantly, they had to pose on top of their car in order to be seen in the midst of the three-foot-tall plants. A farmer near Kirkjubæjarklaustur told me that sandstorms used to force the roads to close many times per year before the lupine cover. Farther east on the national road, it seems that lupine seeds were—at some point—tossed into the moss-grown Eldhraun lava field, the one formed by the cataclysmic 1783 Laki eruption.

At this point, every Icelander has gazed upon a field of purple. And many are lupine lovers. The allies of the lupine are particularly enamored with before and after photographs. Some extol the virtues of the flower as a reforestation tool—trees planted alongside lupines benefit from the enriched soil. Once large enough, trees steal light from the almost-foot-high flowers, and over the next twenty-five to thirty years, once the soil is fertile enough for other things to grow, the lupines naturally recede. At least in theory.

The regreening of Iceland has become a balancing act: we want to retain the renowned splendor of our naturally occurring volcanic deserts, but we also need to revegetate what we've lost. The lovers and the haters each have valid points.

Today, the Alaskan lupine covers 0.5 percent of Iceland's land surface, according to estimates based on aerial footage. That may sound meager, but considering that the country's forests amount only to less than 155 square miles, it's a lot of lupines. And while planted forest cover is predicted to reach about 1.6 percent in 2085 at the current rate, the purple flower coverage could potentially soar into double digits, aided by climate change and human activity. "Exponential growth is

the nature of invasive species," says botanist Pawel Waso-
wicz, who is the lupine expert at the Icelandic Institute of
Natural History. The growth curve, he estimates, will see a
dramatic peak sometime in the next two decades.

According to the Institute, invasive species have enormous
potential to edge out existing flora in Iceland and spread into
the highland interior, which is currently too cold and dry for
most plants. This naturally occurring lunar landscape could,
simply put, disappear. In about thirty years, under the current
rate of climate change, the lupine could colonize much of the
highland, suggests a research paper published in the journal
Flora in 2013. Naturalist and former member of parliament
Hjörleifur Guttormsson, who is eighty-six and one of the earliest opponents of the plant, says, "Everything but the glaciers
are potential lupine land."

Few countries are as vulnerable to global warming as Iceland. Glaciers have retreated by about 850 square miles since
the end of the nineteenth century, when glaciers covered the
greatest amount of landmass since Iceland's settlement, according to the Icelandic Meteorological Office. Almost 309
square miles of that has occurred just in the last twenty years.
The glaciers are melting so quickly that the National Power
Company of Iceland, which is owned by the Icelandic state
and processes 75 percent of all electricity nationwide, is preparing for a future without any of the powerful glacial rivers
used to operate hydroelectric dams, the current source of 70
percent of Iceland's electricity. In 2019, the warmest summer
on record in Reykjavík, mosquito spray sold out all over due to
a sudden explosion of biting midges. Meanwhile, offshore, fish
species living in the ocean's pelagic zone are swimming ever
farther north to keep up with temperature changes. In recent

years, the Atlantic mackerel has entered Icelandic waters, while capelin and herring have begun to shift their grounds to above the Arctic Circle, upsetting the ecosystem of seabirds and whales. Even invasive flowers such as the lupine are threatened by other, taller invasive species such as cow parsley, a flower that reduces biodiversity and does little to enrich the soil. As lupine and cow parsley displace heath, Iceland's only native bee—the heath bumblebee—is at risk of serious decline.

The purpling of the landscape is the most visible evidence of how quickly human activities are changing the face of Iceland. But it may herald even more drastic changes to come.

❀

The area where the astronauts trained is a boundless Icelandic desert, shaped by volcanic eruptions. Named a UNESCO World Heritage site in 2019, as part of Vatnajökull National Park, the Askja region is essentially a black desert. When they arrived, the astronauts traveled on Land Rovers, much like today's visitors—the roads haven't improved much. The most common tour to Askja is via Herðubreiðalindir on Route F88, east of Lake Mývatn. Some three hours on the rocky road, crossing two rivers, will eventually lead you to a middle-of-nowhere campsite at Drekagil canyon. Three cabins line the canyon mouth, their pitched roofs amid the barren landscape looking like the mansions of a James Bond villain. The newest wooden house is from the Vatnajökull National Park. It has a very casual information desk, open whenever the ranger is not out and about. "Some people think we are a coffee shop or a restaurant. That would be a tough business up here," says park ranger Sigurdur Erlingsson, who is stationed at the hut every summer.

The astronauts were there specifically to receive geological training. Most were originally trained as pilots; astronaut Jack Schmitt was the only scientist who walked on the moon. Because gathering samples was a priority, and nobody knew just how long Apollo 11 would be on the moon, astronauts had to learn how to collect the right samples and do it quickly.

To do this, local geologists Sigurdur Thórarinsson and Gudmundur Sigvaldason invented the Moon Game to bolster astronauts' skills. In the Moon Game, astronauts were divided into pairs, placed in a field location with almost no information about the place, and told to pretend that they were on the moon. Astronauts then had to collect the best rock samples and record their reasons for selecting certain rocks on hand-held tape recorders. NASA geologists would analyze the rocks and their reasons and award points based on the samples. Competition was healthy.

This crash course in geology was crucial at a time when geologists simply did not know how the moon was formed, or what it really looked like up close. "The irony was," recalled Al Worden, an Apollo 15 astronaut, "many of them disagreed profoundly about how the moon's features were formed. For every geologist who said the moon's craters were mostly formed by volcanoes, there was another who believed they were created by meteor impact."

When I visit, on a sunny day in July, the Drekagil base camp has a steady stream of visitors. A German couple is drying bright beach towels at the campsite. They have just completed a hike to Víti, a crater lake fed by geothermal hot springs. Just next to Víti is the Askja caldera, the largest in the volcanic belt, which stretches 112 miles along the Vatnajökull glacier.

Apollo 14 astronaut Edgar Mitchell recalled the place clearly: "One of my most memorable trips was to the volcanically active and very remote region of central Askja, Iceland, in July 1967. Known for its volcanic craters called calderas, this region had a very rocky terrain with black volcanic sand, as well as a large lake and hot springs. It was a misty, surreal place unlike anything I'd ever seen in my travels. And because we were there during the summer it seemed like the Sun never set."

But I was headed away from the scenic route, toward a neighboring canyon, one that was without a name when the astronauts first visited half a century earlier. It is now called Nautagil, a play on words that alludes to the canyon's history: Naut—as in "astronaut"—means "bull" in Icelandic. Sigurdur, the park ranger, joins me on this special "moonwalk" through the canyon.

I try to locate some photographs from the time, wondering why this site doesn't see more visitors. Its significance to the actual moon landing may be small, yet it's a rare opportunity to step back in time, akin to holding an object from the mission. We climb up a steep slope for a better view of the area. "I like to think these tracks are from the NASA years," he says, pointing to a faint but broad line in the landscape. It's possible—the cold and stark landscape takes incredibly long to heal, hence the hefty fines for any off-road driving. Armstrong and the crew may have driven just there, as they practiced entering and exiting the lunar module to build muscle memory.

Today NASA is making fresh tracks in Iceland's interior, preparing to explore the fourth rock from the sun: Mars. The prototype of the Mars 2020 Rover was tested on the subglacial terrain of the interior, which theoretically resembles what Mars looked like before it turned into the inhospitable Red Planet. Modern Iceland's glaciers, volcanoes, hot springs, and iron-rich rocks mirror the surface of Mars as it looked three billion years ago, when water flowed on the surface of the planet. Dormant volcanoes and geothermal sites in Iceland, often located close to the coast, have thus been analyzed by expedition leaders as they attempt to determine which part of Mars might be most likely to provide evidence of extraterrestrial life. Specifically, NASA is after fossilized microbes. If found, they would be the first-ever sign of life beyond our Blue Marble. Beyond similarities in rocky terrain, Iceland and Mars have caves formed when the lava moves beneath the hardened surface. Iceland's longest caves, called lava tubes, are formed this way and can be easily accessed from the ground. Scientists hope lava tubes can serve future missions in the race to shelter equipment and humans once there is a way to survive the thirty-four-million-mile journey and minus 100°F. In the meantime: Welcome to Iceland, Earthlings!

❀

The space race between the Soviet Union and the United States was driven partly by national security concerns, and partly by metaphor. Reaching the moon first was a powerful symbol of technological and ideological superiority. The race really kicked off on August 2, 1955, when the USSR responded to a US announcement, saying that it would also be launching satellites into space. So began fourteen years of urgent strides skyward.

For much of the race, the Soviets seemed to be winning. They were the first to launch a satellite, with Sputnik in 1957. They also sent the first human into space when Yuri Gagarin launched on April 12, 1961.

President John F. Kennedy hadn't been interested in the space race until Gagarin's flight. With that triumph, Kennedy began to realize the growing concern and even fear on the part of the American public about falling behind. He announced that the United States would put a man on the moon before the end of the decade.

But the USSR continued to rack up firsts: the first woman in space; the first spacecraft with a three-person crew; the first flight with cosmonauts working in shirtsleeves and not their space suits (though this was actually very dangerous, and only happened because the cabin space was extremely small). A political turn of events may have changed everything: Leonid Brezhnev deposed Nikita Khrushchev a day after the Voskhod 1 landed, and the Soviet focus changed to reaching the moon. This meant they essentially took a two-year hiatus to develop the Soyuz spacecraft, canceling the Voskhod program. The Soviets achieved their very last first—the first spacewalk—in March 1965, just a few months before the first American astronauts landed in Iceland.

And why was Iceland helping the United States, anyhow? As we have seen, their partnership dates back to World War II, when the British had invaded Iceland in 1940 despite its neutrality. The United States then took over the occupation, and after the war, Icelanders received by far the most aid per capita from the United States via the Marshall Plan. Despite dissent, protests, and even riots, Iceland eventually joined NATO—in part to ensure against any rising communist movement.

Meanwhile, the Americans began to catch up. They became the first to change a craft's orbit, the first to dock two spacecraft, and they set a record for human spaceflight of fourteen days.

As both sides drew closer to their goals, a series of disasters set them back. In the United States a fire swept through a spacecraft cabin during a ground test. It killed three pilots, including Virgil "Gus" Grissom, who had been a favored choice to make the first piloted landing. A few months later, Vladimir Komarov, who had commanded Voskhod 1, became the first spaceflight fatality.

As Armstrong and his crew went to Iceland, the USSR made a successful unmanned circumlunar flight. Things heated up further: in September 1968, Zond 5 made a circumlunar flight with two tortoises aboard, and returned them safely to earth. This spooked NASA, as it took them a few days to realize it hadn't been piloted, because the Soviets had transmitted voice recordings from the craft en route. The race appeared to be neck and neck. In December, the United States put people into lunar orbit. The Soviets tried to launch their N1 rocket—it failed, and crashed, destroying their facilities. Neil Armstrong, Buzz Aldrin, and crew raced along, training until just before the scheduled launch day. They climbed into Apollo 11. Their trip to the moon took three days. They landed. They waited about six hours. And then, at last, Armstrong took those famous steps, witnessed by about one fifth of the earth's population—and one young sheep farmer out in rural Iceland, Ingólfur Jónasson, who listened to the landing described via

radio, swelled with pride as he recalled taking that same man
fishing.

❀

Nine of the twelve people who have ever walked on the moon
came to Iceland first. On July 24, 1969, Apollo 11 landed back
on earth with a geological sample—a slice of the moon. In total, Apollo 11 brought back almost forty-nine pounds of moon
rocks and lunar dust. The samples helped determine the age
of the moon and its surface—4.5 billion years old. In 2013, scientists reanalyzed samples, including some Apollo 11 moon
rocks, and discovered trace amounts of water brought by
comets and meteors striking the surface. All of this helped
scientists conclude that the moon formed from great chunks
of earth, blown away by a cataclysmic early impact. The
geological similarities between the moon and Iceland were,
however, mostly superficial.

When the Indiana Jones–like forestry director Hákon
Bjarnason returned from his Alaskan endeavors in 1945, fresh
off the plane, he told a reporter that with some effort, Iceland
could look a lot more like coastal Alaska, with tall trees and
lots of blueberry bushes. The two places did have a strikingly
similar climate. But, again, it turned out the similarities were
superficial. In hindsight, the overconfidence is understand-
able. In 1945 and the decades that followed, we were on a
technological roll; it was an era in which we thought we could
conquer nature, even defy gravity by launching men to the
moon. No one could foresee the tenacity of a pretty flower and
a purple Iceland.

According to a local joke, when the astronauts were leaving

the country, a Reykjavík resident asked them to deliver an Icelandic message to the man on the moon: Við ætlum að leggja
landið undir okkur hægt og rólega, ekki treysta neinum lo-
forðum um annað. The astronaut, oblivious to its meaning,
memorized the sentence and later repeated it for the aliens in
space. It means: "We're going to gradually take over this place;
don't trust a word we say." Jokes always contain a grain of
truth, and this one was no different. It reflected a rising resent-
ment. In Reykjavík, sentiment toward the ever-growing American military base was polarizing the nation. The Americans
had arrived during World War II to "protect the population,"
and then had found many reasons to stay. It was gradually
turning the country of ice into a transatlantic Cold War base.

The Cold War

Iceland from 1970 to 1980

Tomorrow he would be in Spain. Sæmi stretched out in his bed in Reykjavík in 2004 and fell asleep dreaming of golf, sunbathing by the pool, and the orange trees in Alicante. Sangria. Sunshine. As he dreamed, a noise began to bubble up—a faint jingling; the bubbly tune of his cell phone ring. . . .

Sæmi opened his eyes and groped for his mobile.

"Hello?"

The stiff voice on the other end of the line asked if he would accept a collect call. From Tokyo. From jail.

Sæmi put on his glasses and checked the clock—it was the middle of the night.

"I accept," he said. The line clicked as the caller connected.

"Yes," said a faint voice. "Is this my friend Sammy?"

"Ha?" Sæmi replied—the Icelandic response for all things confusing.

"This is Bobby," said the voice. It breathed deep. "I've been kidnapped!"

Bobby Fischer, the American prodigy, pushing an IQ of

180, who'd once stood at the front line of a Cold War proxy battle was the lone superstar who had humiliated the Soviet chess machine. Fischer was a chess grand master, considered by many to be the greatest chess player of all time. He became the US chess champion at the tender age of fourteen and at fifteen, the youngest ever grand master. But it was not simply his prodigious talent that had cemented his place in the cultural consciousness; it was the World Chess Championship of 1972, a match known as the Game of the Century, which functioned as a proxy Cold War battle between the United States and the Soviet Union, one which, for a few months, captured worldwide attention. Here was a man who'd been roundly praised by the free world until his beautiful mind grew erratic, who then dropped into obscurity for twenty years; the eccentric genius Robert James Fischer, calling his old friend Sæmi Pálsson in the middle of the night from a prison at the outskirts of the Tokyo Airport, back again, paranoid, furious, missing a tooth from a fight with the guards; his friend, Bobby.

But now it was 2004. The Cold War and its games were long over. What do you say when your friend, the genius, rings you in the middle of the night after thirty-two years of silence? Do you go back to sleep? Do you express condolences that his international warrant has finally caught up with him? For Sæmi, there was no hesitation. A friend was kin. He told Bobby, "Call me back on country code +34."

Sæmi's Spanish number was on Fischer's speed dial during the fraught weeks to come. Fischer rang him regularly, asking for help and protesting his treatment. He wanted out, he said; he wanted also to avoid extradition to the United States for violating an international embargo on Yugoslavia almost two decades earlier when he'd played a match there.

"If I help you," Sæmi said to Fischer, who was facing up to ten years behind bars, "you might have to move to Iceland."

At this point, all other options for political asylum had been exhausted—not even Iran would extend a welcome—yet Fischer, on the other end of the line, refused. Iceland was too cold!

Sæmi cleared his throat and thought for a moment. He remembered something he'd recently read in an airline brochure. "Well," he argued, "the average temperature in January is lower in New York City than in Reykjavík."

Fischer, born in Chicago and raised in Brooklyn, dismissed the claim. He didn't like the cold. He wouldn't go. He stayed in his cell. Days passed, then weeks. His beard grew long and scraggly.

At last, one afternoon, Sæmi's vacation was interrupted again.

"I called an American weather station to verify your earlier statement," Fischer said stiffly. There was a long pause. "I think Iceland might be a good option."

And so Bobby Fischer was once again embroiled in a political contest, the center of an ideological tug of war. This time, though, the battle was not a matter of capitalism versus communism. Now it was a battle over Iceland's own future, and its alignment with Fischer's despised home country, the USA.

❀

In the seventies, the political landscape of Iceland was largely shaped by one particular issue, one that continues to affect the way we read and write about Iceland. I'm talking, of course, about the letter Z. The debate was a largely existential one: Should *Z* be included in the Icelandic alphabet at all? Phonetically it sounds the same as the letter *S*, and it appears in its place seemingly at random. An arbitrary swap. A touch of alphabetic alchemy.

The role of *Z* was already a long-standing point of contention. The first essay on Icelandic spelling, by a scholar in the thirteenth century, describes *Z* as a Greek letter hanging out in the Roman alphabet, a sort of Trojan horse. And what do we do with infiltrators? Outlaw 'em. (I'm paraphrasing, here.)

Thus it was not entirely out of the blue when, some eight hundred years later, an official petition to remove the letter *Z* from the Icelandic language—cutting it out of our lives forever!—gained majority support in parliament. A center-left government, led by the Progressive Party, decided that *Z* belonged with the other foreign signifiers, *C*, *Q*, and *W*, in the trash bin. The new guidelines on Icelandic spelling swapped *S* in for *Z* everywhere, changing the spelling of thousands of words. The letter *Z* was officially abolished! No more awkward *z*-based typos! No more *Z* versus *S* memorization exercises, a drain on the minds of children! No more trips to Zanzibar via the Suez Canal: now they would memorize the Sues route to Sansibar. The word *pizza* was a notable exception, as nobody could get excited about a hot slice of pissa.

But as it turned out, about half the population carried a great passion for the twenty-sixth letter of the alphabet. They weren't happy about the change. *Morgunblaðið*, a conservative newspaper rarely in favor of civil disobedience, rolled out a rhetorical war for *Z*. The backlash was so strong that for a moment, it seemed the government might have to walk back the regulation.

Of course, this wasn't merely a matter of alphabetic alle-

giance. Often, niche issues like this one end up being shibbo-
leths for people's stances on larger questions. The *Z* versus *S*
debacle was no exception. The Icelandic language is a kind of
protected cultural site for many; that's part of why words that
have been lent are less common in Icelandic than in other languages. *Telephone*, for example, is *teléfono* in Spanish, *téléphone*
in French, and *Telefon* in German, but it is *sími* in Icelandic, a
very old word meaning something like "long thread." The new,
curtailed Icelandic alphabet was in fact a battleground for a
cultural war—a question of whether the country was headed
toward conservatism or radical change, aligning with the An-
glophone superpowers or going its own, idiosyncratic ways.
People's position on the *Z* question was a strong indicator of
where they stood more generally in politics, and especially of
how they felt toward the second-most divisive issue in Icelandic society: should the US military stay or go?

During World War II, America moved some forces over,
planted them squarely in the capital, and proceeded to occupy
the country as a transatlantic stronghold. This all seemed
well and good and temporary; the US government had promised to withdraw as soon as the war ended, a deal they acknowledged on VE Day in 1945. American troops, most of
them happy to leave Iceland, set sail and waved the V-sign
from the deck "like idiots," according to one bystander watching from the harbor.

The gum chewers and chitchatters were gone. At last it was
possible to watch films at the theater without their talking,
talking, talking.

The agreement, however, hadn't mentioned anything
about American forces not being allowed *back*. Just months
after the war ended, Iceland was once again debating a

proposition that would allow the United States to establish a military station with a ninety-nine-year lease in Keflavík. It would be a "defense force" against the looming threat of Russian invasion, a claim unfounded by intelligence reports or facts. The Icelandic government denied the lease request, but some still feared the threat of incursion, pointing to communist Yugoslavia, Hungary, and Romania, all of which had gone the same way as the People's Republic of China.

Communists, communists, communists! They were going to want this prime Icelandic real estate. The Reds could pop out from behind any fjord at any time. Better not lower your guard!

The North Korean invasion of South Korea—the beginning of the Korean War—sealed the deal. World War III seemed to be around the corner, and Iceland, once again, had to pick a side or risk invasion. Iceland had just recently joined NATO, and NATO was nervous, wanting Iceland to have a tangible defense force. But Iceland didn't have the resources to create its own armed forces. Thus, in 1951, Iceland welcomed the Americans back to the Keflavík base (Naval Air Station Keflavík), this time under the label of the Iceland Defense Force. According to the bilateral defense agreement, Iceland only had to provide free land—a massive gravel strip on the southwestern corner of the island—and the United States would take care of the rest: building and maintaining one of the world's largest airports, four radar stations, and a gated military base, and eventually housing for up to five thousand American servicepeople.

Within a few years, Stalin died and the war in Korea cooled down. Fears of another world war faded. Many expected the Americans to leave Keflavík. Instead, some cheery yellow apartment buildings began popping up to house even more navy servicepeople. Icelanders began to question the benefits of this "Iceland Defense Force" composed almost entirely of Americans: How was a massive military station located forty miles from the capital and halfway between America and Russia going to make Iceland *safer* in a time of nuclear missiles?

US military bases elsewhere in Europe always faced at least some opposition, if only on a grassroots level. In Iceland, however, the issue defined the political landscape. Independence had just recently been achieved, and national consciousness was both strong and sensitive. But the country needed foreign investment and infrastructure, and the base provided an enormous flow of foreign cash, money the government had grown to rely on—the Iceland Defense Force provided up to 5 percent of the country's GDP. Supporters saw the base as a necessary evil in a turbulent world, an important contribution to Western cooperation, and, yes, a lucrative enterprise employing hundreds of people near Keflavík.

Among those employees was Sæmi Pálsson. From a young age, growing up in occupied World War II Reykjavík, he had admired the prosperous and friendly US soldiers. He'd grown up poor and the soldiers had often given him gum and candy. In return, he taught them a few phrases in Icelandic, like Já, takk. When the opportunity arose for him to work at the base in Keflavík, he repeated the words: "Yes, please."

The Keflavík base was a state of its own. It had theaters, bars, radio, and TV stations long before Icelanders had even seen a television; it had grocery stores that offered an impressive range of tax-free products. Suddenly, Sæmi had multiple candy bars to choose from. On top of that, he befriended a young GI named Bill and got exclusive access to rock 'n' roll records. He went on to lend the records to Icelandic musicians, and he learned to dance the twist with remarkable aptitude. His performance on the dance floor was so impressive, in fact, that it made him famous nationwide, earning him the name Sæmi Rokk.

As much as Sæmi was enjoying his new position and the music that came with it, the contractor position at the Keflavík base was unstable and provided no pension. So when he saw an ad for eight vacancies in the Reykjavík police force, his mind went spinning. Here was stability, authority, a new career. In his autobiography, Sæmi suspects that being a respected rock 'n' roll dancer helped him to stand out among the other 513 applicants.

In addition to his rock 'n' roll twisting, one more character trait would change the course of Sæmi's life forever.

On a summer evening in 1972, Sæmi's superiors put him on duty outside Vogaland 10, a three-bedroom house owned by the DAS lottery, vacant until its winning ticket sold. Sæmi, they knew, spoke some English from his time at the base—enough at least to communicate with a strange young chess player who had come all the way from America. He was to be the foreigner's bodyguard.

"Don't," they instructed, "let Mr. Fischer out of your sight."

They had reason to be concerned. For months, Bobby Fischer, America's greatest weapon in the cerebral proxy war, had threatened not to partake in the match against World Champion Boris Spassky. His requests were peculiar and extensive. Increase the prize, he demanded. Rebuild the chess board. Place lead inside the chess pieces. Order a new chair. Increase the prize again. Carpet the stadium. Turn the film cameras away. Reserve the front row in the airplane. Squeeze fresh oranges in the stadium's front row, "so I can see them." No reporters on arrival.

After having delayed two passenger planes, only to have his ticket canceled, Fischer at last checked in aboard a flight with Loftleiðir (known today as Icelandair) to Iceland. He had already made up his mind about the nation. In an interview with *Life* magazine a month before arriving, he said Iceland was a "primitive country." Elsewhere, in a letter arguing for a higher winner's prize, he made a rather bizarre (and false) argument: "For the US forces," he claimed, "Iceland qualifies as a 'hardship location' and GIs are compensated extra for serving there." This is true today of, say, South Sudan, but unfortunately for Fischer's argument, not of Iceland.

But as he flew over the Greenland ice sheet, he could no longer complain about money. The plane was heading to the most expensive head-to-head sports event in history outside of boxing. American millionaire James Slater had moved things forward by doubling the original pot. The final nudge came when US national security adviser Henry Kissinger called Fischer on the telephone to personally urge him to beat the Russians. As recalled by Fischer's lawyer, Kissinger opened with, "Greetings, this is the world's worst chess player speaking to the world's best."

Sæmi was waiting outside the DAS house, sitting in his car by the curb, when a young man stuck his head out the door. The kid had a wide mouth and hawkish nose, a flop of brown hair; when not occupied by chess, he had a habit of nervously flinging about his long hands. "Are the journalists gone?" Fischer called to his new bodyguard.

Sæmi rolled down the car window. "Yes."

Fischer came down and asked for directions downtown. Upon receiving them, he promptly wandered off in the wrong direction. "Mr. Fischer," Sæmi called, mindful of his order to keep the grand master in sight, "what do you say we go for a drive?"

The genius and the dancer drove away from downtown, out of the city, and up into the mountains. The buildings dropped away. Iceland's dramatic landscape opened up before them. Look, they pointed, sheep! "We ran after them," Sæmi recalls, "like children."

Lying in the grass on a bright summer night, the Chicago-born chess master seemed to appreciate the solitude and quiet energy of his new travel companion. Sæmi's eager-to-please characteristics empowered Fischer's confidence. On the route home, he tested the loyalty of his new pal by pressing his buttons as they drove: Can we drive faster? What are they talking about on the police scanner? Can you take me to a tailor tomorrow morning?

They arrived back at the lottery-villa around six in the morning. The two had a connection—a friendship was blossoming. They met up again the very next day.

❀

The Match of the Century turned Reykjavík upside down. For the first time in history, the city was packed with foreign press! Each of the two hotels in Reykjavík were fully booked! Some locals even made money by renting out their houses.

Meanwhile, in America, the chess matches would be aired in bars—beer-sipping patriots could look up and watch not the Mets or the Yankees, but the tightly focused face of young Bobby Fischer, sitting rapt in his leather chair.

The new interest in Iceland was flattering. While chess has always been considered a noble exercise for the mind, in the twentieth century, Iceland was the only Western country where grand masters were state supported. The game's local popularity made the tournament itself even more exciting. Everyone wanted to see the world's best chess players, and like true fans, everyone picked a side to root for.

Fischer was up against Boris Spassky, another child prodigy—he had learned to play chess on a train escaping Leningrad at the age of five, and had qualified for the World Championship at just nineteen; he was a man as meticulous as Fischer was erratic. He always arrived at matches on time, dressed in his signature vest, surrounded by Soviet chess advisers and his wife. He never said anything mildly controversial. Even his vest was gray.

With his bouffant hairstyle and reserved manner, he looked rather like a friendly late-night talk show host who had fallen on hard times. Icelanders adored him. According to local rumors, Spassky never once had to pick up his wallet during his stay in Reykjavík.

The mysterious Fischer, meanwhile, was dressed in tailored suits and accompanied by a random local policeman, his only friend. A number of Fischer's biographical writers suggest Sæmi was the older brother he never had; with their height, high cheek bones, and long noses, the two even looked like brothers—but the similarity was only skin-deep. Fischer was dour and capricious. Sæmi was sincere, open-minded, and eager to please. Just as Fischer was gifted with an extraordinary spatial recognition and photographic memory, Sæmi excelled in emotional intelligence.

"They were both childlike, just in different ways," Gudmundur Thórarinsson, chair of the Icelandic Chess Association at the time, recalls in Sæmi's biography. "But I said it then, and will say it again: Sæmundur [Sæmi] saved the match of the century by getting to Fischer when everyone else had failed."

Fischer was, indeed, just as difficult after he arrived in Iceland. After he lost the first match, he refused to show up at the next one unless all film cameras were removed. When they were not, he kept his furious word and didn't show, forfeiting the second game. The match was thus far 0–2; that's a pretty significant margin in chess. Fischer began to consider boarding the next plane out of Iceland. Meanwhile, the match was moved away from the paying audience, and he was promised an even larger share of the gate fees. *The New York Times* wrote: "The match has gone to the ashes, and Fischer is the arsonist." Kissinger called Fischer once again.

The national security adviser's effort to intervene in a game between two grown men signifies the political importance of the match. And Kissinger, in particular, understood the incredible potential that sports could have in easing Cold War tensions: just a year before, he'd made a secret trip to Beijing as tensions thawed as a direct result of what would later be called ping-pong diplomacy.

Just as with the tech and space race, Cold War rivalries had been playing out in sporting arenas for decades. Sports provided a way for the nations to demonstrate and assert their dominance without risking actual war. This led both sides to invest in sports training, though the Soviet Union was particularly dedicated: athletes who won Olympic medals or broke records were promised cash and other rewards. Soviet sports and training programs received huge investments; between 1960 and 1980 the Soviets doubled the number of stadiums and swimming pools. Successful athletes were celebrated as heroes in Soviet propaganda.

Matches served as staging grounds for minibattles reflective of the larger ones. In 1956, for example, the USSR invaded Hungary, deposing the reformist leader and killing thousands of Hungarian protesters. Two weeks later, the Summer Olympics kicked off, and the two nations ended up facing each other in the water polo semifinals, in what would become known as the Blood in the Water match. Tensions ran high. Players traded insults and blows. With a minute left in the match and Hungary leading 4–0, a Soviet player struck Ervin Zádor in the head and left him bleeding from a gash over his eye. The match was called off. Hungary progressed, and ended up winning gold.

The Spassky-Fischer match was occurring in the summer of 1972, at the cusp of a period known as détente, when relations between the Soviet Union and the United States were improving. A breakthrough had first occurred the year before during the World Table Tennis Championships in Japan, when a nineteen-year-old self-identified hippie named Glenn Cowan got on the Chinese national team's shuttle and tried to make friends. Their best player, Zhuang Zedong, gave him a silk-screen picture of the Huangshan Mountains. Cowan gave him a T-shirt with a peace sign and the Beatles' song "Let It Be." The American team wasn't very good—the men's team was ranked twenty-fourth in the world—but when they were invited to China, they suddenly became the most important diplomats on earth. They visited the Great Wall and played a few friendly exhibition matches. The effects were immediate: within weeks, Nixon announced that the United States would ease travel bans and embargoes. Months later, Kissinger made his secret visit, and in February, Nixon became the first American president to visit the Chinese mainland.

Tentative signs of a thaw continued, as all nations stood to gain from increased trade and less nuclear proliferation. A few months before Fischer's game, Nixon also became the first US president to visit Moscow, where he met with Brezhnev and they signed a few agreements on arms control and space exploration. Games were now treading territory somewhere between ploys to gain political advantage and means to forge common ground. Directly after Fischer and Spassky's chess match, a "friendship series" was scheduled between the USSR's and Canada's ice hockey teams. A few months later, the US and Soviet basketball teams would face each other in the summer Olympic finals. Sports had become a venue for ideologies to compete, or as Mao himself put it: "The little ball moves the big ball." And likewise, Fischer and Spassky's pawns were about to move much larger pieces.

Fischer was a superpower's pawn in a global intimidation game. Chess was to Soviets what baseball was to Americans. Grand masters were state sponsored, and for decades no player outside the Kremlin had so much as qualified for the World Championship. The Soviets had held the title for twenty-four years—nearly as long as Fischer had been alive. It would be a huge blow if the "Soviet chess machine" was not even able to beat the twenty-nine-year-old American who had learned to play using instructions bought from a candy store.

Fischer agreed to continue playing—in a small room backstage. The game was on, and so began six weeks of chessboard war.

Fischer and Sæmi by this time had become such fast friends that the chess player spent most evenings at Sæmi's home. He neglected his house and instead kept company with the bodyguard and his family. When GIs at the Keflavík base wanted to invite their fellow American over for a welcome dinner, he declined the offer, saying he had promised to babysit at Sæmi's so he could take his wife, Asa, to the movies. A rather prestigious babysitter that was.

He may not have been a perfect houseguest: in addition to his expansive mind, Fischer had some voracious appetites. While staying at Sæmi's house, he drank so much orange juice that the family began buying it in bulk, straight from the wholesaler. After eating like a competitive runner, he often stretched out on the couch and ruminated long into the evening. Sæmi recalls that Fischer was always fiercely competitive, even when he was playing against Sæmi or his children, whether in chess or another activity. "I was a better swimmer than him," Sæmi recalls, "but sometimes I let him win, you know, to keep him in a good mood."

All this moodiness came long before Fischer's paranoia ballooned into serious mental illness. According to Sæmi, during the time he knew him he never mentioned "the Jews," a topic that would eventually grow into an obsession (despite Fischer's being Jewish himself). The Cold War was, after all, a time when paranoia simply meant being political. In fact, everyone partaking in the match was allowed to be paranoid— ought to be paranoid!

Fischer had begun to build momentum, and the Soviets were getting flustered. They had a sample of Fischer's orange juice sent to the KGB for an examination. Fischer accused the KGB of stalking him with the aim of hypnotizing him. The CIA was accused of having "hijacked" Spassky's mind with radioactive transmitters. To investigate the accusations, police swept the hall, and a few Icelandic carpenters were hired to disassemble Spassky's chair and examine the entire premises. Air samples were taken from the hall. Both players' chairs were x-rayed, swabs from the chairs' leather were taken for lab tests, and all 105 glass panels from the special lighting system (which Fischer had insisted on) were removed and examined. They found, in the end, a grand total of two dead flies.

The bizarre accusations of sabotage were taken seriously in part because people wanted a rational explanation for the poor performance thus far of the two grand masters, Spassky's in particular. After the first ten games, Fischer had won six and a half matches. Games fourteen through twenty were all draws. This was, as it turned out, only the Match of the Century when it came to viewers, media coverage, and political weight—not in terms of game quality.

Two months into the match, the twenty-first game was held. The match would be called when the first player reached 12½ points, and Fischer was leading 11½ to 8½. Fischer played as Black and opened with the Sicilian defense. After fourteen moves, the game looked equal. But then Spassky began to flag. He missed an opportunity to draw, and found himself at a disadvantage. The game was adjourned after forty moves. The next day, when the game was meant to resume, the arbiter announced that Spassky had resigned by telephone. Fischer was victorious. For the first time, America could boast of a Chess World Champion.

Spassky's career never bounced back.

Back in the United States, Fischer received a hero's welcome. New York City hosted Bobby Fischer Day to herald the grand master's return. Fischer appeared on the cover of *Sports Illustrated* and a Bob Hope TV special; he received endorsement offers worth millions. Sales of chess boards soared 20 percent nationwide, and membership in the World Chess Federation shot up thirtyfold. The influence of Fischer's success went far beyond the popularity of chess. In Fischer's own words, the United States had "an image of, you know, a football country, baseball country, but nobody thought of it as an intellectual country until the World Championship in 1972."

Fischer wouldn't play another public match for decades.

The Cold War continued. If anything, the championship only made matters worse. In the ice hockey friendship series held right afterward, tensions got so high that a Canadian player slashed and fractured a Soviet player's ankle. During the Olympics a couple months after that, the Soviet and US basketball teams competed for the gold in what would turn out to be one of the most controversial Olympic games ever played: the Soviets won 51–50, but the US team refused to accept the silver (and still haven't). Reagan assumed the presidency. Détente ended. The Cold War stretched on for years.

But in fact, there was a time—a single day in a stark, white, haunted house on the coast of Iceland—when the two great world powers were a mere moment, a sentence, a single word away from changing the course of history: an afternoon when Mikhail Gorbachev and Ronald Reagan very nearly agreed to eliminate all nuclear weapons.

❦

In 2014, Anna Andersen interviewed ex-president Vigdís Finnbogadóttir for *The Reykjavík Grapevine*. In between asking about her opposition to NATO and her thoughts on gender equality, she asked an unusual question: "What is the Icelandic way of thinking?"

Vigdís theorized that the Icelandic way of thinking was linked to nature. The pressing needs of fisheries and farming and extreme weather meant that Icelanders are impatient and stubborn and dedicated "to what they think is the truth." They are a pragmatic people, in part she says because there is not a heritage of philosophy in Iceland.

"The Nordics—except for the Danes who have Kierkegaard—don't have philosophers. Say you're with six French friends and nobody agrees—the arguments are very intellectual: 'Remember what Pascal said,' someone will say. 'No, you can't say that because Schopenhauer . . .' another will say. They can always refer to ideas. We don't refer to ideas and so our discourse can become very harsh."

The Icelandic way of thinking, then, is very practical-minded. A people who get things done, rather than getting bogged down in abstract discussions. Perhaps it is no coincidence, then, that at the Reykjavík Summit in 1986, Gorbachev and Reagan made more concrete progress than anyone had expected.

The summit began when Gorbachev sent Reagan a message asking for a "quick one-on-one meeting, let us say in Iceland or London." The proposed location was significant. They weren't meeting at any of the more typical venues, like Geneva or Vienna, because both leaders wanted to avoid the pressures and formalities of a full-scale summit. They didn't want to signal that they were about to sign a major treaty: it was meant to be just a helpful working meeting, only the second time the two leaders met. It ended up being, in many ways, the most dramatic summit meeting of the Cold War.

REAGAN PICKED REYKJAVÍK, the conservative *Morgunblaðið* announced with pride in a front-page headline.

The meeting was held at Höfði House, a large, somewhat grim-looking white house built in 1909 for the French consul and later used for the British consulate. It is also, incidentally, very haunted. Memoirs of an early occupant report the presence of the ghost of a young drowning victim. A British envoy who lived there in the 1950s was so shaken by the ghost that he insisted the British consulate be moved; he even applied for special permission from the foreign office to do so. Today the Icelandic Foreign Ministry's official line states, "We do not confirm or deny that the Höfði has a ghost."

Ghost or no, specters certainly hung over the shoulders of Reagan and Gorbachev as they arrived on a blustery October day for the hastily called two-day summit. Gorbachev, for his part, couldn't handle dealing with both economic reform and the arms race. He'd already proposed eliminating all nuclear weapons within fifteen years. Conservative figures in the United States, meanwhile, were bugging Reagan, worried he would agree to something just for the sake of an agreement. To reassure his backers, he reportedly told an adviser, "I don't want you to worry about that. I still have the scars on my back from when I fought the communists in Hollywood."

But both leaders went in unencumbered by big negotiation teams. And face-to-face, they made an astonishing amount of progress.

Gorbachev came out and immediately "laid gifts at their feet," as one attendee recalled, proposing a package that exceeded American expectations. He offered to destroy the intermediate-range nuclear weapons threatening Europe and to cut half of all the USSR's long-range bombers and missiles. All night the delegations worked on the details as guards stood outside in the dark on the fall-colored lawn.

In the morning, Gorbachev clarified that there was a restriction: he wanted US research for the Strategic Defense

Initiative (SDI)—the program for the militarization of outer space—confined to labs for the next ten years. Gorbachev said he wanted this in order to strengthen the Anti-Ballistic Missile Treaty, a treaty signed years earlier and ratified by the US Senate on the day that Fischer and Spassky were playing their tenth chess game.

But Reagan refused. He'd made a promise to the American people about SDI, he said. He told Gorbachev he would share the results of the research, but Gorbachev didn't believe it. He challenged the Americans to make a concession.

Reagan, for his part, pledged to abide by the treaty banning space defenses for ten years, and said both sides should scrap all long-range missiles. Gorbachev, not to be outdone, said, Why not go ahead and eliminate all nuclear weapons?

"They were carried away with the historic ideas they had presented to each other," recalls Alexander Bessmertnykh of the USSR foreign ministry. At one point, Reagan painted a picture for Gorbachev of returning to Reykjavík ten years down the road, as aged, respected leaders, to personally watch as the world's last nuclear warhead was dismantled. They were talking about the elimination of nuclear weapons with an ease that would become unthinkable just a few years later.

Still, the restriction—confining SDI research to a lab for ten years—remained. In frustration, Reagan asked Gorbachev if he would turn down a historic opportunity because of "a single word," that word being the requirement about laboratories. The Americans asked for a time-out. Sitting in a side room, Gorbachev voiced the opinion that if they agreed to the deal that afternoon, the world could change forever.

Reagan, meanwhile, asked an adviser if their research could be done in a lab. The adviser said no, that it wouldn't be possible. Turning to another, Reagan said, "If we agree, then wouldn't we be doing it just for the sake of agreement?"

And just like that, the deal was off.

They'd come so close—closer than anyone had expected. But it was over. As they said goodbye, heading for their separate flights, Reagan said, "I still think we can find a deal."

"I don't know what else I could've done," Gorbachev replied.

On his way to the airport to fly out of Reykjavík, Reagan sat slumped in the back seat, steeped in anger. He knew how close they'd come.

Even years later, Gorbachev recalled: "Reykjavík was the top of the hill. And from that top we saw a great deal."

The deal had failed. But in the long term, most consider the talks a success. The leaders had boldly tackled the issues and proposed serious changes. Gorbachev agreed to on-site inspections. Human rights were agreed upon as a subject of productive discussion. And, crucially, both sides learned what the other was willing to concede. It led directly to the Intermediate-Range Nuclear Forces Treaty they signed the next year.

And it also, incidentally, put Iceland on the map as a meeting place for international dialogue. Fischer, all the while, had dropped off the map.

⚜

After becoming World Champion, Fischer popped up occasionally in circumstances that matched his own eccentricity. In 1977, he handily beat an MIT-built computer program. In 1981, he was arrested in Florida because he met the description of a bank robber; he responded by publishing a fourteen-page diatribe detailing alleged abuses at the hands of police and calling the arrest "a frame-up and setup."

That same year he stayed with former grand master Peter Biyiasas, whom he proceeded to beat seventeen times in a series of speed games. Biyiasas later said, "It wasn't interesting. I was getting beaten, and it wasn't clear to me why. . . . He honestly believes there is no one for him to play, no one worthy of him. I played him, and I can attest to that."

Miloš Forman, the director of the film *Amadeus*, said that he wanted to make a documentary about Fischer. When he managed to get in touch with him, the prodigy was living "with some nuns in some kind of a cult." Fischer went through a cloak and dagger routine before finally meeting Forman at "this little, dingy hotel. Bobby Fischer came in the room. I tried to say hello and he put a transistor radio on the table and put it on full blast. Then he started talking. He was paranoid and thought they might be listening on hidden microphones somewhere. Very strange character."

There's been speculation about Fischer's deteriorating mental condition, but he was never formally diagnosed. One specialist has suggested Fischer was schizophrenic. Another psychologist named paranoid personality disorder. Magnus Skulason, a chess player and the head doctor of Sogn Mental Asylum for the Criminally Insane, was another Icelander who befriended and tried to assist Fischer, and said he wasn't schizophrenic but "had problems, possibly certain childhood traumas that had affected him."

Fischer, by this time at the edge of madness, competed in a major chess match just one more time. It was a $5 million rematch with Boris Spassky, played in Yugoslavia in 1992. Even before the match, US authorities warned that playing would violate the embargo on Yugoslavia, the Balkan state then brimming with chess ambition, ethnic nationalism, and self-destruction. In a subtle diplomatic move, Fischer responded to the warning by holding up the letterhead in front of the international press and spitting on it. He proceeded to win the match against Spassky. Back in the United States, federal officials drew up a warrant for his arrest.

After the Yugoslavia game, Fischer never returned home, and US authorities chose not to pursue an international manhunt. Neither did the feds go after the journalists who'd covered firsthand the Fischer-Spassky rematch in Yugoslavia. In fact, no one else at all faced legal consequences for violating sanctions on Yugoslavia—not even arms dealers, as noted in Bill Clinton's autobiography. The lingering question then becomes: why did the US government go after Fischer more than a decade later?

The answer lies somewhere in Fischer's frequent appearances on radio, where he gave voice to unhinged rants about Jewish conspiracy and displayed an increasing antagonism toward the country he once represented. Responding on Radio Philippines to the destruction of the Twin Towers and the deaths of nearly three thousand people, he said, "This is just wonderful news." The cold case against him was reopened.

On July 14, 2004, while checking passengers onto flight JL745 to Manila, Philippines, the airline staffer at Narita International Airport outside Tokyo looked up from the computer screen and drew the passport closer to her lap.

"Mr. Fischer," she said, "please have a seat." And then she called security.

The mentally ill chess genius Bobby Fischer was going to die of old age in a jail, penalized for moving small pieces of wood on a checkered board in Yugoslavia, a country that no longer existed. Certainly, Fischer deserved a hand from the country he had "put on the map" when he played the most internationally watched sports (and politics) event in Iceland's history.

This, anyway, was the case made for Fischer's asylum in Iceland.

Fischer had kept in poor contact with Sæmi after their famed friendship in 1972, when he'd somewhat exploited the rocker's willingness to work long hours without pay. But Sæmi was willing, once again, to drop everything to help his old friend.

He immediately began arranging meetings with representatives from the Ministry of Justice and Ministry of Foreign Affairs. Iceland seemed truly to be his only hope. Germany and Switzerland had dismissed Fischer's asylum appeal because he had become a Holocaust denier, even though his own mother had moved back to the United States from France in 1939 to flee anti-Semitism and the impending Nazi invasion.

That March, Sæmi drove past the old yellow apartment blocks, gradually bleaching in the Icelandic sun. He was headed to the international airport in Keflavík. He'd bought a ticket to Japan with money out of his own pocket, and was now headed to Tokyo to try to free Fischer himself.

At this point, Fischer had been held at Ushiku, the immigration lockup in Japan, for almost nine months. He was allowed outside for forty-five minutes a day, five days a week. When Fischer's attorney asked a Japanese official when he would be released, the official reportedly responded, "We can keep him as long as we like. We can eat him if we choose to." Fischer celebrated his sixty-second birthday in jail.

Fischer needed support and he needed it soon, but his

continued hate speech did little to garner sympathy. According to a Gallup poll, only 30 percent of Icelanders were in favor of granting him citizenship. This bizarre chess player was
an American problem; at least he certainly wasn't Iceland's.
And that could have been where the story ended, had it not
been for Davíð Oddsson.

A round, pink-faced man with a graying cowlick, Davíð
had already ascended from mayor of Reykjavík to prime minister, a post he held for a record-breaking fourteen years. He
was a man of eclectic interests—a libertarian-leaning, forceful politician, who also aspired to be an actor as a child; in
fact, he supplemented his income as a young man by playing
Father Christmas at children's balls and by writing plays for
the theater. Even as PM, he continued to moonlight as an artist, writing several psalms as well as a best-selling collection
of short stories.

But first and foremost, Davíð Oddsson was a politician, one
so cunning that he admired chess almost by default.

In late 2004, he left the position of PM in a sudden cabinet
shakeup and briefly took the position of minister of foreign
affairs. And suddenly, Fischer began to find more outspoken
supporters within Iceland's ruling Independence Party. Davíð
was backing Fischer's gambit for Icelandic asylum because he
wanted to show Americans that if they really left Keflavík,
they could forget about any favors from Iceland.

In a move that could be called the David and Goliath on a
chessboard, Mr. Oddsson invited the American ambassador
in Reykjavík to a meeting. But the meeting was all about optics, how it looked from the outside: What was that American
ambassador doing in the Foreign Ministry? Was he trying to
push Santa Claus around? The US ambassador's presence in

the ministry only made it seem, in the eyes of the public, as though the United States were trying to use diplomatic pressure to manipulate domestic affairs, throwing its weight around and threatening Iceland not to provide any kind of haven for the fugitive Fischer. And just like that, all the remaining skeptics in the Independence Party now wanted to move Bobby Fischer's case forward.

⊛

Private person though he was, Fischer always did have a good head for showmanship. Stepping down off a private jet with a brand-new, dark-blue passport in his pocket, he had not shaved his gray beard for ten months. He looked like a man who'd been kidnapped. He was escorted once again by his friend, Iceland's beloved dancing policeman, Sæmi Rokk.

As he walked onto the tarmac just before midnight in the rain, hundreds of fans greeted him at the airport, cheering and holding signs that read "Welcome Bobby!!!" Some had been waiting for hours, as his plane had been delayed by fog. The arrival was broadcast, live, on national television. Fischer, in his yellowing whiskers, sweater, and rumpled blue jeans, graciously accepted a bouquet of flowers before being whisked into a limousine (as the airport was also shared by NATO and the US Navy base, there was a theoretical chance he could be arrested upon landing). Did he expect this kind of reception? someone asked. Fischer leaned toward the microphone and answered, "Yeah."

The battle for his release had created a cultlike following among a group of retired professionals and chess enthusiasts. "The Icelanders treated him almost as seventeenth century royalty," writes Frank Brady in the biography *Endgame*. "What they didn't expect was that the king would respond to even the smallest failure with an 'off with his head!' attitude."

If Sæmi expected Fischer to meet his extended rescue efforts with gratitude, he was sorely disappointed. After his release was secured, it was as though Fischer no longer believed Sæmi was playing on his team. He rationalized his moves against Sæmi by accusing him of profiting from a documentary by Fridrik Gudmundsson about Sæmi and Fischer. Why was he still making the film? It was supposed to be about his kidnapping! The group surrounding him sent out a press release, condemning the film and cutting Sæmi off.

Fischer's choice to swap friends during his final years in Iceland is perhaps most handily explained by a fundamental change in his already unstable character. Chess no longer occupied his restless mind. He was absorbed by ideas of world history and philosophy instead of pawn positions and moves; he'd traded an interest in wooden kings for an interest in living ones. His unusual trajectory as a child prodigy meant he'd received virtually no formal education, and like many autodidacts, he sought to prove his competency through debate. Agreeable Sæmi, then, may not have fulfilled Fischer's hunger for friction—and thus he looked elsewhere to meet his compulsive need to debate.

"Bobby Fischer," Sæmi wrote in 2002, "impacted me more than any man in my lifetime." He was ready to put everything aside—money, family, years of his life—to aid the world's greatest chess player, and he was ultimately rebuffed. Reading Sæmi's biography, written by journalist Ingólfur Margeirsson, it sounds as if he resented the group surrounding Fischer more than he did his old friend. They kept him in the dark when Fischer became seriously ill and was put into a hospital.

Fischer grew gravely ill with kidney failure, though in a truer sense, it was his mental illness that destroyed him. Fischer, mistrustful of doctors, refused surgery and medication, despite repeated warnings that such refusals would be fatal. In the end he defeated himself. On his deathbed, true to his anticamera nature, he requested no press at his funeral. Bobby Fischer died in a Reykjavík hospital in January 2008.

❀

During the winter of 2008, I was working at the local newspaper in my hometown, writing hard-hitting stories such as "Drunk Hearse Driver Kills Three Sheep," "Transport Authority Suspends Last Lighthouse Keeper," and "Local Plumber Catches First Salmon of Season."

International news rarely made it to my desk. At best, some famous person might dine at the renowned lobster restaurant in nearby Stokkseyri (in fairness to local journalism, vital to every healthy community, I did write a handful of stories covering public discourse and exposing political corruption). On the morning of January 18, I was woken early and told to grab a camera and drive to a cemetery on the outskirts of town. Fresh footprints led to an unmarked grave, piled high with soil and flowers. After his incredible life, Bobby Fischer was laid to rest in between a horse farmer and a local sheriff. The photographs garnered widespread interest, and the gravesite became an instant shrine for chess enthusiasts. A farmer living next to the church said that for the first few summers, the grave received visitors daily, most of them foreign.

In town, chess enthusiasts established the Bobby Fischer Center, an exhibition of his career with memorabilia from the 1972 championship, including the original chessboard. The center focuses primarily on Fischer's legacy as a genius chess player, despite his de facto retirement around the age of thirty (the age when chess players typically peak). His "escape" from Japan is proudly featured, but little of his madness, paranoia, and aimless years in retirement as an Icelandic citizen. The truth is that Bobby Fischer hated living in Iceland. He couldn't travel abroad with the United States still pursuing a case against him. While Sæmi had boasted of warmer-than-New-York winter temperatures, he didn't mention that Iceland feels much colder due to the constant wind. His baseball cap would blow off his head. And then, unlike in Japan or the Philippines, everyone would recognize him. It was suffocating.

In fact, Fischer's feelings somewhat parallel those of navy men at the Keflavík base, according to their journal entries. None of them really enjoyed their stay on the wind-lashed strip, supervising a fort the enemy never bothered with. Once the base was large enough to provide for daily needs and recreational activities within its fences, Icelandic and American authorities reached an agreement to limit the movement of GIs outside the base. This was arranged in order to temper a backlash against their presence. In particular, the Americans were blocked from the nightlife in Reykjavík, supposedly to preserve the well-being of Icelandic girls who were easily lured by men in uniform. Whether under capitalism or communism, the women of Iceland hadn't gotten much of a say in policies like these. To remedy that, they would need to embrace a newer movement: feminism.

Gender Equality

Iceland from 1972 to the Present

> I'm not going to breastfeed the Icelandic nation; I'm going to lead it.
>
> —VIGDÍS FINNBOGADÓTTIR AT A CAMPAIGN MEETING, WHEN ASKED IF HAVING ONLY ONE BREAST AFTER A CANCER TREATMENT MIGHT AFFECT HER QUALIFICATIONS AS PRESIDENT.

> My time will come.
>
> —JÓHANNA SIGURÐARDÓTTIR, IN A CONCESSION SPEECH, TWO DECADES BEFORE BECOMING THE WORLD'S FIRST OPENLY GAY PRIME MINISTER.

Two Icelanders walk into a London pub. It's the 1980s, and beer is still banned in Iceland, so naturally they order two—I think. The details of this story are a bit fuzzy. Gulp, gulp, gulp! They order another round, and soon begin educating the other patrons about Iceland, a service we Icelanders are often happy to provide outside Scandinavia.

What are Icelandic women like? Why, they're the prettiest women on earth! Proof: Iceland won the Miss World competition in both 1985 and 1988, when Hólmfríður Karlsdóttir and Linda Pétursdóttir were crowned the "world's most beautiful women." And what about the men, you ask? The strongest alive! Our national sport is the World's Strongest Man competition. What is that? An international competition—yes, just like the Olympics, only without all that tedious drug testing—at which strongmen lift boulders the size of a Greek sculpture and pull coach buses with ropes. Icelander Jón Páll Sigmarsson won the title of World's Strongest Man a record four times, and his catchphrase is a popular saying when you complete something difficult: Ekkert mál fyrir Jón Páll—No problem for Jón Páll. During one competition an audience member called him an Eskimo. He shouted back, "I am not an Eskimo. I am a Viking!" right before lifting a cart weighing more than 1,102 pounds.

The bar is about to close. Rounds are bought, shoulders are clapped. Someone praises Britain's Margaret Thatcher. Ah, politics! Did you know about our leader, President Vigdís? She is a single lady with an adopted child, and lots of power, and also the world's first woman president. Impressive, isn't it? As last call is sounded, the Icelanders sit back, satisfied: school's out.

President Vigdís Finnbogadóttir was the first woman to be elected head of state in a direct vote. That means she was not elected as a party head, or by a parliamentary vote. The people chose her as a leader. The people of a drunken-sailor nation, with their particular enthusiasm for Strongest Man and Most Beautiful Woman competitions, threw their political support behind a single, divorced, unemployed mother.

The results of that particular election were announced around six a.m. on June 30, 1980. Later that morning, after a few hours of sleep, Vigdís threw on a woolen sweater and stepped outside onto the balcony facing quiet Aragata Street. Thunderous applause met her. A massive crowd stood around her house.

"Words are our only weapon [as a nation]," she told the crowd. "But with words alone, we can have a lot to say."

The crowd cheered "Madame President!" Two words that had never been heard to ring out side by side in democratic history after a direct vote. A cameraman had to look away from the viewfinder to wipe his tears. Those who witnessed this moment, on a quiet street in Iceland, got to see a rare instance of change in politics. Even the woolen sweater had a dimension of significance. It had been hand knit by a supporter in northern Iceland, and a grateful Vigdís had promised to wear it upon victory.

"I hope she sees me on television," Vigdís said about her sweater-knitting supporter in an interview with the afternoon paper *DV* after the speech. The subject of her clothing had been one of the first questions, noted in the fourth paragraph on the newspaper's front page. It was still, after all, 1980. That same morning, as Vigdís inspired the crowd outside her house, the legendary newspaper hawker Óli, locally famous for occupying downtown's busiest street corner for forty years, cried out the day's headline: Single woman in the Bessastaðir residence! Single woman in the Bessastaðir residence!

Vigdís had made history with a margin of just 1,911 votes.

❀

At the turn of the 1970s, Iceland was a homogenous village at the end of the world. People threw snowballs at musician Hordur Torfason, the most outspoken "homosexualist" in Reykjavík, who was eventually driven into anonymity in Copenhagen. All the Muslims living in Reykjavík would have fit comfortably into a Volvo station wagon. A black person resid-ing on a farm to learn about agriculture was a front-page story in the papers, solely due to the novelty of his skin color.

The year Vigdís was elected, beauty pageant contestant Unnur Steinsson was a media sensation after coming in fourth in the Miss Young International competition. And certainly, part of the population would have preferred that to be the competitive focus for women: women were good at running households, not nations, they'd argue. Up until 1983, only twelve women members of parliament had been elected to the Alþingi. When some pushed for affirmative action initiatives, other legislators took to the podium to claim there was no need for any additional laws on equality—after all, the coun-try already had one. According to Law 60 from 1961, it was il-legal to pay women less than men for equal work. So gender equality, they explained kindly, is already in place.

How handy.

Despite that, trouble was brewing for the patriarchy, and had been for some time. To say no one saw Vigdís's victory coming would be to dismiss the incredible work of feminist activists before her. The movement literally began under-ground, in the basement of the Nordic House, the elegant cul-tural house designed by Finnish architect Alvar Aalto.

The women who gathered at the first meeting worked as teachers, secretaries, nurses, housewives, librarians. On the agenda was a news story from Denmark that told of a new group of women organizers called the Rødstrømperne, the Redstockings. The group had made headlines parading down Strøget, Copenhagen's main pedestrian street, carrying enor-mous breast sculptures, large hats, and fake eyelashes, all of them dressed in red socks. That Danish group, in return, had been inspired by the original Redstockings of the Women's Liberation Movement in New York City, spurred in turn by the 1968 Revolution, a worldwide wave of protests for civil rights and peace. To trace this back even further, you could argue that all of this began poolside, by a new swimming pool at a university campus outside Paris. There, a French minister, invited to preside over the opening ceremony, was heckled by a student who wanted to know why the pool could not be open to both sexes. "If you're having sexual needs, go take a cold shower," the minister told the student. Rather than shower off, a group of students took over the university campus a couple months later. The movement spread like wildfire, and the rest is history, more or less. By 1970, it had inspired some middle-class ladies in Reykjavík to walk out of that basement as a movement. The Redstockings movement, or Rauðsokkahreyfingin, marked the beginning of modern feminism in Iceland.

Around the Western world, women were mobilizing in growing numbers and seeking a life outside the home. The birth control pill had arrived in Iceland four years before the Redstockings movement, allowing more women to obtain a higher education without being forced to drop out due to pregnancy. The number of female university students had grown exponentially, and women now made up roughly one third of the labor force. The female labor surge was in part made possible by technological progress in housework. By one estimate from economist Jeremy Greenwood, the average US household spent fifty-eight hours a week on housework in 1900, including meal preparation, laundry, and cleaning. By the 1970s, that figure had dropped to eighteen hours.

The workday for women was still incredibly long. After

work ended, they were expected to resume household duties and childcare. Their pay was about 70 percent of what men received (despite Law 60), and even in female-dominated workplaces like fish factories and shops male employees received a higher pay on average. Redstockings activists demonstrated the inequality by going grocery shopping and offering the cashier 70 percent of the tagged price. Shopkeepers called the police.

Exposing the imbalanced power dynamics of society is thankless work. Especially when that work targets values, for instance by exposing how the views and actions of men receive more respect than women's. The movement turned its attention to sites where consumer culture and sexism were working in concert. Beauty contests made an obvious target. Outside the venue for the Miss Young Iceland beauty pageant, the activists arrived with a milking cow that they'd dressed up in a colorful cloak, with a crown and a banner that read "Miss Iceland."

The organization kept a flat structure, with no elected leaders, only "Cells" and "Central Coordinators." The founders had been middle-class women who wanted women to be considered equal to men. Others, younger and more progressive, wanted the movement to focus on the situation of working-class women and "female issues" like domestic violence and abortion instead of fighting to be part of the boys club. Both visions were apparent in an idea put forward at the organization's first official summit in Skógar, the southern village backed by an enormous waterfall, ahead of the 1975 "International Women's Year" touted by the United Nations: a day-long labor strike to honor women's contributions to the national workforce.

Due to the organization's anarchical structure, it remains unclear who initially pushed for the idea—scholars say the notion had been brewing for some time leading up to the Skógar summit. The two factions, radicals and moderates, agreed on methods but not optics: the young wanted the campaign to be called "Women's Strike," while the moderates wondered how to reach women beyond their base. How about "The Women's Day Off"?

Regardless of name, they were calling for a complete national shutdown.

On October 24, 1975, all morning flights from Keflavík International Airport were cancelled. The flight attendants didn't show up. Bank executives had to make their own coffee and then sit in as tellers. Students showed up to empty classrooms. Men dragged their children to work. Assembly lines ground to a halt. Phones at reception desks rang unanswered, until an overwhelmed male voice picked up.

An astounding 90 percent of female workers had decided to "take the day off," and the strike didn't just include paid employees: housewives, too, were urged to take the day off and rally with paid workers at two p.m. at a square in the heart of Reykjavík with a landmark clock tower. By noon, the organizers knew the campaign had made a splash in Reykjavík but really had no idea how many women would actually participate in the afternoon rally. By one p.m. the answer was clear to anyone standing on a downtown rooftop—a lot.

Some twenty-five thousand people attended the Reykjavík rally, and many more rallied elsewhere in the country. An iconic *Morgunblaðið* front page photograph, taken from the top of a nearby office building, depicts the rally filling Lækjartorg Square, the crowd so large that the lens can't capture it all. The picture became an international sensation, inspiring women around the Western world to copy Iceland's success.*

Everyone remembers where they were that day. Anthropology professor and former parliamentarian Sigridur Dúna Kristmundsdóttir once told me that the smell of burned meat always reminded her of that day in 1975; she was just twenty-three years old and was walking home through her neighborhood where all the husbands were struggling in their kitchens. The air smelled of over-cooked beef.

And the effect was powerful: by the following year, parliament passed a bill granting women three months of paid maternity leave and made its first steps toward legalizing abortion.

Had the 1975 Women's Day Off never happened, the search for a female candidate for the presidential race five years later would have been considered a radical idea. Early in the race, three men threw their hats into the ring. First, there was alpha male Albert Gudmundsson, a former finance minister who entered politics after retiring as a footballer for Arsenal. Second was Pétur Thorsteinsson, a life-long diplomat who had served as Iceland's ambassador to both the Soviet Union and the United States—a man who could not name his favorite color without walking on thin diplomatic ice. And finally, the favorite to win, a stoic academic and the president of the University of Iceland, Gudlaugur Thorvaldsson.

---

* The "Women's Day Off" has been repeated five times since 1975, always on October 24. Instead of taking the entire day off, women have left work in the early afternoon, symbolizing the time of day when women have, on average, completed their pay in comparison to men. In 1985, the event began at 2:00 p.m., in 2005 at 2:08 p.m., in 2010 at 2:25 p.m., in 2016 at 2:38 p.m., and in 2018 at 2:55.

The problem in the movement for a female candidate was the organization's flat structure. Though the structure had its advantages, it meant they lacked an obvious leader to support, and the most prominent activists were too controversial to stand elections. A poor outcome could even damage the cause. The list of viable candidates was indeed limited to the few who could boast of a fancy job title. Vigdís Finnbogadóttir was the artistic director of Reykjavík's City Theater, a small but respected enterprise, about to step down after a successful tenure. When a reporter asked what she would do next in her career, she threw her hands in the air and said: "I hope Iceland has something for me to do."

❀

Once, on the radio, I heard an interview with a shopkeeper who was bragging about his fine shelf selection. He talked about the way that foreign companies often give Iceland the first stab at new products, in order to gauge interest. The population, he said, was known to be receptive to change, and it was a place where word traveled fast—new products became mainstream within weeks instead of months.

A popular product that catches on tends to have the highest purchase rate per capita in Iceland. Unofficially, Icelandic consumers store in their closets a record-breaking number of Clairol Foot Spas, Sous-vide cooking gear, and eight-hundred-dollar 66°North parkas. More than 70 percent of the population are Costco members. Pop singer Ed Sheeran sold about fifty thousand concert tickets to his show in Reykjavík in 2019, meaning he attracted 15 percent of the population. The remaining 85 percent, of course, were at home reading Halldór Laxness's *Independent People*, listening to pianist Víkingur Ólafsson's latest Bach album, or watching the subtle Icelandic comedy about sheep herders, *Rams*—or so I like to believe.

This is all to say that ideas and trends travel fast in a place where everyone is part of the same conversation. It is, you might say, the upside of homogeneity.

Before Vigdís announced her candidacy, her name—a beautiful name meaning "war goddess"—was already known, as she had spent one winter cohosting an educational program about the French language. That's not because Icelanders particularly love educational programming—everyone who appeared on television at that time became an instant celebrity. The public broadcasting service RÚV had a monopoly on TV and radio, and its approach to television was like that of a wholesome parent—not too much. Programming was limited to prime-time hours, and they took Thursdays off. And also every July, when the station closed its entire operation. People were, therefore, pretty grateful for just about anything that was on television.

And Vigdís excels on television. She's charismatic, she lights up on camera, and she's so memorable, as noted in her 2009 biography by Páll Valsson. She speaks calmly and follows her sentences with a faint smile. She is of average height and has delicate features, with blonde hair and simple makeup. I note all this, of course, not to reinforce the attention paid to the physical appearance of women in politics, but because rising access to television meant that personality and image did matter in politics, more than ever. Vigdís's image, her makeup and clothing, were scrutinized and rehashed relentlessly in the public eye. In an interview about a 2014 exhibit of her clothing at Iceland's Museum of Design, Vigdís recalls, "I realized early on that it's not enough for a woman to be intelligent. Intelligence has to have a modern 'coiffure,' as they say in French." In speech and appearances, she mastered the art of giving local trademarks a cosmopolitan vibe—on her first official visit to Denmark, she appeared in a completely white sheepskin coat tailored at the South Iceland slaughterhouse co-op tannery (whose best-selling product today is a hot dog). In sharp contrast, Queen Margrethe II greeted her in a completely black dress.

In person, Vigdís strikes the perfect balance of energy and calm. She's confident and attentive. I interviewed her twice for the Associated Press, and she got me thinking about the quality of being a good listener. Her strength, I think, lies in her sincere curiosity about other people, making her quick to establish a personal connection. Our conversation was natural and engaged, until I turned on the tape recorder and the answers became routine, verbal press statements. My questions were on threats to the Icelandic language—"We must adapt the language to digital technology"—and the Me Too movement—"It will change the attitude of both women and men." On both occasions she spoke diplomatically, relying on decades of experience talking about delicate subjects. After years of invasive scrutiny, she has, out of necessity, developed a politician's protective veneer, which is perhaps no surprise considering how much the role of president revolves around being a good figurehead.

The president of Iceland is principally a symbolic figure, expected to unite the nation.

Halldór Laxness, the great Icelandic author who won the 1955 Nobel Prize in Literature, was a larger-than-life persona with an enormous talent for stirring controversy. When once asked, before upcoming presidential elections, if he would consider running, he replied in his deadpan manner: "Is that a good job?"

The answer depends on who you are. For someone animated by public debates, as was Laxness, the role of president is very restrictive.

The office has little formal authority in a country ruled by the Alþingi, which is composed of sixty-three legislators divided, on average, between five political parties of various size. Never in history has one political party gained a majority in parliament, and thus every election is followed by coalition negotiations to form a ruling government with a prime minister steering a cabinet of ten to twelve ministers. The center-right Independence Party (Sjálfstæðisflokkurinn) almost always dominates the negotiations as the traditionally largest party, typically aligning with the centrist Progressive Party (Framsóknarflokkurinn). The president mediates the coalition negotiations but is not expected to take sides. The only definite authority held by the president is a veto; laws passed by parliament have to have the president's signature to take effect. But in the history of the republic, only one out of six presidents has ever exercised this right. All the others have considered their personal opinion not heavy enough to outweigh the democratically elected parliament, and instead have used their influence to champion good causes like public health, forestry, and international business relationships.

In other words, political experience is not crucial for fulfilling the role. Charisma is. Anyone without a criminal record can run for president, as long as they are above the constitutional age limit of thirty-five, which is (as everyone knows) the age when one finally starts acting more presidential—the age when one can hear the words *open bar* without waking up hungover behind a dumpster the next morning.

Voters typically favor candidates around the age of fifty, someone with whom they'd be honored to shake hands and share a coffee. Fundamentally it has to be someone who can appear on CNN and address the United Nations without accidentally reminding everybody that Iceland is a small island nation where the pool of presidential candidates is just 150,000 people—a number that includes women over the age of thirty-five. That pool felt significantly smaller, though, in February 1980, four months before the elections, when no woman had ever made the bid.

The first public endorsement for Vigdís was a paragraph-long letter to the editor from a woman known for helping troubled youth. Days later, on talk radio, a listener called with a similar claim. The idea snowballed, without Vigdís ever expressing a willingness to run. "I became shy, even embarrassed, when the issue was brought up," she said. "I felt like being part of some joke."

According to Vigdís, the people who ultimately tipped her decision to run for president were the crew on board the *Guðbjartur*, a trawler fishing for cod north of Iceland. It was four months before the election and the crew, via radio, ordered a telegram for number 2 Aragata, in Reykjavík, her home.

"We urge you to run for President," the telegram read simply.

The support bewildered her. Sailors were well outside her regular circle of actors and professionals.

"To begin with, I felt so shy, embarrassed, even, of being

mentioned as a possible candidate," she said in an interview. "The telegram made all the difference. Suddenly the support was real."

She met with her circle of friends on a Monday evening, the day off for theater actors, to draft her announcement. She was still nagged by self-doubt. Successful or not, the bid would follow her for the rest of her career. Pomposity was not ladylike and boasting of your own qualifications for a task went against her character. When she arrived home that evening, she took out the vacuum and started madly cleaning the apartment to get her mind off things. She slept only a little, and called her friend first thing in the morning, just after seven a.m., to tell him that the whole thing was off.

"I am afraid it's too late. The reporters are already coming to your house at nine," he said.

She hung up and walked into the bathroom—and fixed her hair.

❀

Back in the day, the trust and respect that people still held toward their government was reflected in the questions they posed to politicians. Difficult questions were rare, and personal ones simply rude, off-limits. This ran so deep that the eldest son of Iceland's first president became a mercenary in the Nazi Waffen SS without that doing an ounce of damage to his father's political career. Vigdís, meanwhile, adopted a seven-year-old daughter after challenging the rules that forbid single parents from fostering children. Any questions? Yes, you in the back, with your hand up, please speak so we can hear you: "Madam," asked an older woman at a town hall in the East Fjords, "are you a virgin?"

So much for off-limits. The question she received most often, however, was about her lack of a male companion. How can she host dinners without a spouse? Whom will she tell her secrets to? If you get elected, will you accept the position?

She usually replied with humor, pointing out that she had, so far, coped just fine without a man. Much later, after her tenure in office, she gave a more straightforward answer: she was able to run for president because she didn't have a husband.

"What sort of husband, of my generation, at that time, would have supported his wife to run for President?" she pointed out. But during her run, her replies simply shrugged off the sexism without confrontation. Feminists found her much too soft; shockingly, no women's organization endorsed her campaign. Vigdís, likewise, did not seek their support. She, the woman pioneer, was after all just "light pink," as the Swedish newspaper *Dagens Nyheter* wrote. She had been raised within the establishment and given a lot of opportunities in life. She sought slow reform, not revolution. To claim that the telegram from the all-male trawler crew was the most important push was politically savvy, not feminist: her aspirations were only lent legitimacy when approved by a group of men—strangers, no less, not the women of her community. She further flattered sailors, saying they understood and appreciated the weight of women, who took care of the home while they spent weeks at a time trawling for fish. She even told one interviewer that her dream job was being a captain. The statement may have been meant to inspire girls and women to enter male-dominated careers—that was her preferred style. Subtle. Her actual career certainly does not reflect that of an aspiring fisherman.

Vígdís was the daughter of a superwoman who raised two children, working as a nurse and leading the profession's labor association. As a kid, Vigdís often wished for the typical stay-at-home mother, one with a spotlessly tidy house and ironed shirts. Her father was an engineering professor, among the first hires at the University of Iceland. They lived on campus.

After Vigdís graduated from high school, her parents suggested that she study abroad, anywhere she wanted. That was a rare opportunity for an Icelander, and even more so for a woman: at the time, a total of just nineteen women had completed a bachelor's degree at the University of Iceland. She picked France, in the southern city of Grenoble. After intensive language training, she transferred as a literature major to the prestigious University of Paris, known as the Sorbonne. Still, the language barrier worked to her disadvantage in school assignments, with professors holding her to a high standard. She had to lower her perfectionist expectations.

"What will the day be called when I can make you a little proud?" she wrote to her parents after discussing her academic record at the close of her first year abroad.

Good grades came more naturally to her brother Thorvaldur, she has said. He was two years younger and about to go to England for an engineering degree when he went camping with friends one evening. Drunk, he wandered off with a friend to a nearby lake. They got into a rusty, wooden dinghy, and excitedly declared they would row across the lake. Midway across, the lock holding Thorvaldur's oar broke and he lost his balance, falling overboard. He was able to swim to shore across the freezing lake, while his friend, trapped on the boat with only one oar, drifted to the other side of the lake. Exhausted from the cold, Thorvaldur walked less than 110 yards from the lake before succumbing to hypothermia.

Her parents had lost their only son, the child destined for great achievements. Some have said that the accident became the backdrop of Vígdís's life. In some ways, she had to step up as a son to her grieving parents, to make them forget and be proud. But like any life story, hers is a series of coincidences. For a while, it looked like she would become a stay-at-home wife. While in France, she had a quasi boyfriend at home who was attending medical school. She left the Sorbonne without completing her degree, in part to be with him and marry a year later. Icelandic physicians have to go abroad to special-ize, and so the two of them moved to Denmark. She attended classes in theater studies—Denmark generously allows Ice-landers to attend their universities for free—but her husband wasn't satisfied with his position in Denmark. So they left for a small town in Sweden. He worked long hours, while she stayed home and tried hard to make it work between them. One night, they went for a drive, and he said their seven years of marriage were over.

Vigdís returned home. She worked as a guide for the Na-tional Travel Agency, a state-funded tour company established to service tourists, developing a concept called "cultural tour-ism," meaning, in modern terms, talking to the tourists. She translated plays by Jean-Paul Sartre and founded an avant-garde theater group. Watching theater was her greatest plea-sure, and when the position of director at Reykjavík's local theater opened up, her friends urged her to apply. It was like that throughout all of her career: she was humble and fulfilled in life, while the people around her urged her to go for more.

❀

Vigdís's victory came at the crest of second-wave feminism, a social movement that had swept the world through the 1960s and '70s.

While first-wave feminism, of the early twentieth century, focused on the fight for legal rights, such as women's right to vote, second-wave feminism focused on the broader experience of women: not just in politics, but in work, family, and sexuality. The National Organization for Women was founded in the United States in 1966 to fight for equal pay. The New York City chapter of Redstockings published its principles in "The Bitch Manifesto" and invented consciousness raising, which helped women to articulate how gender shaped their daily lives.

It's important here to note that this was not simply a neat new addition to the left-wing ideology. Some of the grossest sexism came from nominally progressive organizations. In 1964, when a resolution was brought up by a woman at a Student Nonviolent Coordinating Committee (SNCC) conference, Stokely Carmichael cut her off by saying, "The only position for women in SNCC is prone."

Much like the Icelandic chapter of Redstockings, the second-wave feminist movement was divided between a moderate and a radical wing. Some of the middle-class professionals wanted to reason with men. Others were sick of trying polite discourse. The question was reform versus revolution, that is, lobbying politicians versus storming in to disrupt legislative hearings.

After a wave of victories, including Vigdís's election, organized activity declined for a time. Partly this was thanks to a sense that core goals had been achieved; it was also due to dissent over things like women in the armed forces and the prominence of abortion rights in the movement.

The emergence of third-wave feminism in the mid-90s was only possible due to the greater economic security procured by women who had fought for greater access and equality in the '60s and '70s. Third-wave feminists conceived of gender as a spectrum, and embraced artifacts that earlier feminists had rejected as demeaning, like lipstick and high heels, in order to reclaim feminism.

Today we're witnessing the development of what you might call fourth-wave feminism. It'll take years to really see what it looks like, but the movement now is more focused than ever on intersectionality: that means recognizing that different aspects of a woman's identity affect her simultaneously. Intersectionality requires that everyone is included, not just middle-class white women; it means attending to race and LGBTQ issues, because we can't bring about meaningful change without recognizing the way injustices are tied together. The Me Too movement demonstrates that progress for gender equality does not just lie in electing female candidates to office or even passing progressive legislation: a whole cultural shift is needed.

Before Vigdís ran for office, it did not occur to her campaign that the election would be historic. Female leaders had, of course, existed before her. The earliest twentieth-century example is Sirimavo Bandaranaike, leader of Sri Lanka, who came into power after her husband passed away; the first nonhereditary female head of state was Khertek Anchimaa-Toka, supreme leader of the Tuva Republic, Russia. Other women, such as Benazir Bhutto of Pakistan and Indira Gandhi of India, inherited their positions as party heads from their fathers. And in Western democracies, women had been elected as party heads, most famously Golda Meir, the Israeli prime minister, and her British colleague Margaret Thatcher. But no woman had ever been elected in a direct national vote. After Vigdís, in fact, it took another ten years for it to happen again: Mary Robinson of Ireland.

The significance of her campaign only became clear when foreign media began dispatching reporters and photographers to follow Vigdís on the trail around Iceland's coastal communities. Vigdís remembers realizing the import when she received a newspaper clip from a Chinese newspaper, with a photograph of her walking all alone outside. She was humbled by the attention. The nation, however, not so much. Cheers to us for being best in the world in gender equality. Business leaders seized the international spotlight to sell their products. Locals happily told foreigners they had voted for Vigdís—even though only a third of them actually did. You could speculate that the constant desire of a small nation to prove itself overcame whatever prejudices some voters still nursed. The 1975 Women's Day Off had, for the first time in modern history, cast Iceland into the world spotlight based on merit—not as a place of volcanoes, US soldiers, and a chess tournament. Now they could have an internationally recognized leader who spoke five languages with the aura of a queen and a good sense of humor to boot.

Vigdís made one of her first trips abroad to London. She received a formal greeting from Margaret Thatcher outside the Downing Street residence. Thatcher invited her inside and, according to Vigdís's biography, as soon as the door shut behind them, Thatcher asked: "So you are against nuclear energy?"

Thatcher wanted a debate, but Vigdís's reply was probably a bit too vague and philosophical to sustain a dynamic dialogue. In a photo snapped of the two leaders, they are looking in opposite directions. Thatcher looks at Vigdís with her mouth half open, while Vigdís is looking stoically off frame with a warm smile. Thatcher eventually left the meeting early to attend to other remote islands in the Atlantic, the Falklands, where a confrontation was brewing with the military junta in Argentina, one that would boil over into war two months later.

Thatcher and Vigdís were two iconic female leaders of the 1980s, both holding office throughout that entire decade. Their legacy couldn't be more different, however. In a fractured age, Vigdís became a symbol of stability, and the closest thing to a universally beloved public figure. She inspired women and children to dream big; she planted trees and spoke to foreign leaders about parenting.

Thatcher, meanwhile, was known as the Iron Lady, a leader with an uncompromising approach. She became one of the most beloved and most hated figures in modern politics. Her administration pushed for laissez-faire economics—antigovernment, antiunion, and proprivatization—in harmony with the Reaganomics on the other side of the Atlantic. This austere economic approach initially saw support when the Swedish Academy honored libertarian thinkers Friedrich Hayek and Milton Friedman with the Nobel Prize in Economics in 1974 and 1976, respectively. But only in 1979, when Thatcher ousted Britain's incumbent Labour government, did the message enter mainstream politics, echoing all over Europe.

In the Nordics, the timing was key: all but Norway were in a recession, and the government, rightfully or not, was blamed for enabling a vicious cycle of inflation. Voters began doubting the Nordic social-democratic model of treating the free market as "a good servant, but a bad master." High taxes and strict regulations were, indeed, good for equal opportunity but bad for robust growth. Instead of making sure the ladder to success was equally accessible, the new economic approach was focused on making the ladder reach higher, beyond any previous limits. The shift toward deregulation saw an explosion of successful Nordic corporations.

In Sweden, IKEA conquered Europe and later the United States with meatballs and BILLY bookcases, while relocating production processes to East Germany, where labor was strikingly cheap (the company has since "deeply apologized" for relying, in part, on political prisoners of the communist regime). Finland turned the rubber boot manufacturer Nokia into the flagship of Finland's "Nordic Japan" campaign, becoming a leader in the innovation of consumer electronics and telecommunications. Norwegians, already filthy rich from discovering oil plus a culture of conservative spending, "freed" its petroleum revenues by establishing the state-owned Oil Fund for market-driven investments, revenue poured mostly into international markets. Denmark, inventors of the hygge lifestyle, brewed more Carlsberg and welcomed tourists to Legoland.

And then there was Iceland. To follow the money, the country followed its fish. Until 1980, the fishing industry was a largely unregulated competition among towns and local fishermen. Despite some conservation efforts, the system—or lack thereof—led to overfishing and, due to the uncertain future of fishing, a lack of investment in more efficient boats and gears. Right-wing politicians championed a new solution: a market-driven quota system. By handing out quotas based on past performances, the fish stock would be protected from overfishing and fishing companies would have a more certain outlook. Brilliant solution, right? The answer often depends on people's personal experience with the system. Many watched their once-vibrant fishing community be devastated by a single business deal: if Fisherman A owns 1 percent of the annual cod license, he can sell the license to Fisherman B, who already owns 2 percent—or 10 percent. With that, jobs move and fish factories merge—unemployment soars in one place and shrinks in another. Thatcher's economics had introduced fishing monopolies to Iceland. Sure enough, three decades after the system was introduced, a few big companies have accumulated most of the quota, using bigger and more efficient vessels than the little enterprises who "refuse" to sell.

Fishing licenses, though, soon meant much more than access to fresh cod. They became Iceland's golden ticket to the world of international finance. From the perspective of a bank, the fishing quotas made for a solid collateral; just as land reform turned "dead capital" into liquefiable assets, having a fishing quota was like being a shareholder in the ocean. When the time came to liberalize Iceland's three major banks, which were state owned until the early 2000s, the fish moguls came running with money—their access to international loans was golden.

By embracing the flashy world of finance, Iceland could suddenly attain the wealth that traditional industries had not been able to provide. Over a span of just seven years, the financial industry in Iceland grew twentyfold through debt-fueled acquisitions abroad. The media frequently referred to aggressive entrepreneurs as "modern-day Vikings raiding foreign shores." These self-made capitalist upstarts had begun their careers driving forklifts in fish factories and selling imported pineapples at a markup. Now they owned Britain's legendary luxury jeweler Goldsmiths, Denmark's flagship department store Magasin du Nord, and the West Ham United Football Club.

Iceland was set to become the "Dubai of the North," all thanks to the bold and brave business Vikings.

But the popular myth of the male entrepreneur genius did, eventually, unravel.

Fast forward to 2007. On the road between Keflavík Airport and Reykjavík, economics professor Robert Aliber watched out the window how Iceland was to become a case study in his field: that of economic bubbles fueled by international capital.

"Too many construction cranes," he murmured. All these cranes rising from the skyline were, the joke went, our new national bird. But they were a sign for Aliber: the country was in a bubble. And one feature of a bubble is that people can't see that they are in a bubble.

❦

The Lehman Brothers bankruptcy threw the United States into an epoch-defining financial cataclysm in 2008.

Now imagine three hundred Lehman Brothers going bust at once.

That, in relative terms, is what Iceland endured during the banking crisis. Over the span of one week, 90 percent of the financial sector defaulted. The International Monetary Fund rescued the state from bankruptcy, the first time in forty years an "industrialized" nation had to apply to the emergency fund. An economic depression followed that saw people lining up for food aid, an unprecedented sight in modern Iceland. Thousands immigrated to Norway, the largest immigration since the nineteenth-century exodus to the New World.

Politicians, businessmen. and the media had told the public, over and over, that everything would be fine, and people believed them. No one expected the country to become known as the failed WALL STREET ON THE TUNDRA, to quote the headline of a *Vanity Fair* article describing a society ravaged by shock and humiliation. Policemen, armed with pepper spray and handcuffs, had to guard parliament from angry protesters; washing smashed eggs off the humble, gray building a daily routine.

There is no agreed formula for restoring a peaceful, democratic society. In Iceland, still a young state, people feared not just for the future of the economy but for the country itself. A long path to reconciliation began, complicated by disagreement over whom to blame. The reckless bankers or years of deregulation and political policies favoring short-term risks? A special investigation committee concluded that the banks had grown too fast and had concentrated their investments around enterprises with direct connection to its biggest owners—the boys' club. Politicians responsible for reacting to warning signs had kept their actions informal and personal; two of the most powerful figures of government finance, the prime minister and the Central Bank chief, were friends since college and spoke casually on the phone about who deserved a rescue.

The claim that the financial crisis would not have happened if the banks had been led by women—sometimes called the Lehman sisters hypothesis—is impossible to prove but certainly persuasive. Of the thirty-one Icelandic bankers sentenced to jail for financial crimes ranging from insider trading to market manipulation only two were women, considerably fewer than the male-to-female ratio of upper-level managers would suggest. Further, a 2015 study by Finnish researchers did find that US banks with female CEOs were less likely to fail during the financial crisis. The women in charge were assessing risk more conservatively, and in fact, according to Sami Vähämaa, one of the study's authors, the difference was significant: "Male-led banks were six to seven times more likely to fail."

The idea became a powerful force in Iceland. Jóhanna Sigurðardóttir, the first female prime minister of Iceland and world's first openly gay premier soon took office. A number of other firsts for women followed in the early years of recovery: first female bank boss, police chief, prison warden, leader of the Glíma Icelandic Wrestling Association, head of the Sheep Farmers Association, bishop. Feminist scholars call this phenomenon the glass cliff: it's the tendency to put women in charge only after male predecessors have failed. The Church of Iceland, for example, was under fire for sexual misconduct accusations and was rapidly losing members when a woman was sworn in as its first female bishop. But women were suddenly entering all kinds of sectors traditionally dominated by men—policing, construction, law, journalism, divinity.

In parliament, the crash led to political instability and a record number of first-time MPs. That in turn ushered in policy changes. Private companies were soon required by law to have the composition of their boards be at least 40 percent women, and to prove with a stringent audit that men and women were being paid the same for comparable work. Strip clubs were banned. Iceland adopted what is now known as the Nordic-model approach to the sex industry, which seeks to criminalize the buyers of sex work while decriminalizing and assisting the sex workers. The most radical measure, which never reached the floor of parliament, was a government effort to block online access to violent porn.

By one year after the crash, Iceland ranked first on the *Global Gender Gap Report*, where it remained for eleven years running. This index takes into account life expectancy, educational opportunities, political representation, equal pay, and other factors, and it ranks the country on a scale of one to one hundred. The Nordic countries are far ahead of the rest of Europe, generally receiving a score of around 80 points, almost double that of Greece and Portugal, for example. Holland is the only other European country that comes close.

Gender studies professor Thorgerdur Jennýardóttir Einarsdóttir* keeps a special folder in her email inbox for interview questions from foreign media, who often ask her to articulate how Iceland has become a paradise of gender equality. Her reply: it isn't. "Between heaven and hell, we are, of course, doing better than most places," she said. "But the best-in-the-world ranking depends a lot on the variables behind each index."

The index measures some important aspects, but it doesn't take into account rates of gender-based violence, or the care-

---

* Icelandic last names are traditionally patronymic but in recent years some people, particularly feminists, have adopted an additional matronymic last name. Hence, Thorgerdur is the daughter (dóttir) of Jenný and Einar.

taker burden of women, for example. Iceland has, by some measures, one of Europe's higher per capita rates of reported rapes. Amid the Me Too revolution, the realization was stark: equal representation does not, by default, eliminate gender-based violence. Thorgerdur says the "myth" that Iceland's record on gender equality makes it a safe haven for women can in fact be a distraction from the steps needed to fight systemic oppression. "One of the biggest challenges now," she said, "is for men to change their ideas about masculinity."

The rise of women has ultimately been the most lasting effect of the financial crisis. Other political movements that emerged from the crisis—EU membership, a new constitution, direct democracy—lost their momentum when the economy bounced back, but political platforms on gender only got more progressive. Abortion is now allowed until the twenty-second week of pregnancy; fathers are paid four months paternity leave just like mothers; fiscal spending is actively analyzed from a gender perspective in a process known as gender budgeting.

Thanks to its image as the best place in the world to be a woman, Iceland often gets credit for policies it did not invent. That image has made Iceland an influential force. According to a recent academic study, based on interviews with veterans in foreign service, "Supply and demand appears to be the main reason for Iceland to choose gender equality as a brand." That image has made Iceland an influential force: under the leadership of Prime Minister Katrín Jakobsdóttir, the government has employed a special "equality unit" within the Ministry of Welfare. It's a team of agents promoting gender-related issues abroad, going around the world to connect with experts and audiences who are eager to learn "the Icelandic magic."

Imagine a foreign agent with their eyes behind sunglasses, quietly assessing an agency's strengths and weaknesses, someone soft-spoken with an Icelandic accent who seeks to overthrow a regime. That's Magnea Marinósdóttir (minus the sunglasses). She speaks rapidly, with great energy. Gender public policy has been on her mind since she became a single mother at the age of twenty, around the same time the government changed the terms for student loans, in turn forcing many single mothers to drop out. The amendment was meant to make student loans more conditional to academic progress and punish students who failed to complete a certain number of credits each semester. The move stripped parents of their flexibility and altogether about 30 percent of parents stopped taking student loans (Magnea completed the degree by taking an extra job). Their fate was a consequence of Thatcher-esque austerity politics, a shift in policy that sought to cap spending.

Revealing and eliminating that sort of hidden, structural gender inequality has defined Iceland's policy work for years, and today many Europeans are taking notice. But not for the reasons you'd think. Other nations are wondering how Iceland maintains an above-replacement birthrate, yet simultaneously maintains the highest rate in the Organization for Economic Cooperation and Development of women working full-time. "European nations tend to view gender equality as a means towards an end, the objective being to maintain current standard of living against a declining birth rate and lower labor participation among women," she said. Yet she insists the Icelandic system is not perfect. For one, the lack of public day care for children under the age of two means many women need to stay at home throughout that time.

Magnea offers a lesson on the benefits of gender quotas in

business, paid parental leave for both parents, and the equal pay audit. "For every piece of legislation, the private sector initially pushes back, fearing hurt profits and red tape," she told me. "But once they come into effect, surveys suggest a swift change in tone. Business leaders no longer consider the laws much of a burden and, more significantly, workers have more trust in the fairness and leadership of their workplace." As it turns out, more gender equality also means a more robust economy.

❀

Vigdís Finnbogadóttir turned ninety in April 2020, at a time when the country was on coronavirus lockdown. Dozens of people gathered outside her house to support her, much like forty years earlier, only this time they had to comply with the new rules on social distancing. Her big celebration at the Vigdís International Centere for Multilingualism and Intercultural Understanding had had to be canceled, and celebrations were moved to social media, prompting an outpouring of posts tagged #TakkVigdís—*takk* being Icelandic for "thank you." One millennial recalled thinking, as a little boy, that the presidency was only for women, which he found strange and unfair until learning the truth. Women leaders thanked her for inspiring high goals and bold moves.

Archival footage ran in the media on her birthday: Vigdís laughing with Queen Elizabeth, taking a walk with Ronald Reagan to chat about acting and theater, holding hands with French president Jacques Chirac. After she was elected, the country had a waiting list of world leaders keen to visit. Iceland had arrived.

Of course, most of this took place long before I had any real political or national consciousness. But I can relate to that sense of national pride when one of ours shows the rest of the world that Iceland is not just a "small, rugged island nation," as typically described.

Earlier in 2020, I stayed awake until four a.m. to watch the Academy Awards live, so I could see if composer Hildur Guðnadóttir would become the first Icelander to win an Oscar. She was nominated for Best Original Score for *Joker*, an award that had never been given to a female composer working alone and which was slotted for late in the ceremony. I was surprisingly excited about her success, despite having absolutely no personal connection to her other than a common nationality.

The music stilled. The celebrities opened the envelope. Sigourney Weaver read: "Hildur . . ." She had won, and in her two-minute speech, Hildur said: "To the girls, to the women, to the mothers, to the daughters who hear the music bubbling within, please speak up. We need to hear your voices."

That's one way to change the world.

AFTERWORD

On the May morning in 1940 when British marines invaded Reykjavík, their top general pulled Icelandic officials aside and warned them that German aircraft might be incoming. Prepare residents to flee into their basements, he said. Limit indoor light to candles and cover the windows. Avoid big gatherings and big buildings—those will be the first targets.

Yikes.

The shocking information called for a major intervention. Urgent directives were sent to protect the nation's precious resources: books at the National Archives.

On orders from higher-ups, archivists packed the nation's invaluable vellum scripts and sagas into a paper box marked FLÚÐIR: the name of a one-hot-spring town in the rural south, safely inland. The boxes were stashed away in Flúðir's community center, where they remained hidden for the remainder of the war.

Having taken care of the nation's past, officials then turned their attention to the nation's future: the youth. They, too, would have to be moved someplace safer. All over Reykjavík, children were uprooted from their city-slicker lives and placed into (temporary) foster care around the country, away from dangerous target zones and sprawling military

construction. Children living in central Reykjavík were prior-
itized; officials told them to pack their bags within days after
Britain's invasion.

My grandfather, age six, living in a basement near the city
pond, had to kiss his mother goodbye and leave aboard a Red
Cross truck headed northeast. He knew the road just as well as
he knew the other passengers—which is to say, not at all. Crossing mountain paths and fording unbridged rivers, the truck
reached its destination after 270 miles and three days of driving. The modern traveler can go to China and back in less time.
Here, at a vacant boarding school near Lake Mývatn, children
of various ages were meant to share the available rooms.

"I cried a lot," my grandpa, now turning eighty-six, recalls
today in his rough voice and matter-of-fact manner. "The
adults didn't know what to do with me."

The Red Cross organizers came up with a solution. A couple living on a nearby farm had offered to foster a child, and
although they had explicitly asked for a girl, the arrangement
was made. The family took Grandpa in. He joined their three
other children living in a turf house. In a black-and-white
photograph of the farm, Grandpa shows me the little building,
made almost entirely from ground material: big black stones,
grass turf, mud. The roof and the entrance had timber support. The entire farm was clustered close together for energy
efficiency, the communal living room situated just down the
hall from the barn—altogether, they lived in four rooms connected by a long, dark hallway.

Grandpa loved it.

"I still remember walking into the house, down the dark
hallway, and feeling so relieved. For reasons I can't explain,
this felt like home," he says. "A place where I belonged."

The farm had goats, sheep, and one horse. Grandpa mostly herded the goats, while the sheep roamed free in the High-lands. In the fall, the animals were rounded up for the slaughtering season. By then, it was time for him to leave. "I wanted to stay, but the farmers said winter was too cold for a boy like me. And I think that was the real reason. The house was getting very cold."

No wonder. The Mývatn settlement sits closer to the High-lands region than any other in Iceland. The town on the edge of the lake features a tundra climate, bordering on subarctic; Grandpa would have endured winter in a turf house with no modern heating in a place where the average high in January is about minus 2°C. Yet despite the cold, the region is gorgeous, teeming with life, surrounded by hot springs and volcanoes. The wide, shallow lake is home to great numbers of waterbirds like the red-throated loon and the whooper swan, while gyrfalcons circle the surrounding moorlands. The wilds all around are strewn with pseudocraters and pillars, with the moors grown over interglacial lava flows. It's a land of burning stone and frozen air.

The next summer, Grandpa returned north. Children were no longer required to leave Reykjavík, as the German Luft-waffe seemed unlikely to get past the lines of British and American air defense along Iceland's coast. But Grandpa longed to return. A year older, his hands were still too soft and small for most of the labor on a farm. He was too weak to mend fences. Too small to wrangle a ram. What would he do to stay occupied?

The farmer had an idea.

Near the farm, there lay a dramatic expanse of rock: lava formations the size of three-story buildings, rising abruptly from the flat ground. The stony towers form impossible shapes, reminiscent of the ancient remains of a vast burned city. The stone is uniformly black, igneous-rock black, as black as the earth can be. The incredible sight seizes the imagination. In Nordic Christian lore, the land was known as the place where Satan landed when cast from heaven, called the Catacombs of Hell. They are indeed as winding and mazelike as catacombs: if you go into the rock field to see particularly striking landmarks like the Church, you need to focus on the shape of the skyline, memorizing it, in order to find your way back out. The place is a labyrinth.

Unless, of course, you have a resourceful seven-year-old to guide you.

My grandfather had found a way to stay busy and even helpful. He would wait at nearby crossroads and offer passersby an hour-long walk to the weirdest-shaped rocks. And they do get weird. Several of the formations in the lava field are in the shape of trolls, the creatures that turn into stone if they stay out past sunrise, and others have caves and gates (lava tubes, to use the technical term). He worked for tips, which ranged from one to ten krona. Over the following years, most of his tour guests belonged to a growing class of affluent Icelanders, ones who drove fancy American cars, thanks to the lucrative war economy.

"I once got a small bus of school children from Reykjavík, and afterwards their teacher collected cents and kronas from each student," Grandpa, the entrepreneur, remembers. "It was good money, you bet."

Today, in brochures, Dimmuborgir is known as the must-see Black Fortress. Formed when lava spread over the marshy sod thousands of years ago, the dramatic spires might be familiar even to those who've never been to northern Iceland, as they served as backdrop to winter scenes in *Game of Thrones*, the TV drama filmed partly in Iceland. Visitors today are required to stay on the designated paths, with signs pointing toward the most interesting spots, like the Cave and the Church. The nearby visitor center has a menu offering Lava Cake (delicious) and Edible Rocks (scones dyed black). The toilet fee is two dollars. Drones are forbidden on the premises. Thousands flock through the fields each year and if you'd like to really soak in the eerie splendor of the lava towers in silence, then, well, the worst time to visit is the summer.

The best time to visit is during a global pandemic.

The winter of 2020 began like any other in northeastern Iceland, with the arrival of snow and travelers searching for the Northern Lights. I was living in Húsavík again, only thirty miles from Lake Mývatn, writing this book, watching the sea, and ensuring that my two-year-old son didn't go for a plunge in the northern waters. Every time it snowed, the one guy in town who owns a snowplow cleared the streets, piling the snow into hills. I asked him how it felt, waking up every morning knowing yesterday's work had been erased by yet more snow.

He shrugged and said, "It's a job." (In the summer, he drives an ice-cream truck stashed both with popsicles in fifteen flavors and with frozen fish fillets to properly fill up the car's freezer trunk, sold on the side.)

I thanked him for the advice, then went and applied it to my own writing. It was a good philosophy. The work seemed endless, but if I kept showing up each day, putting in the hours, eventually a path would be cleared.

After dropping off my son at day care in the mornings, I usually headed to the Húsavík Research Center, where I got to use an empty desk among the local experts in seabirds, baleen whales, and local gossip. The research center, a renovated fish processing plant, sits next to the shipyard, the place where my old friend Captain Hordur spends his winters fixing his fleet and coming up with tasks for people passing by. His latest project is an electric schooner, ideally one with a propeller that can also work as a turbine when there is enough wind to rely solely on the sails.

"In no wind, we can sail electric," he declared to me in excitement. "Good wind, we can recharge the batteries. We'd never, ever have to stop!"

Usually, I was able to walk by without having to hold a bucket of tar for him or splice a rope. But still—just in case I was looking for something to do—one day Captain Hordur recommended some dense history books to me. One of them proposes a theory that the early battles of Iceland's first settlers were in fact fought along ethnic lines, with the Celts losing. I checked it out from the local library. I walked, I read, I wrote. Winter ticked by. Like the local snow plower, my days appeared predictable, steady, and soon enough—surely—spring would come, and things would get a little easier.

It snowed. Come January, a series of storms caused power masts to break from the weight of the ice. Inside became as dark as outside, and sunlight hours up in the north are about an hour shorter than in the south. The Ring Road closed. Cut off from the outside world for days, the town's grocery store ran out of milk. This may not sound like a serious problem, but the store services a good number of farmers from the region; their bodies are 90 percent milk.

"Water," as one told me, "is for bathing." My son was less upset; chocolate milk was still available.

It kept snowing. In February, the town's ski area closed "because of snow." A multiday blizzard had dropped so much snow that the lifts were buried.

On the very last day of February, as the massive snowdrifts dwindled, as the ski lifts got set to open again, a man in Reykjavík returned from a holiday in the Alps. He had a low-grade fever. A cough. Sick.

Icelandic COVID patient zero had arrived.

Over the winter, I had written the book while in isolation from the rest of the country. Now, suddenly, impossibly, we all had to go even deeper into isolation—from the rest of the town. From everything, from everyone.

The following months were, of course, strange and frightening. But ultimately, Iceland weathered the coronavirus pandemic without resorting to the near-total social and economic shutdowns enforced in many other European countries. Our son's preschool remained open. Most workplaces kept operating, following social distancing rules. Infected people, and those they'd been in contact with, were quarantined, but the rest of the population was not forced to stay inside, only advised to be careful. Iceland's testing capacity was its greatest strength: over two months, Iceland managed to test almost sixty thousand people, more than 15 percent of the population, the biggest chunk of any country in the world. Additionally, civil defense authorities set up a contact tracing team, which included police officers and university students who used legwork and phone calls to identify the people who had come into contact with infected individuals. Iceland's success was partly thanks to its tiny population, but it also reflected decisive action by authorities. As *The New Yorker* put it, "The country didn't just manage to flatten the curve; it virtually eliminated it."

But once Iceland had tamed the outbreak, it had to self-isolate from the rest of the world. That meant economic suffering for the thousands of people who make a living from tourism, many of them migrants in low-wage service and cleaning jobs. Visitor numbers have quadrupled over the past decade, making Iceland's economy among the most tourist-dependent in the Western world. Without immigrants, the growth would have been impossible to sustain: every second job added to the economy in recent years has, eventually, been filled by someone not yet living in the country. Before the pandemic hit, a new foreign resident arrived, on average, every hour via the international airport, calling the country home for long or short periods of time. In total, 15 percent of the nation is now foreign-born, roughly fifty thousand people, approximately the same number of people living in the country eleven hundred years ago, after a century of Viking-led settlement.

At the turn of this millennia, when the Icelandic population was only 2.5 percent foreign-born, few envisioned that Húsavík, a traditional port town, would be home to twenty-six different nationalities only twenty years later: a Polish chef with a passion for sushi, a German economist moonlighting as a whale-watching guide, a Kenyan bodyguard selling tickets at the public pool, a French-Icelandic ornithologist fanatically against cats, a Republican diehard from southern California, a Danish folklorist with a passion for old wooden houses, a yoga instructor with an accent from somewhere. . . .

These are exciting times to be in Iceland, suddenly the land of opportunities.

Once the country gradually welcomes tourists again, I drive to Lake Mývatn on assignment for *The Lonely Planet*.

My mission is to find and interview the rare traveler, those willing to be virus-tested twice upon arrival.

It is winter—again, already!—and I am reminded what Grandpa meant by Mývatn's freezing temperatures. Driving down the narrow road to Dimmuborgir lava field, I stop at a parking lot resembling an ice rink in both size and slipperiness. My notebook in hand, I slide toward five people eating sandwiches next to an out-of-business café. They are international students at the University of Iceland. "We still have to attend classes remotely," says Moira Smets, a Belgian student of linguistics, "and that is precisely what we are doing. Very very remotely."

They have just completed a walk between the lava rocks and enjoyed it. The paths, they warn, are buried in snow with few footsteps to follow. "Be careful and bring a phone maybe," one says. I thank them for the advice. The rocks are casting a shadow in the setting sun, so I better get going and cross that parking lot again without breaking a bone. I slide away, to the rock formations, probably about to get lost and discover Iceland.

ACKNOWLEDGMENTS

Takk is the pan-Scandinavian word for thanks. It's a mono-syllabic word, spoken from the tip of the tongue, cognitively on a level with primate communication: very snappy, very simple. Not the sort of thing to say to someone who has, over and over, helped and encouraged you through a death march of a project. This book, in fact, would not make any sense without all my collaborators, and I cannot thank them enough. But, for the sake of trying, imagine a big hailstorm falling down on cars and roofs on a cold spring afternoon, beginning slowly but soon impossible to ignore: takk, takk to . . .

My agent Michelle Tessler at the Tessler Literary Agency in New York.

My editors at Penguin Books: Patrick Nolan, Matthew Klise, and Sam Raim who made sure this book included only a limited number of bad jokes. And, further, the entire team at Penguin Books including Brian Tart, Kate Stark, Lindsay Prevette, Mary Stone, Ciara Johnson, Nora Demick, Elisabet Stenberg, Sharon Gonzalez, Matt Giarratano, Paul Buckley,

Roseanne Serra, Lauren Monaco, Andy Dudley, and Travis DeShong.

American novelist and friend Delaney Nolan. As reader number one, she helped me turn a messy idea into a book proposal, and her encouragement and advice on everything from structure to style have shaped this book more than she knows.

Hólmfríður María Ragnhildardóttir, Claire Kowalewski, Marc Nieson, Alexandra Yingst, Jude Isabella, Meg Matich, and Bjarni Harðarson each read early parts of the book and provided advice on how to tell a fairer and more accurate version of history. My brother Gunnlaugur, a baritone with a degree in Icelandic, wrote the phonetic spellings.

In Húsavík, thanks to everyone at the Þekkingarsetur Research Center, North Sailing, and the Public Library.

Gregory Katz, my editor at the Associated Press. He passed away after a fight with cancer while I was incommunicado writing this book. He oversaw Iceland coverage from his chair as the London bureau chief and hired me as a stringer when that position didn't exist. His spirit is all over the pages of this book; contemporary topics like the banking crisis aftermath, climate change, and the Me Too movement were initially reporting assignments.

Above all, and as ever, my heartfelt thanks and admiration to my partner, Sigrún.

INDEX